THE

UPPER DERWENT

10,000 YEARS IN A PEAK DISTRICT VALLEY

THE UPPER DERWENT

10,000 YEARS IN A PEAK DISTRICT VALLEY

BILL BEVAN

TEMPUS

Frontispiece: *A nineteenth-century bridge across the River Derwent now lies submerged in silts on the bed of Derwent Reservoir.* Courtesy of the PDNPA

First published 2004

Tempus Publishing Ltd
The Mill, Brimscombe Port
Stroud, Gloucestershire GL5 2QG
www.tempus-publishing.com

British Library Cataloguing in Publication Data.
A catalogue record for this book is available from the British Library.

ISBN 0 7524 2903 5

Typesetting and origination by Tempus Publishing.
Printed and bound in Great Britain.

CONTENTS

ACKNOWLEDGEMENTS

Thanks is given to the many people who contributed to the archaeological survey of the Upper Derwent and the production of this book. Many thanks are given to the Upper Derwent Officer Working Group and the organisations which commissioned the survey: the Peak District National Park Authority (PDNPA), Forest Enterprise, the National Trust and Severn Trent Water. Albin Smith of Forest Enterprise, Judy Merryfield, Ken Smith and John Thompson of the PDNPA, Stan Hitch, Mike Innerdale and Geoff Nickolds of Severn Trent Water, and Sophie Milner, Mark Newman, Leigh Rix, Simon Wright and Steve Trotter of the National Trust have given valuable help and encouragement throughout the project and writing of this book. I also thank other landowners and farmers who gave permission to survey their land, and often provided valuable historical information: Jeremy Archdale of Moscar Lodge, Peter Atkin of Rowlee, Maurice Cottrill of Hayridge, Mr Fryer of Old House, Michael Jolley of Ashes, Mr Wainwright of Upper House, Mr White of Two Thorn Field, Mrs Wild of Blackden View and Mr Wood of Crookhill. Thank you also to all members of the parishes who have given support to the project.

Paul Ardron initially alerted the Peak District National Park Archaeology Service to the archaeological richness of the area, identified many of the archaeological features on the moorland and in the woodlands and provided information on his collection of artefacts. My interpretation of the area has greatly benefited from many fruitful conversations with Paul and with Mark Edmonds, Ken Smith, John Barnatt and – for Tin Town – Professor Brian Robinson. I thank everyone who has helped with survey, fieldwalking, documentary research, excavations and post-excavation over the years: Kenny Aitchison, Paul Ardron, Paul Ash, Pauline Ashmore, Dave Ashton, John Barnatt, Pauline Beswick, Paul Buckland, the Byford family, Derek Cater, Vicky Cooper, Chris Cumberpatch, Gavin Davies, Mark Edmonds, Ashley Edwards, Kathryn Ellerby, Rowena Gale, Pru Goodman, Jill Gorvett, Ann Hall, Danny Hind, Tracey Hulme, Miles Johnson, Barbara Jones, Chris Jones, Robin Keech, Liz and Nick Landon, Mike Lea, (the appropriately named) Derwent Levick, Stella Maguire, Melissa Peet, John Roberts, Frank Robinson, Phil Sidebottom, Paul Smith, Pam Staunton, Gill Stroud, Alice Ullathorne, Helen Ullathorne, Arthur Wilson, Hugh Willmott and Jo Woofitt. I'm especially grateful to those who have patiently put up with questions about artefacts, conducted fieldwork in fog, rain, gales, thunder and lightning, and those who have repeatedly walked up and down hills.

Thanks also to members of the Peak Park Ranger and Information Services: Dave Ashton, Gavin Bell, Jozef Hegyi, Brian Jones and Bob Young, who have helped carry equipment, unearthed local information and provided cups of tea in the Fairholmes Centre. Alison Foster, Angela Johnson, Anne Loy and Gary Short have given technical help over the years. Ray Manley is responsible for the following beautiful photographs: cover, **4**, **5**, **6**, **10**, **21**, **25**, **31**, **32**, **47**, **48**, and **81**, and Steve Fox for the reconstruction drawings. Photographs used in illustrations **64**, **68**, **69** and **70** are from the Brian Robinson collection at Eyam and are reproduced by courtesy of Prof. Robinson. Photographs **3**, **12**, **56**, **60**, **77** (left), **78**, and **79** are courtesy of the PDNPA Collection, **8**, **53**, and **58** are courtesy of the National Trust Collection, **66** is courtesy of the Severn Trent Water Collection, and the remainder of photographs, as well as all the site plans, are by myself.

The following have read and commented on drafts of the text, and suggested many improvements: Dave Ashton, John Barnatt, Mike Innerdale, Georgia Litherland, Stella Maguire, Judy Merryfield, Ken Smith, Steve Trotter and Simon Wright. Any mistakes, omissions and bad puns are solely my responsibility. Georgia has had to put up with return visits to the Upper Derwent and endless ramblings about this or that of 10,000 years of history whilst giving support in return. It is to her and to G.H.B. Ward of the Sheffield Clarion Ramblers (the Upper Derwent's first landscape archaeologist) that I dedicate this book.

I am grateful to Peter Kemmis Betty for giving me the opportunity to publish the Upper Derwent's landscape history, and to all at Tempus who have worked on the book.

The Upper Derwent Archaeological Survey and publication of this book has been kindly supported by the following organisations:

THE NATIONAL TRUST

This way to the Upper Derwent. Photo by Bill Bevan

ONE

INTRODUCING THE UPPER DERWENT

Ripples in time

The Upper Derwent sits in the gritstone moorlands of the Peak District National Park, a remote upland area north of Bamford village separating the cities of Sheffield to the east and Manchester to the west (**2**). Here the River Derwent starts high up on the moors as one of many small streams that cut through the blanket peat (**3**). As it descends similar watercourses soon join it to form patterns that look like the roots of giant trees. These streams have eroded through the bedrock to form steep-sided, narrow valleys that are known locally as cloughs. In places the river quickly courses over slabs of stone and water-worn pebbles while in others it slows down to idle through deep pools. It is this river that has bitten deep into the rock over many millennia to create the steep-sided, v-shaped valley of its upper reaches. The river widens by the time it reaches Bamford and takes a determined course for many miles along the broad valley it has created, changing direction where stubborn rock has not been so susceptible to erosion (**4**). Some of this rock has formed cliffs which overlook the river from the east, their updraughts ingeniously used in the medieval period as natural bellows by lead smelters but now less welcomed by climbers who chase routes up the edges. At Chatsworth, a succession of gardeners has worked since the sixteenth century to turn a swathe of the valley into an idealised pastoral idyll. Further south, the river became one of the engines of the industrial revolution. Mill owners followed in the footsteps of Richard Arkwright and diverted some of its waters to cotton mills in the eighteenth and nineteenth centuries. Where the river cut a deep gorge through the limestone, Matlock Bath was built as Derbyshire's landlocked Victorian 'seaside' resort. The city of Derby grew up along its banks on the site of the Roman fort of Derventio. Beyond Derby, the river joined with the River Trent, and the waters that flowed south for over 55 miles turn northwards to continue their journey to the Humber and finally, the North Sea.

There is a long story to be told of the people who lived alongside its course. Since the glaciers retreated at the end of the last Ice Age 10,000 years ago, generations have been born, lived and died in the country to either side of the river. This is a story of ordinary people, who looked much like you and me but who have perceived the world in very different ways to us. Over time these people shaped the rocks, soil and vegetation to form the landscape we know today. We can tell something of their story from what survives to be read; the changes they made to the landscape, the material objects left behind and, for more recent times, written documents which catalogue and describe various aspects of their lives.

I first discovered the Upper Derwent in 1994 when I began an archaeological survey of the area on behalf of the Upper Derwent Officer Working Group. Since then I have come to know the area well through walking across it many times during survey, from the enclosed spaces of the valley woodlands to the exposed, relatively featureless tops of the moorlands. You learn the importance of navigation when travelling by foot away from the footpaths, how a good knowledge of

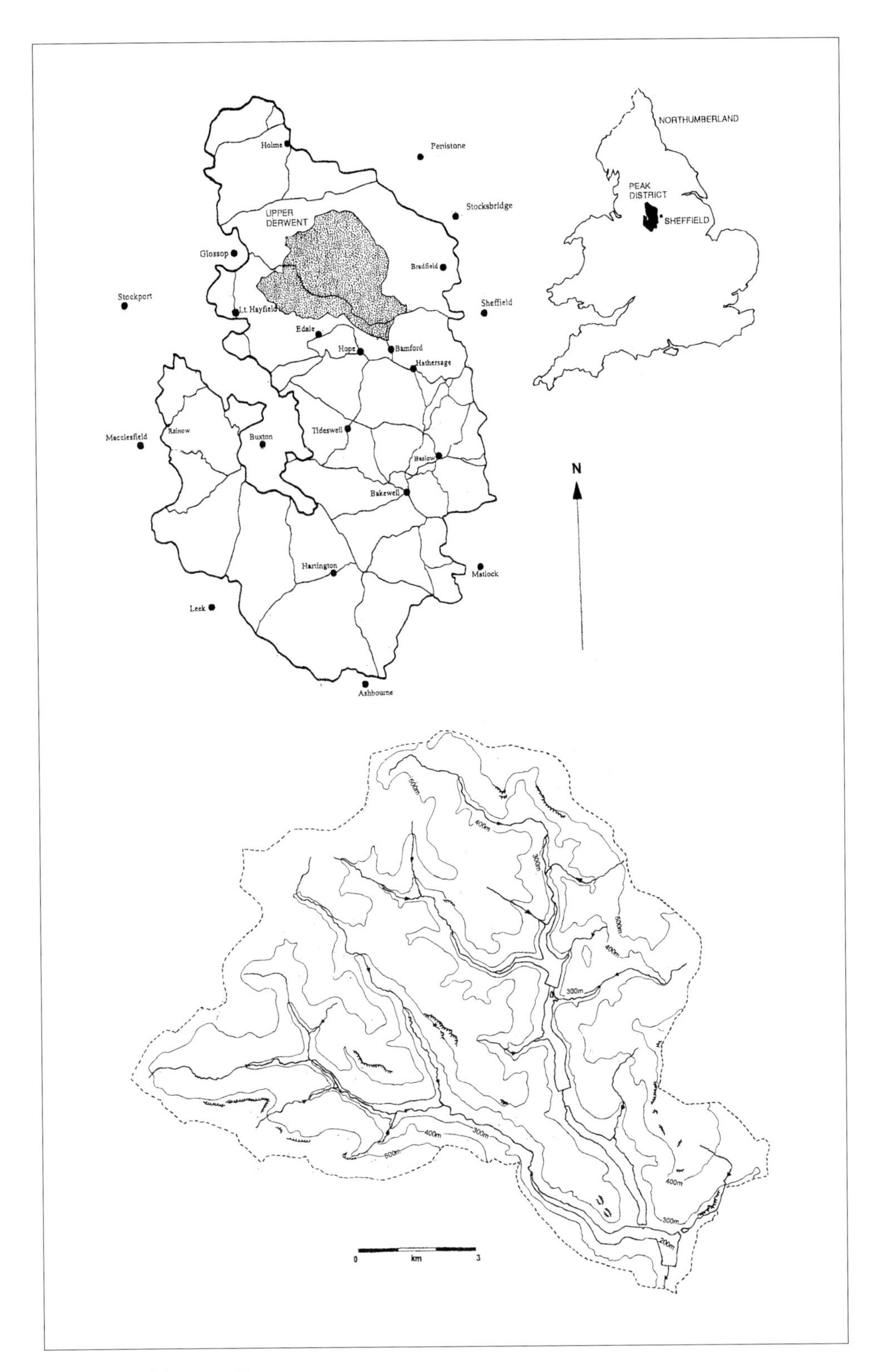

2 *Location of the Upper Derwent*

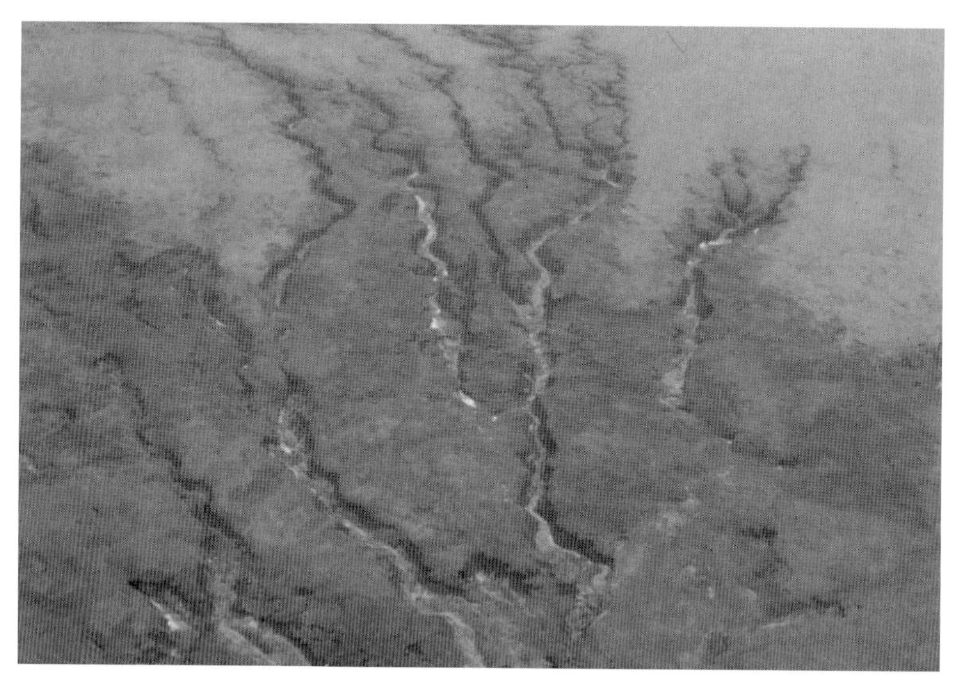

3 *Source of the River Derwent. The Derwent River begins high on the moorlands as narrow watercourses cut through the peat.* Photo by Ray Manley

4 *Looking north along the Derwent Valley from Frogatt Edge with Bamford village in the distance. The Upper Derwent lies amongst the moorland hills beyond Bamford.* Photo by Ray Manley

the area or little decisions can drastically reduce or increase the effort required to get from one point to another. One wrong turn may take you to the cul-de-sac of a scree-covered steep slope. Setting off a few degrees from your intended direction can bring you to the edge of a deep clough rather than the flat land beyond its source. Maps do not help in these sorts of landscapes and you quickly realise how important it is to take your bearings from features until you get to know an area well. These are also very physical landscapes where you feel your journey in your legs and lungs. Distance is not measured by metres or yards but by time and landscape features seen ahead, then passed. When spending time at one location for survey or excavation you get a different sense of landscape, what it is like to dwell in a place – so it is perhaps apt that much of our more detailed work has been at the sites of dwellings and burial places. For the archaeologist it is important to get some understanding of what it means to inhabit a landscape. This helps to interpret land use in the past from the human perspective rather than just from maps or the distant landscape view. The map is a relatively recent and privileged view of a piece of land, land where access was, initially, restricted to landowners and those in positions of authority.

The history of the Upper Derwent, like any other landscape, has not simply waited to be discovered by teams of modern time travellers. Archaeologists do not just dig into the soil and uncover buried truths about the past. Understanding the past, whether that of Mesolithic gatherer-hunters or nineteenth-century farmers, requires the wide range of evidence to be identified, sorted, described and interpreted. Some of this evidence may be obvious, such as the burial barrow on top of the hill, the pattern of farmsteads and their surrounding fields or the estate map. Other evidence is more obscure, the scatter of flint tools eroding out of the side of a footpath or the microscopic pollen grains preserved for thousands of years in the peat bog. This is the challenge to archaeologists: to identify what is the relevant evidence and to interpret it in ways that do not simply transplant our modern understanding of the world onto the past. We cannot assume that different societies at different times perceived and occupied the landscape in the same way we do today.

A landscape biography

This approach to archaeology is a landscape-based one. My definition of landscape is the physical world of places within which people act out their lives through time, and which is populated with buildings, objects, animals, plants and other people. The idea of land*scape* is a culturally specific modern Western concept, originating in sixteenth-century Renaissance theories of form and perspective where people objectively 'view' the landscape from a distance. Landscape ideals came to be most obviously applied in painting and the garden designs of the landed gentry. Tourism was also born out of these principles. Members of the aristocracy toured Britain and Europe to observe scenic places that the more literary published as some of the earliest travel writings. The Peak District was a stop on the 'Grand Tour' of these early travellers and in 1636 the first guide to the region was published with the title *The Seven Wonders of the Peak*. Thomas Hobbes, the author, described seven natural and human-made marvels which the discerning tourist should visit to be astonished. Chatsworth House, seat of the Dukes of Devonshire, diplomatically headed the list followed by Peak Cavern, Eldon Hole, the Ebbing and Flowing Well at Barmoor, Mam Tor, Poole's Cavern and St Ann's Well. While visiting the Peaks on his own seventeenth-century grand tour, Daniel Defoe subsequently and scathingly criticised all but Chatsworth and Eldon Hole as 'mere trifles'. This reminds us that people's perceptions of the same landscape can vary enormously, and that archaeology is as much about how we interpret features as it is about dryly describing them.

This formalised view of the land as landscape can be contrasted with the routine lives of people and communities that have close working relationships with the land: farmers, miners, foresters, etc. Through dwelling, working and travelling, people inhabit the land; give it meaning and form close connections with places. The landscape is not simply a backdrop to their lives. This is where landscape archaeology includes interaction with the geology and topography of the land, with buildings and other structures, vegetation, objects and with people. The numerous structures and artefacts that survive from different periods did not exist in isolation but represent the interconnected elements of past landscapes that have survived to the present. Some are redundant and seen as relics of other times, while many more continue to be incorporated into the fabric of today's working and living landscape. The interpretation of their inter-relationships helps to give an understanding of the varying uses and perceptions of the landscape, and how this landscape has developed through time.

In this approach we have to take into account that people live within, and experience their world across different spatial scales, travelling packhorse routes to neighbouring market towns, tending stock in fields or entering the interior of a house from outside. Social interaction with other people varies from everyday close association with family or well-known neighbours to less frequent contact with comparative strangers from further afield.

People who share common social connections with each other and who see themselves as belonging to the group form communities. These may be based on where people live, the language they speak or the social class they belong to. Any individual is aware of their own identity, a sense of 'who you are' based on gender, bloodline, age, prowess at certain tasks, and even unusual traits such as height and colour of hair. These are personal factors that are understood through the relationships formed with others, relationships that take place within the landscape.

Individuals live in societies that hold social ideals or beliefs. Anyone living in a particular community, whether connected by kin, gender or task, requires the skills and competence to give and understand the implicit and explicit signals to effectively join in and be a part of that community. We become exposed to these social signals throughout childhood. Certain ways of doing things are more expected than others. They are reinforced through the day-to-day living together and the rituals we conduct in the presence of others. Often people agree with those beliefs and maintain the status quo. Sometimes people act in ways contrary to what is considered the right way to behave. This may result, on the one hand, in condemnation and punishment or, on the other, in the adoption of new ideas and social change. It is through this interaction between individuals and widely agreed social beliefs that societies are maintained or changed from one generation to another. As a result, the nature of societies has varied enormously over time. In the Upper Derwent, we find the mobile kin group of the Mesolithic, the bonded tenants of the medieval grange and the navvies of the early twentieth century. Same landscapes – different worlds.

We perceive the passage of time at different frequencies. There is the immediacy of a single event, the daily round of routine jobs to attend to and the passage of seasons. There is the lifespan of an individual, the succession of generation after generation, and more persistent traditions and long-lasting institutions. We may feel that we control some of these, while others are just the way things are done.

Archaeologists also have more than a passing fascination with time – it structures their subject. Prehistory is divided into chronological periods first created in the nineteenth century to sequence finds based on technology; Stone Age, Bronze Age, Iron Age. The problem is that technology has come to define societies and provide an evolutionary index of their place on the road to civilisation. However, it is not only tools that define social complexity, which includes much wider ideas about how to understand the world. People's lives, and major changes to the way the landscape is used, do not conform to definite boundaries. For example, many prehistoric burial barrows and stone circles were built during a period covering the later Neolithic and early Bronze Age. These ages are convenient terms created by archaeologists to organise the huge time spans we study.

I aim to bring out these different scales of space and time, in effect to write a biography of the Upper Derwent from the end of the last Ice Age to the modern day. The subjects are the people and their interaction with the landscape. This of course presents some problems. The evidence is huge; it comprises a large number of varying types of material; built structures, objects, written documents, maps, oral history, pollen preserved in peat bogs and the structure of the soil itself. These have to be studied in the context of each other, looking at the numerous connections that may have been made between different places, and how those connections may have changed over time. Yet only a small proportion survives of what has been built and used over the millennia since the last Ice Age. What we have are small windows into the past. At times these windows are thrown fully open and we can see enough to be able to interpret the detail of peoples' daily lives. At other times the windows are firmly shut and we can only glimpse the occasional activity in passing, or for some periods we may even think there is no one at home.

Lie of the land

The Upper Derwent comprises two valleys, the Derwent and the Ashop, and their surrounding catchment areas (**colour plate 1**). The former is mostly lost under the three reservoirs built in the first half of the twentieth century by the Derwent Valley Water Board to supply Sheffield, Derby, Nottingham and Leicester. The latter valley, also known as Woodlands, forms an impressive sight for those motorists with time or thought to look as they travel along the winding Snake Pass between Sheffield and Manchester (**colour plate 2**). Derbyshire and Yorkshire also meet at the Upper Derwent – the county boundary runs across moorland and along the River Derwent.

The two valleys have narrow bottoms where deeper soils lie. In places, level ground fringes the rivers before the valley sides climb steeply up, interrupted here and there by areas of gently sloping land. Small cloughs pour their contents into the rivers directly off the valley sides while larger cloughs form tributary valleys such as the Alport and Westend (**5**). Soils are thin and the underlying gritstone outcrops in places above the valleys to form large edges such as Derwent and Howden Edges, and weather-worn tors such as Rocking Stones and the Salt Cellar. The underlying rock mainly comprises a coarse, hard, sandstone called Millstone Grit that is interleaved between bands of softer shales. These were laid down over 400 million years ago as sediments carried by rivers from the north-east when the Peak District was a shallow sea surrounding a limestone reef. Landslips have formed where hard rocks lie above shale on steep slopes. These can be seen at Alport Castles, along the north side of the Ashop Valley and the east side of Alport Dale where landscapes of irregular hummocks have formed below steep cliffs of exposed rock.

To the north, east and west of the two valleys the land rises to heights of over 600m above sea level. Here the land forms a broad, undulating, featureless plateaux interrupted by deep cloughs which create barriers to easy movement. Unless you know this landscape well or can read the few natural landmarks it is easy to get lost. Further east and west the moorlands eventually drop down towards the lowlands. The high moorland continues to the north as part of the Pennines which meet the Cheviot Hills in Northumberland. To the south lies the remainder of the Derwent Valley, the Hope Valley, the Eastern Moors and the limestone plateau.

A landscape of different characters

The modern landscape of the Upper Derwent is characterised by a number of different zones dominated by certain landforms, vegetation and land use (**6**). These are instrumental in how we perceive the landscape today. They also have significant impacts on the visibility and survival of archaeological remains, and

5 *Alport Dale looking north. A typical Pennine valley with enclosed and improved pasture giving way to rough pasture, woodland and open moorland.* Photo by Ray Manley

thereby inform us how the area's history can be written. They are the result of the decisions people have made over time about using the landscape in relation to its topographies. In effect then, they will form the conclusion to our story, so without spoiling the end, we will look at them in brief here.

Moorland

Many visitors describe the area as rugged, and since the nineteenth century, walkers have been attracted to its open moorlands, the skyline sometimes broken by outcropping edges and tors (**7**). The moors are often perceived as wilderness, untouched by human hand. This is very much a false impression and largely derived from the perspective of those escaping the confines of modern city living. Those who live and work on them perceive the moorlands differently. They are viewed as an integral part of the agricultural economy, essential grazing land for farmers, and heeded for the difficulty of terrain and surprise changes in weather. The moorlands are a human-made landscape, created through the prehistoric removal of woodlands in tandem with climatic changes following the last Ice Age.

Heavy rainfall caused peat to form, while woodland was prevented from regenerating by grazing sheep. Over time, tree cover was lost and blanket peat spread.

Moorland is not intensively used so a great number of archaeological features survive from all periods, many of which are visible above the blanket peat. However, peat will have also covered features pre-dating, and contemporary with, its formation that remain hidden. Peat first formed during the Mesolithic in large hollows where water collected from surrounding slopes. About 7,500 years ago peat began to spread further during wetter conditions and was almost as widespread as it is today by the end of the Bronze Age. Since at least the medieval period the moorlands have been primarily livestock pastures, sources for quarried stone and peat fuel for domestic fires. The latter two uses have potentially the greatest impact on earlier archaeological features and artefact assemblages.

Erosion of peat provides tiny windows into this buried landscape within which artefacts and structures are occasionally found. Ramblers and members of archaeological societies have made most finds of artefacts, recording the locations and notifying archaeologists. These have contributed greatly to our understanding of prehistoric land use on the moors

Farmland

From the medieval period onwards the valleys, lower valley sides and favourable locations at higher altitudes have been enclosed into small fields and woodlands bounded by dry-stone walls (**8**).

For most of the medieval and post-medieval periods farming in the area has been predominantly pastoral with limited arable. Many archaeological features have been preserved under pasture and are visible as a variety of earthworks. Damage and destruction of some features will, of course, have taken place over time, for example, by ploughing for arable or grass re-seeding and by the re-use of stone for building. Levels of damage increase with age because the chances of it being swept away by later generations are greater. This means that there are more features preserved from the historical period compared to prehistory. From later prehistory onwards people probably re-used many of the same areas most favourable for agriculture and associated settlement. Areas better suited to more recent arable, such as the gentler valley sides and valley bottoms may often be the areas where earlier settlements and field systems were located. Use of the valleys for arable may have been limited until metal-tipped ploughs capable of dealing with heavier soils were introduced during the Iron Age. Very few artefacts or cropmarks of buried sites are found within pastures because ploughing and arable crops are extremely rare at present.

Conifer plantations

During the twentieth century extensive conifer and deciduous plantations were created around the reservoirs (**6** & **9**). They have had a major impact on the

6 *Looking south over Howden Dam. The Upper Derwent landscape is characterised by its twentieth-century reservoirs, fringed with plantation woodlands, in the valley bottom, open moorland and enclosed farmland.* Photo by Ray Manley

7 *The Derbyshire-Yorkshire county boundary snakes across the moorland as an earthen bank in an area where its line was contested between landowners who wished to incorporate the high pastures into their estates.* Photo by Bill Bevan

8 *A National Trust waller rebuilds one of the dry-stone field walls in the valley.* Courtesy of the National Trust

9 *Dense conifer plantations of the lower valley sides not only dominate how the landscape looks but also hide many archaeological features.* Photo by Bill Bevan

10 *Water cascades over the top of Derwent Dam, constructed in the early twentieth century during the flooding of the valleys.* Photo by Ray Manley

survival and identification of archaeological remains. In places they correspond to areas of ancient woodlands, which were themselves managed for timber and charcoal, remnants of which survive. Ploughing for tree planting will have destroyed many features while the dense tree cover, especially of immature plantations, masks much of what remains. Where plantations occupy the gentler valley sides they have had more impact on the survival of archaeological sites than those situated on the steeper upper valleys. This is because people are more likely to have lived and worked on the more moderate slopes.

Reservoirs

Most of the bottom of the Derwent Valley and part of the Woodlands Valley now lies below the twentieth-century reservoirs (**6** & **10**). They hide a potentially large number of archaeological features because they cover land that was the most used and densely populated. The drowned village of Derwent is a good example.

The areas nearest to the high water level are exposed periodically due to fluctuating water levels and are often subject to erosion through wave action, weathering and visitors. Erosion from the reservoir sides not only damages archaeological features but also produces silt that masks archaeological remains lower down (see frontispiece).

THE PATH

The group left their camp by the river. They had been settled there for two full moons and the days were becoming longer. Days before, the elders had decided it was time to leave the lowlands and the forest, but not everyone agreed, and the leaving time had been delayed much to the annoyance of some. The young girl was only partly aware of the lengthy debate, but she distinctly remembered the raising of voices one night around the hearth. Some wanted to stay because it was a sheltered place to be, with plentiful food nearby. She too wondered why they should leave when fish from the river, and birds and new shoots from the trees were providing for all. The arguments of those wanting to leave became dominant, many of the elders concerned that the spirits of the waters would turn against them if they overstayed their welcome. They remembered and told those who cared to listen how during their younger days the river turned from its normally strong and deep flow into a narrow thread and the fish had deserted them. They also argued that they required time to hunt and prepare the deer they needed for the gathering. Everyone knew that the deer were easier to find on the more open higher ground as spring approached. Vocal support for moving came from some of the younger kin who were eager to demonstrate their prowess at the wait and the chase of the hunt. One boy was especially eager, it would be the first hunt he was to be actively involved in and could not wait to cleave away from the children who irritated him more and more as the days of debate dragged on.

She helped with dismantling the camp soon after sunrise. Some of the women lit a torch from the fire to carry to their new camp, laughing and shouting as the flames took to the tar and bark. Then they solemnly buried the remainder of the hearth with its ashes and burnt stones in a pit while the rest of the group watched. The shelters were taken down – their skins and cloth rolled into bundles around wooden poles. Flakes of flint crunched underfoot, and she paused to reflect on the tools she had made there, some coming out of the stone with ease while others had to be forced and encouraged out. One of the elders had laughed at one effort to produce one of the blades used for cutting, telling her that when she did not handle the stone well it would not release its shape willingly. And maybe she had been right for the blade was awkward to use and sometimes snagged.

One of the elders led the way along the path that followed the river as it climbed, trees crowding against either side. As they continued the trees thinned out and changed, there were more of the lighter-skinned ones used for making bindings. It would not be long before they were away from the thicker forest and two of the younger children wanted to race ahead. If they made their customary good progress then they would have plenty of time to set up their new camp before dark.

As she did this she remembered they would soon go to the gathering where the day begins by the joining of the rivers. There were four other groups whom they regularly saw and who included close kin amongst them. Others were not so familiar but brought with them stories of places she had not seen. Last gathering, one of these men talked of a group that had beasts kept in one place and encouraged to breed with each other. They had another area encircled with bushes and wooden poles where they grew their own plants that they crushed and added to water then cooked on the fire like meat. She was fascinated by these stories but the elders simply shook their heads and muttered bleakly that these upset the ways of the ancestors.

TWO

MOVING THROUGH THE MESOLITHIC FOREST

After the ice

Stories about the past hold a fascination for us, whether of prehistoric cultures we think of as far removed from our own or of how the well-remembered shops of a town's High Street have changed over a lifetime. The human story of the Upper Derwent stretches back for approximately 10,000 years, or put another way about 333/400 generations if each generation is taken as 25/35 years. That is a lot of grandparents between us living in the twenty-first century, and those people who lived amongst the forests and alpine scrub just after the last Ice Age.

The Peak District was on the southern limit of the glaciers during the last Ice Age, a period that spanned about 65,000 years. Many glaciations froze what was then a promontory attached to north-west Europe under huge ice sheets. The last of these was at its height approximately 18,000 years ago when northern Britain was covered by glaciers that slowly expanded and moved southwards as new ice formed to the north. These and much earlier mighty sheets of ice had a dramatic effect on the landscape by scouring valleys, making them wider and deeper while depositing the eroded material elsewhere as moraines, tills and alluvium.

The region was probably not covered by the last of the ice sheets but would have been an area of tundra and thick permafrost, characterised by the types of vegetation and animals typical of Lapland and Siberia today. Only a handful of palaeolithic artefacts dating from this period have been found in a number of caves in the Peaks and none in the Upper Derwent. The climate warmed about 10,000 years ago, perhaps taking as little as 150 years to rise from subarctic to temperate conditions, and as the ground thawed thousands of tonnes of water were unlocked. On the higher ground this would have run down slopes and collected into rivers and gullies, carving out new courses and enlarging existing ones. In places huge chunks of rock and earth sheared away, slipping to gather in large piles and mounds, leaving bare rock faces behind. New types of vegetation colonised the area from further south, new species of animals moved with changing habitats and people found new opportunities within their rapidly changing world.

The interpretation of pollen preserved in peat bogs tells us something about what the Upper Derwent would have looked like. John Tallis, from the University of Manchester, has done most of this work in the Dark Peak and believes that trees colonised the areas which had been tundra to form forests dominated first by birch, hazel, pine and willow, and later by oak, alder, ash and lime. Mixed forests filled the valleys and spread on to Crookhill and parts of Derwent Moor up to about 425m above sea level. Above this the woodland began to thin out and land above 500m was covered by hazel and birch scrub. The Upper Derwent would have been wooded like this for about 3,000 years with even the high plateaux around Bleaklow, Margery Hill and Kinder being covered with scrub. At this time Britain basked in the best climate of the last

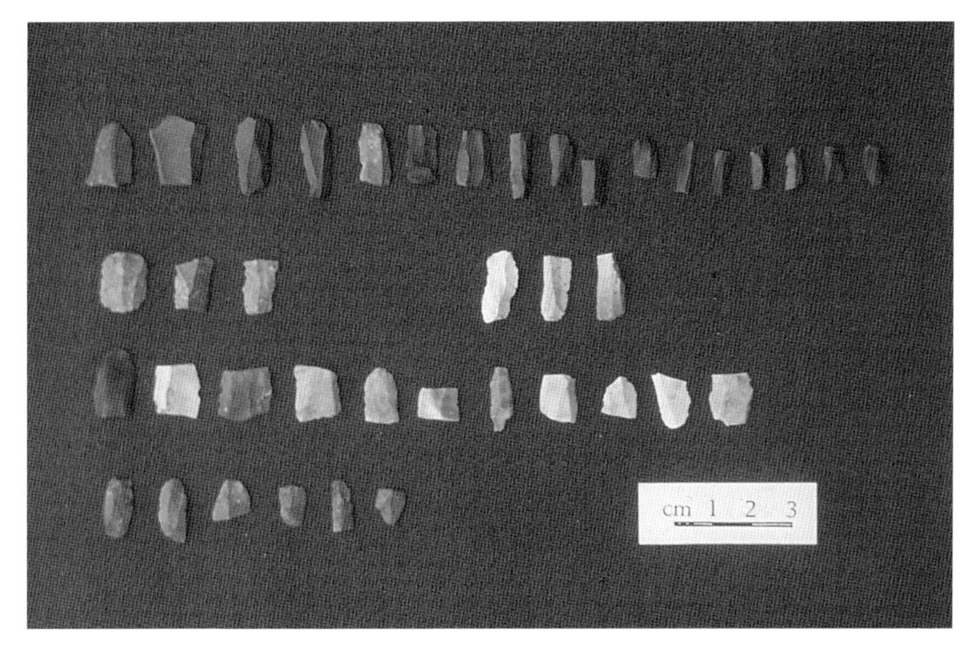

12 *Flint and chert tools such as these are typical of Mesolithic assemblages found in the Upper Derwent and elsewhere in the Pennines.* Courtesy PDNPA

20,000 years and enjoyed its most extensive woodland cover. The sodden peat moorlands we are familiar with today were still to develop, and in places they have preserved stumps of these post-glacial trees.

Enter people, stage left

The earliest evidence so far that has been discovered for the presence of people in the Upper Derwent is from the period which follows the Ice Age known as the Mesolithic. Stone tools and the waste from their production have been found across much of the Peak District, turned up by the plough, washed onto the sides of streams or eroded out of peat (**12**). Walkers, through their diligence in reporting discoveries, have made possible many of the finds and this has been instrumental in piecing together a picture of life after the ice. Many are located across the higher ground of the moorlands where the disturbance of vegetation has exposed the soils lying below. The network of rights of way heavily influences the locations of finds, how the wind removes peat from the tops of valleys or the favourite spots sheep choose for shelter. Distributions of artefacts are, therefore, only partial; they certainly show where people were present but by no means are these all the places that were visited.

The first thing which stands out is how many more finds there are for this period compared to earlier ones. Could this be the first time that the region was extensively inhabited by people? Also, very different types of stone tools were being made than before. Known as microliths, the most characteristic of the stone artefacts are small, carefully shaped points and barbs made from flint and chert. It is known from rare surviving objects in peat in Northern Europe that a number of them were attached to wooden handles and shafts to make composite tools such as arrows and saws. Archaeologists divide the Mesolithic into two phases, early and late, turning around 8,600 years ago when smaller and more geometrically shaped tools were introduced. There is also a change in the main materials chosen to make the tools. Earlier assemblages are dominated by flint from the chalk lands of the Yorkshire and Lincolnshire Wolds while those of a later date mainly comprise fine-grained black chert, a similar material to flint from the limestone plateau of the Peak District. There is, of course, some continuity across this divide, as there is between all archaeologically defined periods.

At this time, people fed themselves by gathering and hunting. Gathering would probably have constituted a major part of a community's daily activity, using a deep knowledge of the landscape and its vegetation to find a wide range of edible fruits, berries, nuts, seeds, leaves, stems, fungi, and animal foodstuffs such as honey, eggs and insects. Gathering also provided medicinal, hallucinogenic and 'technical' plants: wood for fires and buildings, birch resin for hafting wooden handles on to stone tools, bark and sedges for baskets, fibres for binding etc. Hunting, trapping and fishing would have taken place to catch mammals, birds and fish. Sometimes visits would have been made to favoured locations where animals had dens or often returned, at other times opportunities might present themselves, such as coming across a deer on a path. Animals also provided pelts and leather for clothing, and leather and sinews for cord. Evidence of fires suggests that people managed their landscape too, creating clearings where lusher vegetation could grow in order to attract herbivores and so provide good hunting places. Dogs were domesticated as hunting companions.

Archaeologists interpret the ephemeral evidence for the period as indicating people lived mobile lifestyles. Well-worn paths may have followed prominent topographical features in the forested hills, though a mobile community's intimate knowledge of their surroundings would have allowed them to range beyond the obvious ridges and edges. To those familiar with or inhabiting the forest, the pattern of its trees, its rocks, notable and well-known landmarks would be recognised and used to orientate. Movement around the landscape would be according to traditional rights of access, possibly linked to the seasonal changes in climate and natural resources or in relation to more immediate needs, such as water. A strong sense of place is created and reworked through the routine inhabitation of the same locations – making and managing woodland clearings, acquiring chert from known seams, revisiting the same positions, travelling the same paths over and over again. With a sense of place so ideals of tenure are established, traditional rights of access which are more than casual associations.

The kin group of extended families who were bonded to each other through birth or marriage, would perhaps be the main community that an individual identified with in the Mesolithic. Any one person might also associate with others according to gender, age or tasks such as gathering and chert quarrying. These would be the people that any individual spent their day-to-day lives with, most probably living in, and travelling through, places they had the right to inhabit through traditional claims passed from one generation to another and reinforced through storytelling and by dwelling there. Social identity, a sense of belonging with others, is developed in relation to where in the landscape you carry out activities together. Over time some areas of the landscape may have become identified with or claimed by one group while other areas might be shared by a number of groups.

It is unknown how big such groups were and their size would not have been static. A group would fluctuate with births and deaths, with members away on designated activities or with people from other groups staying to visit relatives. Contact with strangers from other kin groups might occur through happening upon each other where their paths overlapped. Perhaps other groups might be expected at specific places at certain times of the year. Members of one community might visit another to call for help or challenge their right to be present at that location. There were probably also formal gatherings of numerous groups, large rituals through which the appropriate use of the land could be argued and agreed, the raw materials for stone tools exchanged and marriages proposed. Through this contact people would see themselves as being part of wider social worlds, of larger clans comprising many individual communities.

Earlier Mesolithic

Sites with tools characteristic of the earlier Mesolithic are rare in the Peak District even though they are more prevalent than sites dating to the Ice Age. There are a number of isolated finds on the limestone plateau while larger scatters of implements have been found by a river confluence at Deepcar, Sheffield, on moorland at Pike Lowe and Mickleden Edge, South Yorkshire, near Marsden, West Yorkshire, and in a riverside cave at Wetton Mill, Staffordshire.

Deepcar is an important discovery because it was here in the 1960s that one of the few structures of the early Mesolithic was excavated. Dating to about 9,500 years ago, quartzite blocks and sandstone flags were arranged in an oval pattern interpreted by the excavators as the possible footing of a windbreak. Within this was a roughly circular setting of gritstone blocks approximately 4m by 3m across and containing three hearths. By sieving the excavated soil the archaeologists found a total of 23,000 flint and chert tools and waste flakes, mostly derived from Wolds flint. These were concentrated in and around the structures. Another structure has been found on Broomhead Moor, just east of the Upper Derwent. A series of five stakeholes appear to have supported a windbreak near to a paved area with flints and hearths radiocarbon dated to about 8,500 years ago.

On higher ground in the Upper Derwent, a walker found a small group of early Mesolithic implements fashioned from flint; a hammerstone and a waste flake (**13**). They were dropped near an edge by someone who was perhaps taking time during a foraging trip to make the tools they were soon going to need, while discarding those that were worn out and beyond reworking. Various tools and waste flakes have been found in the valley too. They are scattered along the eastern bank of the River Derwent, showing that people were occupying or moving through the thickly wooded riverside. People were moving between the higher ground and the valleys, at home in the forest and the lighter scrub, using the resources both have to offer. The amount of early Mesolithic material is so

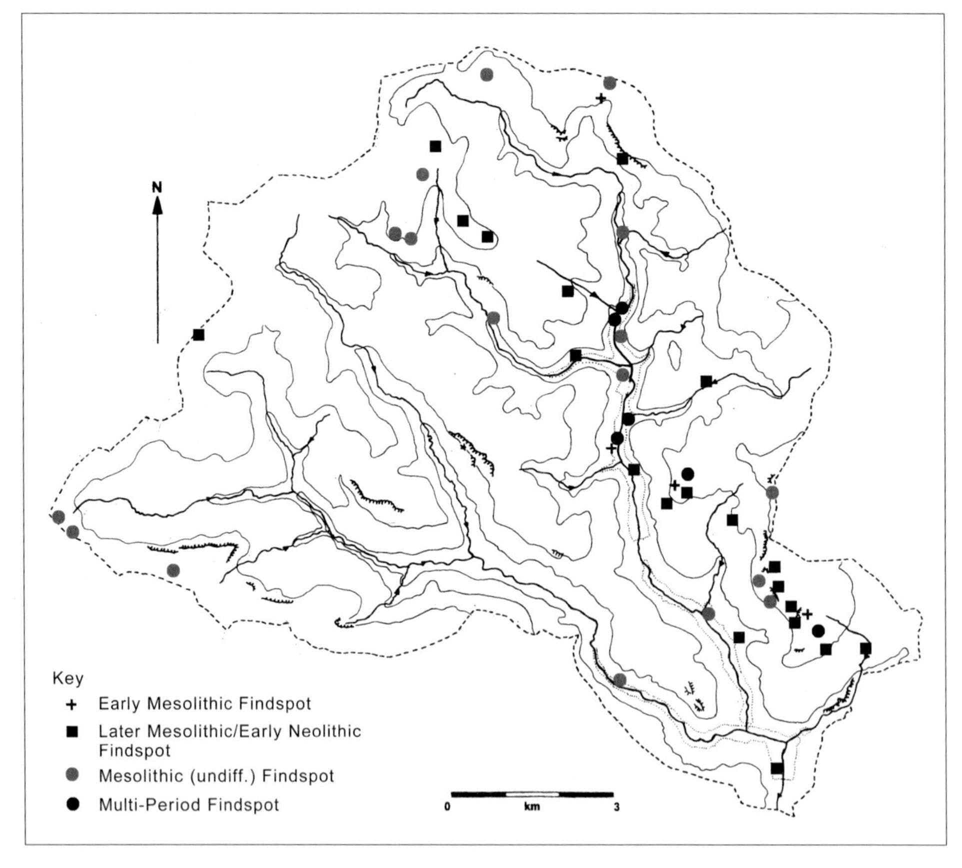

13 *Locations of mesolithic to early neolithic findspots in the Upper Derwent. Gently sloping ground and level terraces on the lower valley sides such as these near Linch Clough were occupied from the Mesolithic to the early Bronze Age.*

small as to make it impossible to interpret in more detail how people would have lived in this landscape; whether there are locations where they would have spent more time and others visited less frequently.

Later Mesolithic

Tools typical of the later Mesolithic and early Neolithic, dating between approximately 7500 and 3500 BC, are much more common (**13**). This is perhaps because there were more people or because the common types of composite tools used more individual pieces than earlier. Small blocks of chert and flint were systematically worked into cores and blades which were carried by people as sources of tools. Blades were used as they were or snapped and trimmed into a wide range of microliths. These appear to be convenient toolkits for life on the move, providing material at hand in an easily portable core or blade that could be worked into tools as and when needed. This characteristic way of working stone suggests life on the move. During the later Mesolithic, tools become smaller, and more geometric, complex and regionally distinct in style. They were also mainly fashioned from more local cherts with distant flints becoming less common. This combination of greater regionalisation which utilised more local sources suggests a gradual reduction in the distances people moved or exchanged items across.

Here we have people who were skilled at fashioning chert and flint. The regularity of microliths shows that there were set ways for their production and final form, that stone-working skills were much respected and passed on as important knowledge. It was a social as well as a practical task. Standardisation of how each type of tool looks also shows that traditions of the correct ways to make tools were becoming more defined. There may have been tool-making specialists, people who produced many of a community's tools and, presumably, spent less time gathering and hunting. If there were specialist toolmakers then it is likely each group had other specialists, people with specific skills and designated tasks, such as basket making, preparing hides and hunting. These benefited the whole community and through participating in them, peoples' social identities were further developed.

Many of the finds on higher ground represent places where a single implement was lost or discarded while being used – a scraper broken when removing bark from a birch tree to make bindings, a blade thrown away in flight from angry bees protecting their honey or a projectile that missed the running deer. Occasionally a group of lithics has been found in one location, where a variety of types of tool such as scrapers, blades and points lie amongst the waste from their production. These are places where people spent more time, tantalisingly suggesting places where camps were set up overnight or for a few days. Such locations have been identified across the higher ground, some by watercourses, some near edges, by tors or below underhangs and some on the more featureless expanses in between (**colour plate 3**). People were moving across this higher ground and in places staying for enough time to make the tools they would need later that day or the next. The known distributions of these finds are in part created by the modern network of moorland footpaths, routes across and bitten into the peat which have brought eagle-eyed walkers to find ancient tools eroding onto the ground surface. The Upper Derwent is a place which has attracted serious searchers for stone tools, people such as Alistair Henderson and Paul Ardron who have walked away from the footpaths in their search for finds. Recording the locations of their finds, they have widened the distribution patterns across broader swathes of landscape. Patterns of erosion are, of course, still instrumental in defining these distributions, as are the favourite haunts where collectors have previously made finds.

Constellations in stone

Moorland locations are typical for discoveries of Mesolithic lithics in England, with most being found above 350m above sea level. The uplands of the Cheviots, North Yorkshire Moors, Pennines and Dartmoor, amongst others, have contributed greatly to our knowledge of life in Britain during the period. The adjacent valleys, however, have largely remained unexplored gaps in the distribution plots caused by the lack of fieldwalking opportunities on rarely disturbed grassland pasture. Derwent, Howden and Ladybower Reservoirs have, however, given archaeologists an advantage because their waters have eroded topsoil and during dry summers the water levels drop enough to fieldwalk along their temporary beaches of subsoil. Here, the accurate recording of the location and nature of every piece of flint or chert has built a picture of later Mesolithic to early Neolithic life near to the river.

There are intermittent finds of waste flakes and implements throughout most of both Derwent and Ashop valleys, background scatters which show the presence of people moving through most of the valley woodland without hinting at the places they settled or gathered. In four places these scatters coalesce into larger constellations of flint, chert and quartzite numbering hundreds of microliths, blades, scrapers, knives, awls and burins as well as the cores they were made from and the waste flakes produced in their manufacture. They are the results of accumulation over time, places where people repeatedly had time to work stone and make new tools.

All four locations have some things in common. They are on areas of naturally gently sloping ground that break up the steep valley sides, near to confluences of the River Derwent with tributary streams yet above the narrow floodplain (**14**). They would have been deep in the thick valley forest and may have become clearings through their use. These are obviously longer inhabited areas than the transient stopping points common on the surrounding higher ground. The nearby river would have provided a range of resources. Salmon and other fish in

14 *Gently sloping ground and level terraces on the lower valley sides, such as those near Linch Clough, were occupied from the Mesolithic to the early Bronze Age.* Photo by Bill Bevan

the water itself, water-washed pebbles are ideal hammer stones, sedges and rushes are suitable for making baskets and water-edge plants provide numerous food supplies. The riverbanks provide habitats for waterfowl and other birds, while the lush forest-edge vegetation is attractive to grazing animals.

It may be that these sites were more sustained settlements where a whole community or some individuals visited regularly or for long periods. A group may have moved between valley and upland to stay at favoured locations in the valleys again and again. There may have been one kin-group or a small number of groups who occupied the Upper Derwent. Neighbouring groups may have met up periodically at these locations, gathering for major collective hunting expeditions or for ceremonies. Alternatively, the area may have been just one part of a landscape inhabited by a group who occupied a much larger terrain, possibly moving between valley, gritstone uplands and limestone plateau. We know from the presence of chert that there was some form of contact with the plateau. This may have involved certain members of the kin group travelling to the dales where chert seams outcropped or the whole group moving with the seasons.

It was not only stone tools which changed in the later Mesolithic. The vegetation altered too. Woodlands and plants, which dominated the uplands after the glaciers retreated, began to decline from approximately 7,500 to 7,000 years ago while blanket peat began to spread. This was the beginning of the peat moorlands we identify the region with today, often seen as the last remaining areas of wilderness in England. However, the peat moorlands are anything but a product of the wild. Human activity during the Mesolithic, in tandem with the onset of a wetter climate, was responsible for altering the vegetation of the area and contributing to peat formation. It seems that people were using fire deliberately to reduce the woodland. Repeated burning of vegetation and ground cover is suggested by the concentrated finds of carbon and charcoal in virtually every palaeoecological sample contemporary with the Mesolithic. There's too much charcoal for it all to be explained as lightning strikes setting fire to trees – and deciduous woodland is very resistant to wide scale burning except during dry conditions. Fine charcoal from fires is found ubiquitously in peat, a background level that suggests the common occurrence of domestic fires across the uplands. There are also concentrations of charcoal alongside streams and the forest edge that suggest attempts were made to improve the attractiveness of the vegetation to herbivores. Creating clearings in woodland can attract large game animals, such as deer, to more abundant vegetation, and therefore facilitate hunting. This sort of forest management is recorded as a common practice of many modern hunter-gatherer communities. Many animals likely to have been hunted for meat or pelts – deer, pig, aurochs (wild cattle), fox, badger and beaver – prefer open canopies in deciduous woodlands with good ground vegetation. Clearings also improve the amount and quality of plant foods by stimulating the growth of nut, seed and berry-bearing species such as blackberries and hazel.

While forest clearance was a sustainable strategy in lowland areas where woodland regenerated easily, this was not so on the uplands of the Dark Peak with high rainfall and thin soils. Open areas eventually became waterlogged due to decreased transpiration of water in combination with increased rainfall. As peat forms, organic material is washed downwards and attacks minerals in the soil. These form soluble iron compounds that are redeposited lower down as iron pan, a hard iron-rich layer. Higher ground and water-collecting hollows would be the most susceptible and the places where the earliest blanket peat formed. It then slowly spreads from these areas until there is mainly peat moorland within which many tree species are unable to survive. Species tolerant to poor soils such as birch would come to dominate and as the variety of trees was lost so did the associated rich ground flora and animals dependent upon them.

The spread of peat was a slow process, possibly not obvious within the lifetime of one generation. Most of the higher ground was covered by the end of the fourth millennium BC while lower altitudes under blanket bog today may have been free of peat until the Bronze or Iron Ages. A cairnfield situated at approximately 300 to 330m above sea level on Derwent Moor is typical of those on the Eastern Moors to the south which are dated to between the early Bronze Age and Iron Age. It was in use before the thin blanket peat formed at this location showing that there were still peat-free areas at lower altitudes well into later prehistory. The valley woodlands also remained.

Expansion of peat reduces the potential of the upland areas to sustain existing populations as habitats change and the amount of food-bearing plants and game decrease. Over-wintering becomes harder due to reduced stores and groups have to range over greater distances to find food. If the Upper Derwent was one part of the area covered by a group or groups then they may have begun to visit it less often or in smaller numbers. These changes occurred over a long period of time and people may not have been directly aware of them except perhaps as stories of the rich woodlands and numerous animals told around campfires and passed down over many generations. How reluctant communities would have been to leave such areas is unknown, they may have been very willing to move with resources though their connection with specific areas could be strong. Also, the potential for conflict with neighbouring groups would be high. People would knowledgeably assess their situation rather than simply react to changing conditions without thought.

Taking or leaving agriculture

Gatherer-hunter lifestyles continued into the Neolithic – the fifth and fourth millennia BC. The start of the Neolithic equates with the earliest dated introduction of agriculture in Britain in approximately 4500 BC, and is roughly when the first pottery vessels were produced and significant changes in the types of stone tools occurred. As with all archaeologically defined periods this does not equate with a new beginning for people living at the time. Hindsight and our desire to assign definite dates give the impression of a sudden transition from one technology and way of living to another. In reality changes took generations, possibly hundreds of years to occur and did not involve the wholesale replacement of the old with the new. As people living in the area came into contact with communities who grew crops and tended domesticated animals they too may have adopted some of these practices over time.

It is likely that different aspects of Neolithic culture, as identified by archaeologists, were taken up at different times rather than as a package for a new way of living, and that many aspects of gatherer-hunter lifestyles were maintained. In Britain, cereal cultivation appears to be adopted in the fifth millennium BC, though 1,000 years later teeth wear from mortuary deposits at Whitwell, Derbyshire indicates a diet that was still largely based on coarse fibrous plants, typical of foragers. Woodland clearance increased in the fifth and fourth millennia and was replaced with grassland, which suggests the creation of grazing land for livestock. Many earlier styles of tools, portable microliths and narrow blades fashioned from well-worked cores, continued in use from the later Mesolithic into the early Neolithic. Danny Hind has studied stone tools from this period in the region and has concluded that the Mesolithic to Neolithic transition is practically invisible in the lithics record. Pottery vessels and new

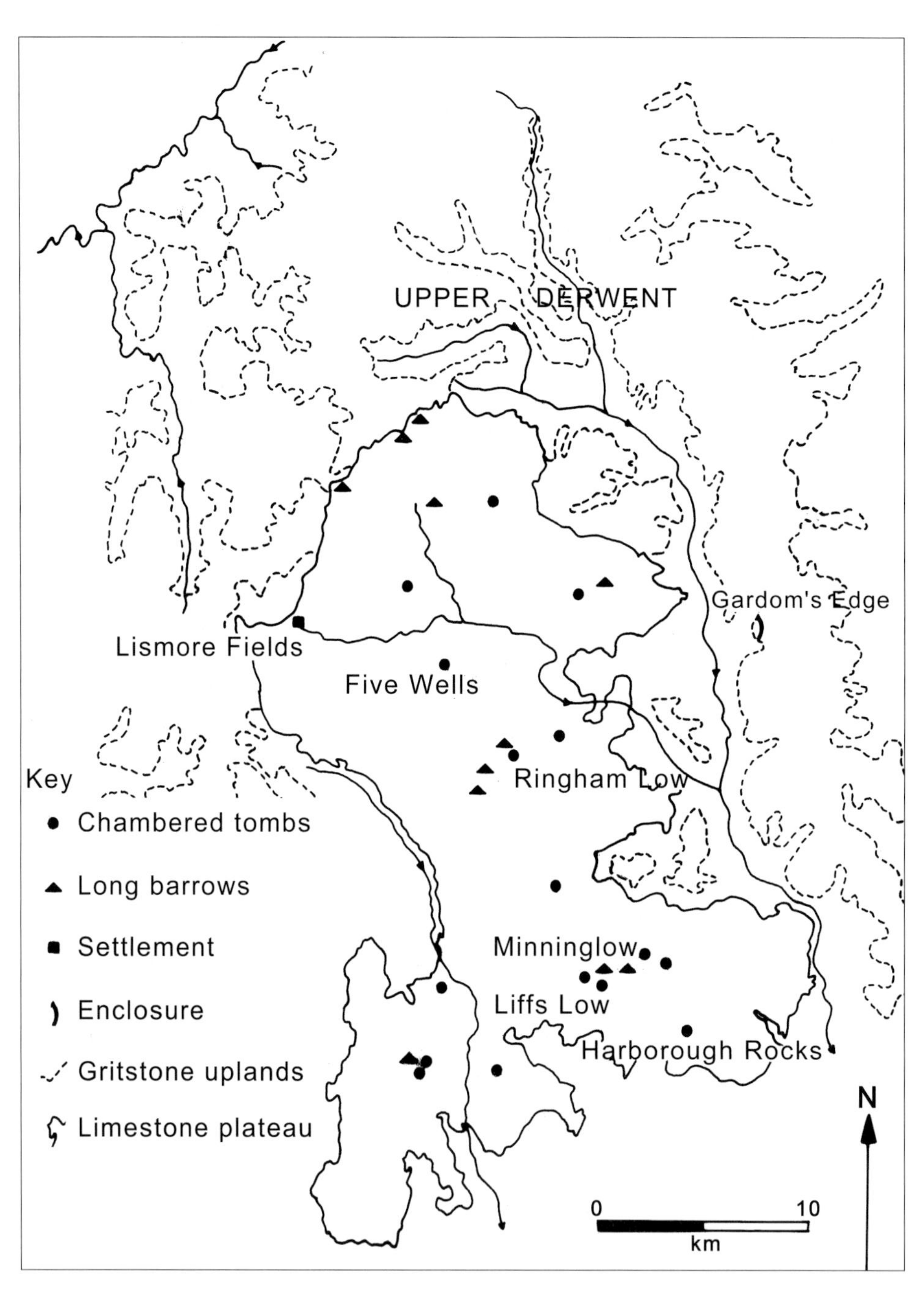

15 *Neolithic monuments and settlements in the Peak District*

types of tools such as knives, stone axes and leaf-shaped arrowheads, along with new ways of working involving bifacial flaking and the fine retouching of edges appear not to have been adopted until some time later.

Evidence for early domestication is found at Lismore Fields near to the modern town of Buxton, excavated by Daryl Garton. Here a site was excavated which sheds some light on settlement during the later Mesolithic and early Neolithic. Stone implements, waste from their production, postholes and pits filled with burnt stones and charcoal are found across the site and have been radiocarbon dated to the fifth and fourth millennia BC. Pollen preserved in a nearby peat bog shows that over this time, people were repeatedly clearing trees in between periods of woodland regeneration in the vicinity, growing cereals and creating grazing areas. Two or three timber-built rectangular buildings were constructed during the early fourth millennium BC and are associated with charred cereal grains and pottery in which residues of beeswax, honey, apples and dairy products have been identified. The buildings did not collapse but were deliberately taken down by the occupants who placed broken pottery vessels into the holes left behind, perhaps to commemorate the act of abandonment. The buildings may have been taken down upon the death of a head of the household or to build other houses elsewhere. While it has been suggested that people settled down to permanent lifestyles during the Neolithic, the evidence is far from clear-cut. Nor are the options just between mobile and permanent. People may choose various types of shifting settlement related to patterns of land-use.

Some of the new tool types are present in the Upper Derwent but only in very small numbers. They appear on the uplands and in the valleys in the same sorts of locations as the more widespread blades (**13**). There is a single sherd of Neolithic pottery, a fragment of a perforated macehead, maybe three polished stone axes and a handful of leaf-shaped arrowheads. This tiny number could indicate that peat formation was contemporary with a dramatic drop in the population of the area, but more likely, it shows that old types of stone working continued into the Neolithic while new types were not widely adopted. People could have continued to inhabit the Upper Derwent valleys much as before, successive generations moving around the landscape to visit the same locations over hundreds of years. Now, however, they may have also pastured domestic cattle or planted small areas of crops in the clearings that had previously been used to attract game.

Through domestication, the ties between people, plants and animals were slowly changing. People were probably still mobile, moving seasonally along traditional paths to settle temporarily at locations they used for pasture, growing crops, gathering and hunting. Agriculture demands a strong awareness of the seasons because it is critical that certain tasks are undertaken at specific times in the year. Deliberate cultivation of crops depends on saving seeds from one year's harvest to the next year's sowing time. Bulls need to be present during the mating season. Community identification and sense of ownership may be stronger with domesticates than with wild resources because herds, flocks and crops have to be protected and tended in much closer fashion than wild plants and animals. New ways of thinking may be required to ensure that the bloodlines of livestock are mixed to prevent in-breeding, crops tie part of a kin group to their growing place through the growing season. However, none of these are such a radical departure from managing clearings for lush vegetation and attracting game, moving across the landscape for different wild resources, being aware of the life cycles of wild plants and animals, or preserving stores for winter. This brings us to one of the big questions of archaeology – why did people stop hunting and gathering in favour of farming? The answer may be that for long periods people didn't, they continued to gather and hunt while incorporating small-scale agriculture into their lives for many generations before completely relying on it. The domestication of animals and plants may have been first perceived as better control of some wild resources. It is with their descendents, possibly grandchildren or great-grandchildren who were brought up living more and more closely with greater numbers of domesticates, that attitudes and values changed. Slowly, as distinctions came to be made between 'domestic' and 'wild' so greater importance was attached to land suitable for pasture and arable.

With these changes, people began to build large stone chambered tombs and long barrows across much of Britain. These were repositories for the bones of the dead and access was maintained so that the bones could be taken out for ceremonies and new individuals could be added. Most of the Peak District's burial monuments were built on the limestone plateau amongst areas which would have been suitable as upland grazing for livestock. They were impressive reference points in the landscape, built by shared labour to give a permanence and ancestral validity to their rights of access to the land. Conducting rites, which invoked the ancestors through the display of their bones, would reinforce a community's links with the land. The importance of fertility, of death and rebirth in the community were emphasised at these locations. Such ideas would not be new, gatherers and hunters are aware of fertility and wild reproductive cycles. However, domesticates require careful attention to ensure successful birth and germination too. This realisation led to stronger ideals about fertility, and the links between the productiveness of the community and its domesticates.

Such monuments would be most appropriate in places where different kin groups shared the same areas of land and so conflicts over access might be greatest. Their absence from the Upper Derwent suggests no such competing interests in an area which may, therefore, have been held by one kin or open to many without contention. If the flints indicate a resident population rather than people moving through the area, it is possible that at least some of the community made the journey to the limestone pastures to tend livestock every summer, meeting with others and sharing ideas. Some of the routes passed may have been in use for generations, taking people to sources of chert or areas providing different gathering and hunting opportunities. They may also have travelled further downstream to a particular cliff, now known as Gardom's Edge, overlooking the River Derwent. Here, archaeologists from the University of Sheffield and the Peak District National Park Authority have investigated a 650m long stone embankment which encloses the top of the edge. Charcoal samples are still to be dated, but the site appears to be a type of Neolithic causewayed enclosure found throughout much of Britain. If so, people from different kin groups from across the region perhaps might have gathered here occasionally to celebrate, tell stories, exchange gifts and negotiate conflicts of interest at a time when relations between groups were flexible and changing dramatically.

She would become an ancestor, their link to the land. Stones had been gathered from the river nearby to build the mound, gifts had been chosen and wood gathered for feasts. The signs were right, her journey into the ground could begin.

THREE

LIVING AND DYING IN LATER PREHISTORY

Digging pits

After a morning's bus journey from Sheffield, during which he watched the shadows of the clouds race across the ever-nearing moorland, the fieldwalker returned to one of his favourite locations. This was a spot he knew well from many visits, a narrow terrace which followed the contour of the valley side on the otherwise steep sloping shore of Howden Reservoir. Today he would start near to where the River Derwent and Linch Clough meet. It was a place which could be relied upon for finds of prehistoric flints or cherts, and conveniently the bus stopped immediately opposite. He walked back and forwards along the terrace, methodically going over the ground. As he stooped to pick up a likely stone he spotted something different, patches of tightly packed pink burnt stones and black charcoal amongst the yellow sands. He felt instinctively that they were old because they lay below where the topsoil would have been if the reservoir waters hadn't washed it away. They were very close to one of the occupation sites defined by large scatters of later Mesolithic to early Neolithic stone tools and production waste. Later he would return with archaeologists from the Peak District National Park Authority to excavate and find out what these features were before the rising waters of the reservoir swamped them again.

During excavation, the features proved to be the bottom 10-20cm of four circular pits, surviving in the heavy subsoil while the remainder had been eroded away by the reservoir water (**17** & **colour plate 7**). Dug into the clay and sand using wooden or stone hand tools, the strokes of the original excavator could be seen in a scalloped effect around the edge of one pit. They were then filled again not long after being dug with burnt stones, charcoal and the soil that had originally been taken out. Radiocarbon dating of the charcoal shows that this excavation and refilling of the pits took place during the middle of the third millennium BC, approximately 2500 BC, within the later Neolithic period.

The charred material was brought from fires situated elsewhere, probably nearby, after it had cooled and the sides of the pits were unscorched. All of the stones were river-worn gritstone cobbles that had been collected from the nearby rivers. The deliberate selection of cobbles and lack of other burnt plants or meat bones suggests that the pits were not simply receptacles for waste from general cooking fires or household hearths. Instead, the stones may have been deliberately heated to cook food in water-filled pots or pits, or to create steam from water-filled troughs in sweat lodges. The charcoal was from a mixed woodland dominated by oak, hazel, hawthorn and rowan with smaller quantities of ash, alder, birch, elm, willow/poplar and bird cherry. Whether the different amounts of each species reflect the actual mix of local trees or whether different species were selected deliberately is unknown. The pits and their associated fires may have been in a clearing, created on the level terrace with access to water below, and surrounded by the woodland that the charcoal came from.

The later Neolithic date of the pits shows for how long this location, with its finds of Mesolithic tools, was revisited and inhabited. Nor are they alone: similar

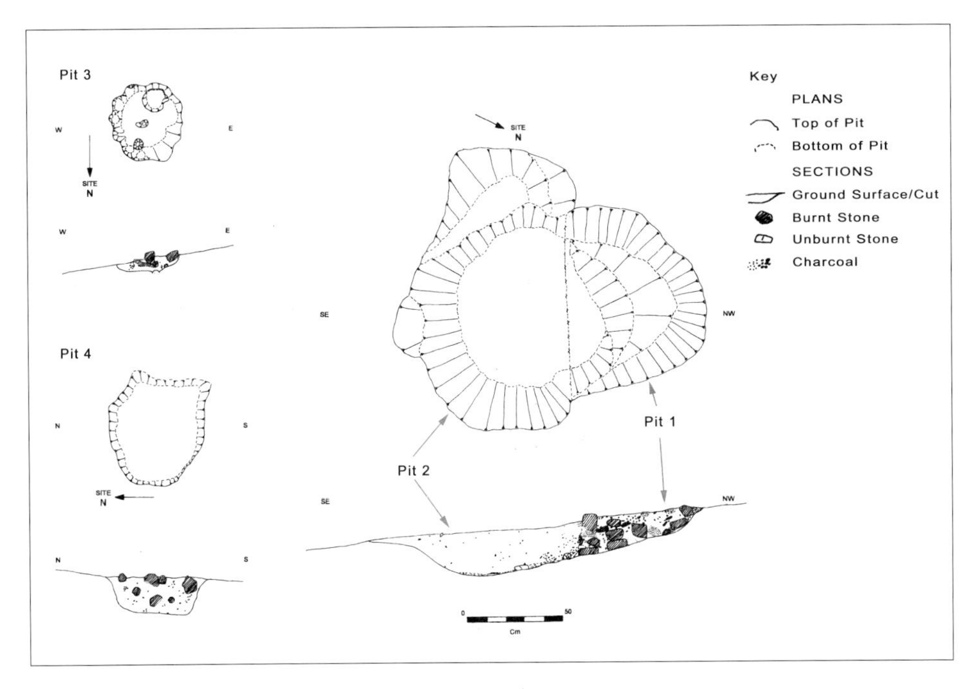

17 *Plan and section of later neolithic pits at Linch Clough*

patches of burnt stone and charcoal have been identified throughout the valley on the exposed reservoir floor and, crucially, many are found at the same confluences where the earlier flints and cherts are found. At two of these locations other structures were built about the same time or within a few hundred years of the pits – mounds of stone and earth in which the dead were buried. These are obviously locations that remained socially important for thousands of years.

Ancestral claims

Two burial mounds, or barrows, survive across the clough from the excavated pits (**18**). One mound is only 100m north of it, just below a terrace on which earlier flints and cherts have also been found (**colour plate 8**). Disturbance caused by water currents in the reservoir has exposed a straight alignment of stones and part of a stone burial chamber or cist deep within the barrow, within which pieces of cremated human bone are regularly washed out. The other is within a plantation woodland on the edge of another level terrace further uphill from the first and has a large hole into its centre, possibly excavated in more recent centuries by prospecting grave diggers or people constructing a kiln to dry wood for lead smelting. Both are on the apex of a sloping ridge created by the confluence between the River Derwent and Linch Clough. Standing on either mound you gain a fine view looking south over Howden Reservoir towards its

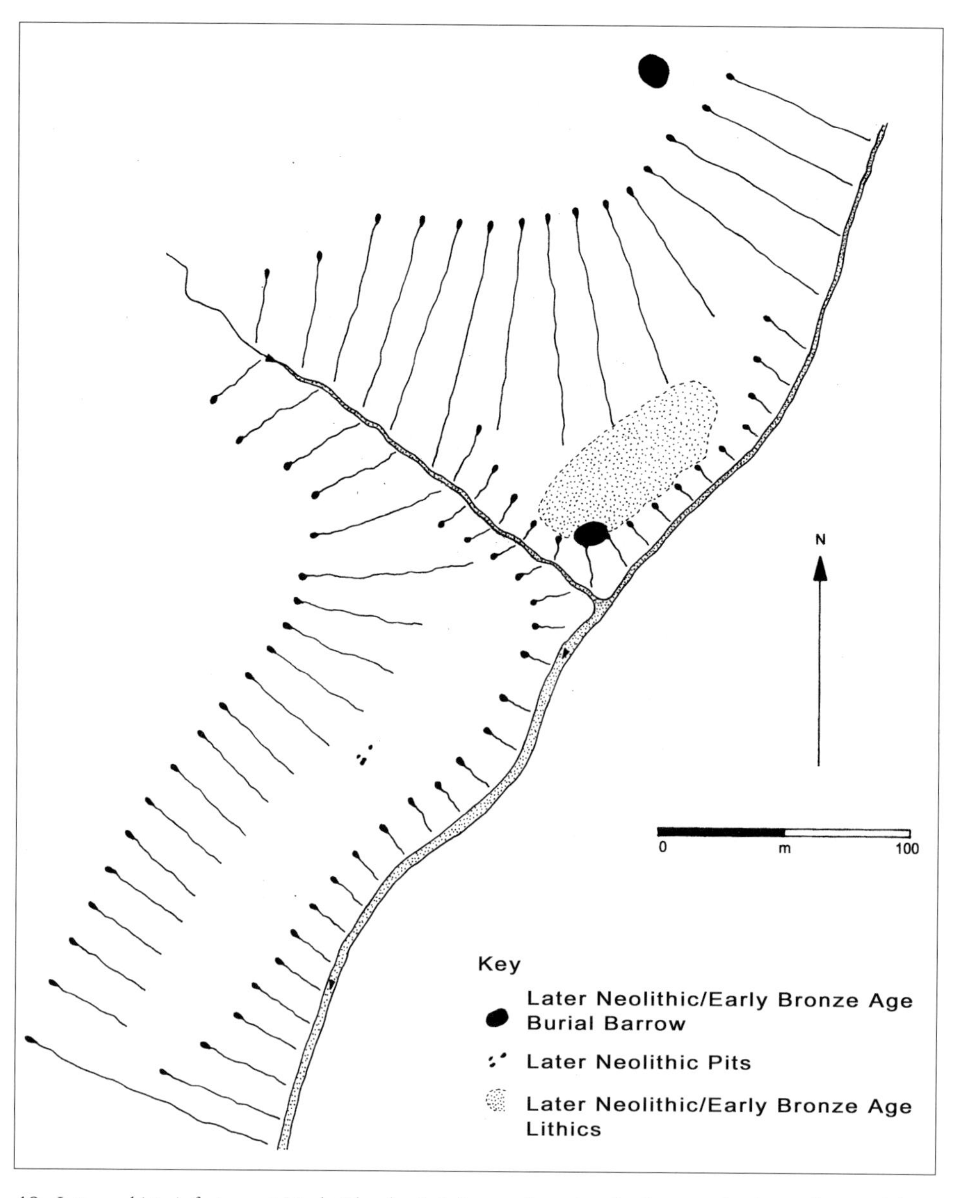

18 *Later prehistoric features at Linch Clough. Activity was focused on level terraces by the confluence of the clough and the River Derwent*

dam which blocks sight of the Derwent Valley lower down. While today the ridge is a prominent topographical feature when approaching it from the south, if the woodland was particularly dense in prehistory it would not have been so obvious.

Further south along the valley another barrow is close to the confluence between the River Derwent and Abbey Brook, this time in a location usually flooded under Derwent Reservoir (**19**). Again, this is near to, but not superim-

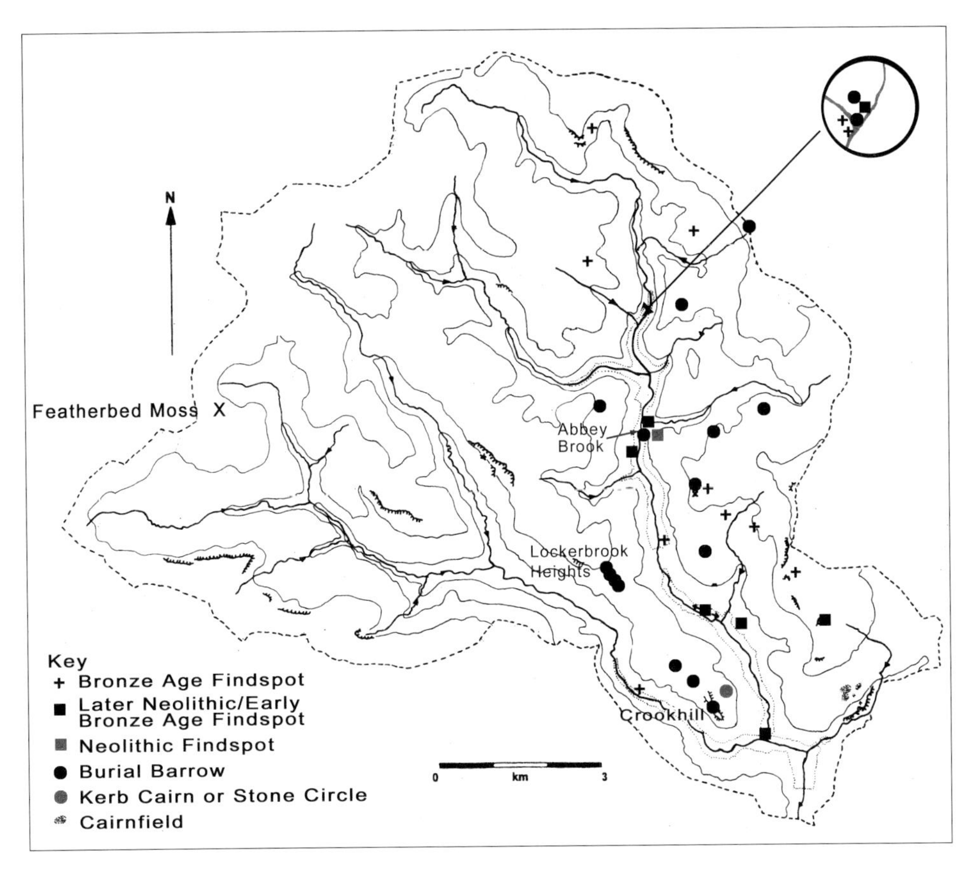

19 *Locations of later prehistoric features and findspots in the Upper Derwent*

posed over, one of the large scatters of earlier lithics. The mound itself is disturbed by water with stone spread outwards and burnt bone washed from a square stone cist. This barrow is located on the edge of one of the largest level areas in the valley, a significant terrace of light sands raised above the normal flood levels of the two watercourses. Relatively level land continues on three sides while the side overlooking the river itself sits above a steep drop. Its location is not very prominent unless you are very close to it, and its position would be visually lost if the forest was anything but a scatter of trees and scrub.

Do these three burial mounds suggest only a lightly wooded valley, or extensive grasslands as has been argued for the placement of barrows at prominent landmarks elsewhere, such as in the rolling downs near Stonehenge? Or were the barrows situated within a wooded valley landscape, possibly in clearings, where they would be hidden from distant view and known only to those who were already acquainted with the area?

John Barnatt has studied the distribution of the region's barrows. On the gritstone Eastern Moors to the south there are many barrows located on the edge of later prehistoric field systems and settlements (**20**). They tend to be small and, like those in the valley bottom of the Upper Derwent, they are usually not placed in highly prominent locations. On the whole, barrows contrast with the larger communal tombs of the earlier Neolithic. Barrows are generally smaller, more numerous, and the dead were buried in separate graves. This suggests a greater concern with the genealogies of individual families rather than the ancestors of wider communities. The Peak District barrows may have been important to the extended families who occupied the settlements, frequent reminders of earlier generations and their community's connections with the place to the living who went about their daily routines in their fields. The settlements consist of cairn-fields and small, irregular fields throughout which round building platforms are

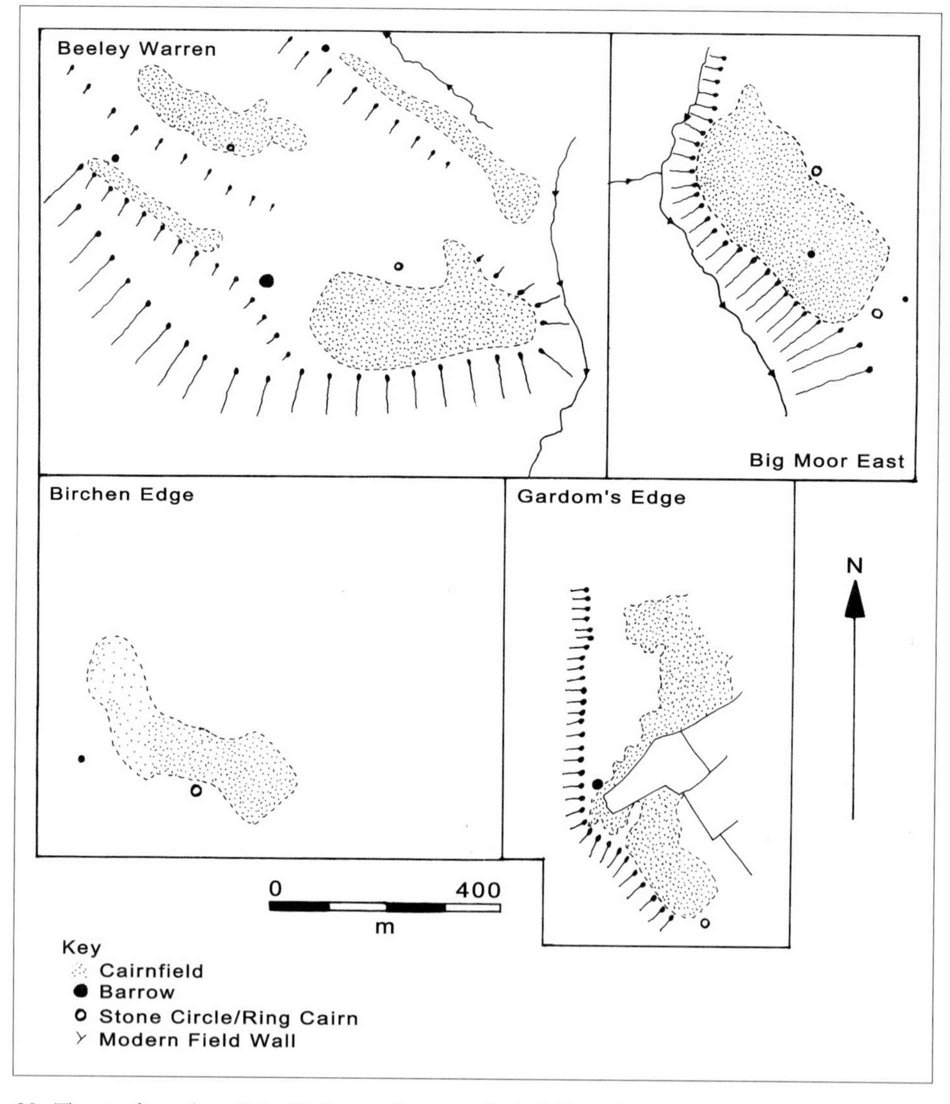

20 *There is often a close relationship between barrows and cairnfields on the Eastern Moors of the Peak District*

scattered. They mainly survive on lower terraces left relatively undisturbed from the early medieval period onwards as moorland common. Each is an island of enclosure and cultivation, separated by less hospitable land at high altitudes or covered in heavy soils that would have provided extensive unenclosed grazing. Evidence from radio-carbon dated charcoal, pollen and artefacts shows that the Eastern Moors were farmed from the early Bronze Age to the Iron Age but the longevity of any individual field system is unclear. Where buildings are excavated they are usually associated with pottery dating from the later Bronze Age and early Iron Age. Those situated in the most favourable locations probably endured for the longest time and the sites of many of these will have been lost to later farming.

Not every field system has barrows nearby and, as was found during excavation of piles of stone cleared from field plots at Eaglestone Flat, not all burials are placed in purpose-built mounds. Even on the limestone plateau, where relatively intensive and continuous farming since at least the early medieval period has removed many less substantial prehistoric features, many of the barrows lie adjacent to locations likely to have been settled in prehistory. The Upper Derwent's valley soils are a varied mix of heavy boulder clays and lighter sands, some originating from the underlying bedrock and others deposited from upstream and upslope by the action of water. Many of the more gently sloping valley sides and more level ground lower down would have been suitable for later prehistoric cultivation. Lines of test pits have been excavated above Gardom's Edge on the Eastern Moors to look for scatters of lithics and pottery. These have shown that later prehistoric artefacts are found closely associated with buildings with little being deposited across the wider landscape. Pottery is nearly impossible to identify from fieldwalking because of this restricted distribution and its very fragile nature means it does not survive for long once exposed to the elements. The terraces of light, sandy soils in the Upper Derwent would have been especially attractive to farmers, and those associated with burials were probably later prehistoric settlement locations. The wide, flat expanse at the confluence of the River Derwent and Abbey Brook was one favoured location and returned to again and again over time.

These are not the only barrows in the Upper Derwent. There are at least another sixteen, mainly located in prominent positions distributed across the high ground above the valleys (**19**). Most have been carefully placed on shoulders of land overlooking the major valleys. These shoulders form small blocks of moorland, separated by deep cloughs and backed by scarps or ridges. Lying 2km south-east of Abbey Brook is the peat-covered summit of Pike Low, a rounded shoulder of land perched above Derwent Valley. The deeply incised Millbrook cuts into the valley side to the east and rising ground lies to the north. It is separated from this by a lower-lying saddle. To get there from the valley you can take many routes, either traversing the steep valley side or taking advantage of slightly more gentle gradients above one of the cloughs. Here, a mound measuring 1.3m high and between 15-17m wide is built near the top of the summit at over 400m above sea level (**21**). In the immediate vicinity, any view of the barrow is blocked by the surrounding ground itself until you climb onto the summit. Moving away to nearby moorland and Derwent Edge, the summit is very prominent and the barrow is sometimes highlighted against the horizon, its profile rising above the gently sloping ground of the summit to draw your attention. From further afield the summit blends into the surrounding landscape and is difficult to pick out, unless standing to the south, whether in the valley, on the flat-topped ridge between the Rivers Derwent and Ashop or from nearly 5km away on the Winhill ridge beyond the Ashop Valley. From here, the summit is at the top of a large bluff of land framed by the dark recess of Millbrook to the right, and Derwent Valley to the left, though the barrow itself is too small to be seen.

Where visible to those moving around the landscape, the locations of Pike Low and of the other ridge-top barrows become exemplars of the wider landscape. The barrows imbue the landscape with ancestral significance. Again, extensive tree cover in the neighbouring valley blocks views of the uplands and the locations of these barrows, except from within clearings (**22**). Even where the tree cover gives way to open ground higher up, they are only visible when nearby and approaching from particular directions. As with the barrows placed in the valleys, their significance is signalled closer at hand to people who already know of the barrows' existence. I feel that their importance lies more in looking the other way round, in what can be seen from them, rather than where they themselves can be viewed. When standing by each barrow, the view is mainly restricted to the immediate Upper Derwent area, including valleys and surrounding plateaux (**23**). The moorland block occupied by the barrow, and all of its topographical boundaries, is visually encompassed. There are also some specific long-distance views, such as Pike Low where the limestone plateau is visible along the Derwent valley to the south. If the barrow builders had wanted the locations of their burials to be visible or give views across longer-distances, they could have placed them on prominent positions nearby. Derwent Edge and Whinstone Lee Tor, for example, are near to the valley and elevated above surrounding moorland. That they were not chosen demonstrates the deliberate and careful selection of these locally known places for burials. From the enactment of the funerary rite to the continuing presence of the barrows, the burials serve to draw this broader landscape into the ancestral past.

These locations are very different to those seen on the more hospitable parts of the Eastern Moors or limestone plateau, and the relationship between barrows and settlement is also likely to have been different. The ridge-top locations in the Upper Derwent would be suitable for hunting and pasture rather than settlement and arable. However, like those near to settlements on the Eastern Moors, they reinforce the feelings of attachment that the barrow builders held for this country rather than conveying messages across large distances from one kin group to another.

21 *Pike Low barrow was built to mark the dead as a prominent feature in the landscape between 2500 and 1500 BC. Barrows like this are placed where there are good views of the surrounding local landscape.* Photo by Ray Manley

22 *Pike Low seems like a prominent hill from open ground in the valley. When viewed from within woodland it almost disappears.* Photo by Bill Bevan

23 *Three views of the surrounding landscape from Pike Low prehistoric barrow. Views are restricted mostly to the adjacent moorland shelf except down the Derwent Valley to the south-east.* Photo by Bill Bevan

A more remote barrow is situated to the north at nearly 550m above sea level on Margery Hill, a high point on a major watershed which divides the Upper Derwent from the foothills and valleys to the east (**19**). Excavation by English Heritage revealed part of a stone cairn which was built over a mound of peat and enclosed within a stone kerb. The preserved remains of three birch trees were found in the top of the cairn, above which, a further peat mound has developed. Vast expanses of exposed moorland, broken only by the lines of watercourses cut into the peat, drop away from the hill in all directions. To walk from Pike Low to Margery Hill you need to pick your way between the cloughs and many watercourses by following known routes along flats and watersheds, perhaps taking four hours to complete the journey. A wrong turn can make the going even tougher by taking you across the watercourses or down the steep side of a clough. Following the watershed makes passage and navigation easier across these highlands and it probably formed part of a routeway during prehistory. Margery Hill is a prominent skyline feature for anyone on this route or the surrounding uplands.

This barrow was designed to be seen by people moving across the landscape, maybe placed to identify traditional claims to hunting grounds or seasonal pastures. This is an interpretation put forward by John Barnatt for the large barrows found on high watersheds and remoter areas in the Peak District. These were places which may have been shared pastures for surrounding settlements at lower altitudes. Where land is not settled as such, there is the threat of conflicts of interest over access, and placing your dead in barrows is a way of staking a claim to the land for your kin through connections of genealogy. As with Margery Hill, both the barrows and their promontories are highly visible over long distances.

Living settlements

The most visually striking geological feature in the Upper Derwent is Crookhill, a pair of distinctive gritstone crags which rise above the southern end of the flat-topped ridge that separates the Derwent and Ashop Valleys just before the two rivers converge (**colour plate 5**). They are not visible over long-distances but in the near vicinity their distinctive topography attracts your attention. The gently sloping land which lies below the crags is no higher than 350m above sea level. It comprises light, sandy soils which are significantly free of peat and it has been a known focus of settlement and cultivation since the medieval period when Welbeck Abbey founded a grange here. Since this time, land-use has comprised of walled pastures and small cultivated plots more typical of the valleys below than the surrounding high ground. Prehistoric activity is betrayed by the survival of two barrows (one placed on the saddle of ground between the two crags), a kerb cairn, three other possible barrows and a small group of clearance cairns. The kerb cairn is 6m in diameter and made of four standing stones, though originally it probably contained five or six evenly spaced uprights, forming a kerb around the circumference of a barrow. Comparable stone settings with internal mounds or platforms are found at stone circles on Moscar and Totley Moors and at Doll Tor on Stanton Moor. Small stone circles in the Peak District are roughly contemporary with burial barrows and are found in similar proximities to settlements, suggesting they were also the ceremonial places of extended families. The barrows and kerb cairn on Crookhill form the densest concentration of ceremonial monuments in the Upper Derwent. Their presence could be associated with the prominent landscape markers provided by the crags which themselves look like huge burial mounds. But there is another possibility, that this area was occupied by later prehistoric settlements and fields which have since been swept away by later farming.

Just such an area of fields survives approximately 2km east of Crookhill on the gently sloping south-east facing side of Derwent Moor. The two areas are not visible from each other and are separated by the Derwent, which forms some of the steepest sides to the valley where it is joined by Ladybower Gorge from the east. Here is a cairnfield at an altitude between 300-330m above sea level on ground typical of later prehistoric settlements on the Eastern Moors (**19** & **24**). Hidden amongst the heather are stone cairns, linear stone heaps, an earthen lynchet and possible building platforms covering an extensive area. The cairns and heaps were created from extensive stone clearance before and during cultivation or improvement of pasture. The date for this particular cairnfield is unknown, however, its similarity to those further south on the Eastern Moors suggests it is broadly contemporary. No burial barrows are obvious amongst its cairns so maybe it was created later, in the later Bronze Age or Iron Age when a direct connection between settlements and barrows was lost. Light, but stony, brown earths were found here in prehistory, before soil deterioration took place. The linear clearance comprises three low banks of stone which were most likely created by throwing stones cleared from the ground against field boundaries. Two of these banks appear to form two sides of a rectangular field. The boundaries themselves are now no longer visible, probably because they were fences or hedges and their lines tend to only be identified where these linear clearance heaps have been formed against them.

While the cairnfield is similar to others on the Eastern Moors, the nature of settlement is very different to Mam Tor, situated only 5km to the south-west. Mam Tor is an impressive bank and ditch hilltop enclosure, traditionally referred to as a hillfort (**25**). It is built on a prominent hill at the northern end of the limestone plateau and overlooking the Hope and Edale valleys. Within its boundary are numerous round house platforms, a spring and two later Neolithic/early Bronze Age burial barrows. Limited excavations by the University of Manchester on platforms and the ramparts suggest the cairnfield was occupied during the later Bronze Age to early Iron Age. This means that it

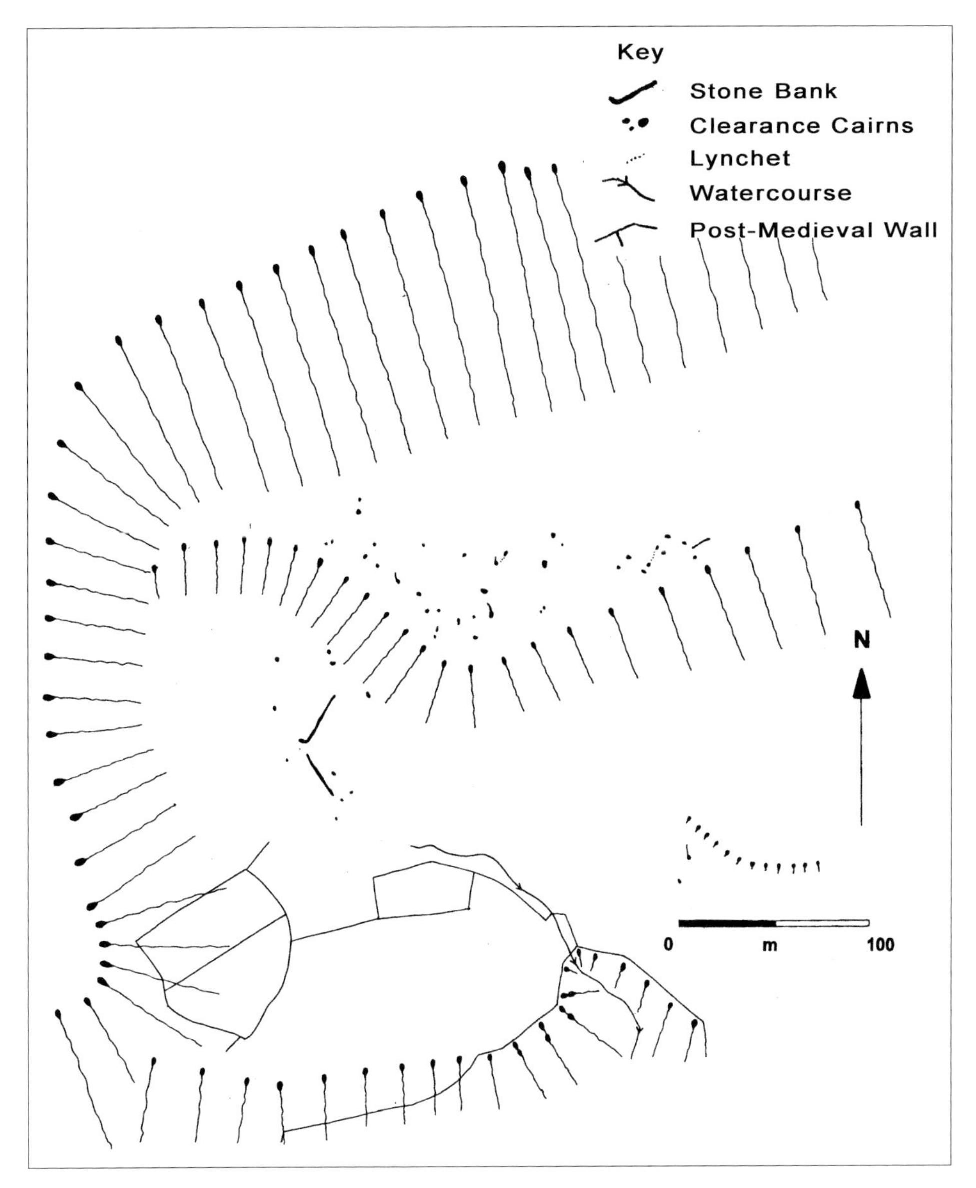

24 *Derwent cairnfield is situated on gently sloping moorland 300m above sea level. It is similar to later prehistoric field systems found across the Eastern Moors of the Peak District*

is contemporary with some of the Eastern Moors fields and possibly the Derwent Moor cairnfield. In contrast to the scattered nature of their settlements, Mam Tor contains a high-density of houses in one location, occupied by people who farmed the surrounding landscape. Without knowing more about the chronology of the platforms, we cannot tell if there was a large, contemporary nucleated settlement, or whether the total number of buildings was an aggregation over time of much smaller populations repeatedly returning to the

25 *The prominent hill-top of Mam Tor was settled and enclosed in later prehistory. Mam Tor is only 5km south-west of the Upper Derwent and can be seen from Derwent Edge. It is likely that the occupants of both would have been in social contact.* Photo by Ray Manley

enclosure. The earthworks would symbolise their community identity, both in the shared labour required for construction and in being visible for miles around. Mam Tor is visible from Derwent Edge, and anyone tending their herds or hunting along this scarp would have seen the impressive hill (**colour plate 6**). The ramparts would also form a deterrent to potential conflict at a time when aggression was small-scale and may have been related to rights regarding land, livestock and kin. The frequency of the unenclosed settlements shows that violent disagreement was unlikely to be common.

What of the lithics that we made so much of for earlier periods? Surely these also show us where later prehistoric settlements and activities took place (**19**). The first obvious thing is how numbers of finds on the higher ground drop significantly over time when compared to the Mesolithic and early Neolithic. Again, the majority of findspots are where a single flint tool was lost while someone was working or passing by: an arrowhead fired while hunting, a scraper dropped while working leather, a knife discarded upon breaking. There are also one or two more unusual finds of stone and bronze axes, tools for working wood and chopping trees as well as items of show and display. Only occasionally are tools found with waste flakes from their manufacture, a common occurrence in the Mesolithic and early Neolithic where small groups of implements and waste flakes are found across the uplands and within the valleys. However, in the valleys there are larger congregations of tools that suggest sites of relatively intense landscape occupation in later prehistory. A series of large assemblages are found along a 900m stretch of the eastern bank of the River Derwent, north of where it is joined by Millbrook. They comprise mostly later Neolithic to early Bronze Age material. In many ways it is difficult to say with certainty whether these represent the locations of buildings, of fields cleared within the surrounding woodlands or of other activities conducted in more remote places. Two scatters which are more likely to represent settlements occur near to the valley bottom burial barrows at Abbey Brook and Linch Clough. The range of implements is almost identical at each – scrapers, awls, knives and plano-convex knives.

The topographical location of Derwent cairnfield is typical of those elsewhere on the Eastern Moors and little different from other areas in the Upper Derwent which have been subject to later farming. It is likely, therefore, that these other areas, such as Crookhill, and suitable land in the valleys, as at Abbey Brook, were settled and cultivated during later prehistory. The fields would have been worked by hand, using wooden ards and spades rather than ploughs pulled by horse or oxen. Farming was probably a mix of small amounts of arable cultivation for family consumption and livestock that would have been grazed both within the fields and in the extensive open land above. Prehistoric buildings were probably scattered amongst the fields as elsewhere on the Eastern Moors. These areas would have been isolated clearings within the otherwise extensive valley woodlands and, therefore, the barrows in the valley bottoms would have been in clearings rather than deep in the forest.

People living in the Upper Derwent during later prehistory were living in a region where some neighbouring communities lived in houses scattered amongst fields and others lived in enclosed nucleations of houses, as at Mam Tor. It may be that these contrasts are a result of varying occupation strategies by different communities related to topography, political leadership or social identity. There must have been social contact between people living in different settlements. While we cannot be sure how this contact took place, we can imagine that gifts and livestock were exchanged, large gatherings held, and individuals married into other communities to cement wider ties of kin. Occupants of the Upper Derwent looking up at Mam Tor may have perceived them as odd for their choice of lifestyle, or recognised them as some form of regional social power. We will return to discuss the changing nature of interaction between communities in the Upper Derwent and elsewhere in the region in following chapters.

The sun rose higher to chase the shadows from the valley. Walls are buried in soil turned downslope by the plough over generations, though this year it is the turn of the cattle to graze the fields. They prepared to eat and sharpened tools, bemoaning the corn they would have to deliver to the Roman tax collector at Navio.

FOUR

FROM ROMANS TO NORMANS

Navigating the Romans

The navvies who built the Derwent and Howden Dams in the early twentieth century are not only part of the history of the area, they have also helped to tell the story of earlier periods. One group of workmen building the road along the valley side near to Howden Dam unearthed two complete Romano-British corn-grinding querns and fragments from five others in close proximity to each other. They had found tools of everyday living that were most likely from the site of a settlement. This was the earliest discovery of a Romano-British community in the valley. Another gang excavating the foundations for Derwent Dam on the 26 September 1905 discovered a strange lozenge-shaped sandstone block. Regular-shaped hollows, two discs, two rings and two bars or ingots, were pecked into one side of the stone. Its antiquity, strangeness and charm were recognised straight away and after its salvage it was displayed in the Derwent Valley Water Board's offices at Bamford Filters where its use and date were sometimes mused upon. It passed with the rest of the DVWB to Severn Trent Water Board after nationalisation of the utilities in the 1970s then to Severn Trent plc after privatisation in the 1980s. As the filters became surplus to requirements it turned into more of a nuisance than an intrigue and was stored away. In the 1990s, Julian Parsons, the then curator of Sheffield City Museum, looked at it and realised what it was – a mould for casting metal objects typical of Iron Age/Romano-British date. In 1996 it entered the archaeological literature as the subject of an article in the Derbyshire Archaeological Journal.

Roman rule

In archaeological and historical terms the Iron Age – prehistory – is only divided from the Romano-British period – history – by the Roman conquest of Britain. This Conquest not only brought dramatic changes to the landscape and to the social contexts in which people lived their lives. It has also become the landmark event with which the school history curriculum in England usually begins, so erroneously reducing thousands of years of pre-Roman history to a footnote. Roman occupation in itself would have been a major event in the lives of many people, but initially much of this may have been at something of a distance as news travelled about the arrival of people who fought, dressed, ate and spoke differently.

People living in the immediate vicinities of forts and roads, or under those leaders who raised armed resistance to the invaders felt the arrival of Roman rule most acutely. In most areas of Britain, major changes to the nature of indigenous settlement or the wider landscape by Roman rule was not immediate. We see a greater impact in the second and third centuries AD when there was a more widespread change in houses and objects. More people chose to live in rectangular buildings rather than roundhouses and wheel-turned pottery became important as a material for household vessels. These were not simply technical innovations welcomed by societies who had previously been unable to make them. These were new ways of living which were adopted by the descendents of those who had first encountered the Romans, the children and grandchildren who had grown up with Roman rule rather than experiencing its arrival.

Rome divided the Empire into local governments known as *civitates*. Different approaches were used in reaction to the local circumstances of resistance or acceptance to Roman rule but, on the whole, Rome preferred to adapt what was already in place through creating *civitates* along tribal lines rather than enforce the reorganisation and relocation of populations. In some places they also created new towns, or *colonia*, of retired soldiers to help populate areas. Veterans could be granted land in the countryside too, as shown by a surviving bronze plaque granting a retired soldier an estate at Stannington, only 3km to the east of the Upper Derwent. Whether native or Roman, the governing *civitas* council comprised the local landowning aristocracy.

When they came into contact with Rome some leaders felt they would increase their local power and influence through the personal wealth and status which could be obtained from Imperial officials in return for service. Others resisted Roman rule and in some societies power struggles developed around differing ideological responses to Rome. With no major resistance to the Roman army evident in the north Midlands during the first century AD it is likely that the existing social order was co-opted with existing leaders becoming local councillors. It is unknown which *civitas* the Peak District lay within. To the south and east was the *civitas* of the *Corieltauvi* with the capital at *Ratae* (Leicester) while to the north were the *Brigantes* with the capital at *Isurium* (Aldborough, North Yorkshire). The Peak District may have been within either or another, though unrecorded, *civitates* with a political centre closer to the region.

Major transformations to people's lives were brought about by the Roman introduction of the market economy, urbanisation and the increasing numbers of people in Britain who were working in non-food-growing occupations. Iron Age and Romano-British tribes were bound together through extended kinship groups or by allegiance of non-kin through complex social relations which were encouraged by displays of wealth, tribute and force. Allegiances to others were partly reinforced through blood ties and exchange. Market economics became another way through which people could develop relations with each other. Coinage and local market centres were introduced to many areas of the islands for the first time. Early in the period, the low numbers and high values of coins suggests they were mainly used in taxation, paying officials or soldiers, for transactions between merchants and within Roman circles. It is not until the third century AD that the presence of lower denominations and greater quantities of coins, including forgeries, indicates their use in more everyday situations.

Increased demands for agricultural produce arose to feed Roman officials and other people working in trades which maintained the Empire. Taxes replaced

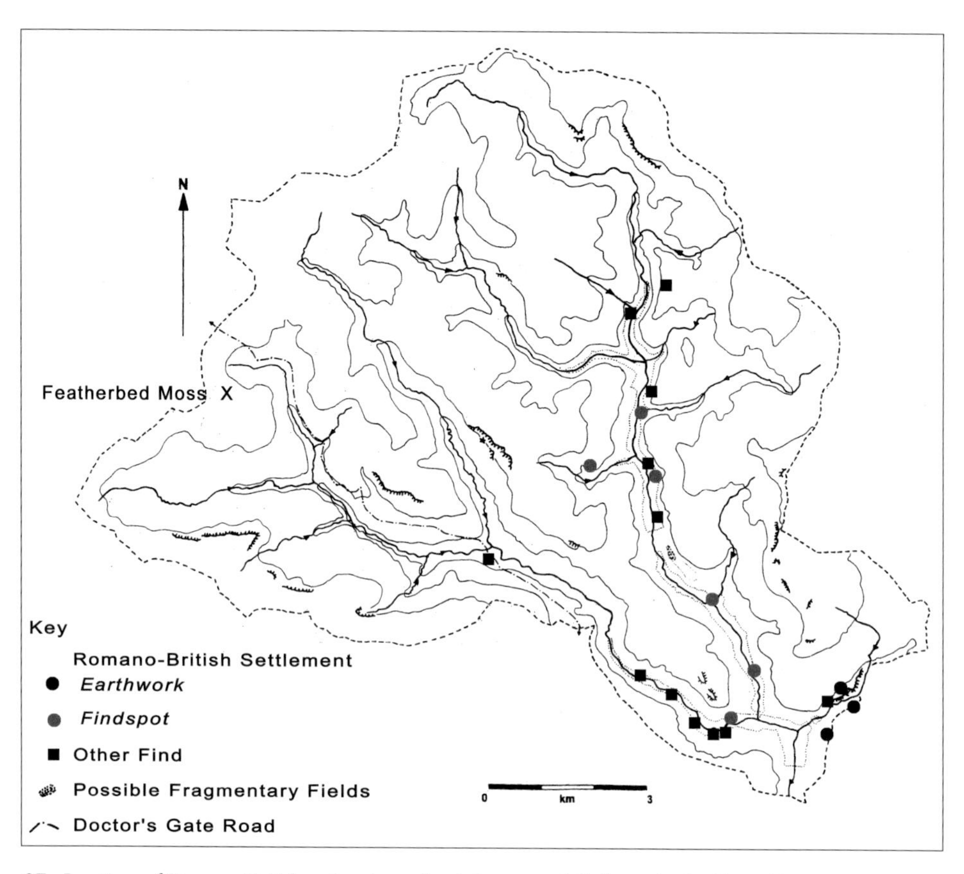

27 *Locations of Romano-British and early medieval features and findspots in the Upper Derwent*

social obligation as the method of collecting wealth from the land, either as produce or more likely as coinage. The impact of taxation may be seen in the quote attributed to Boudica, that it is much better to be slain than to go about with a tax on our heads. Markets became important places where agricultural goods could be sold, where people could meet and exchange news, and where they could acquire new types and forms of material possessions. Goods were imported from across the Empire and through their ownership people could maintain or enhance social positions. Markets and consumer objects were the means through which someone living in a place like the Upper Derwent could interact with Rome.

Settling and cultivating the land

Three small settlements sit high up above the valley on the edge of the Upper Derwent. Each comprises a series of two or three small, irregular enclosures bounded within dry-stone walls (**27**). Two of these are located on narrow

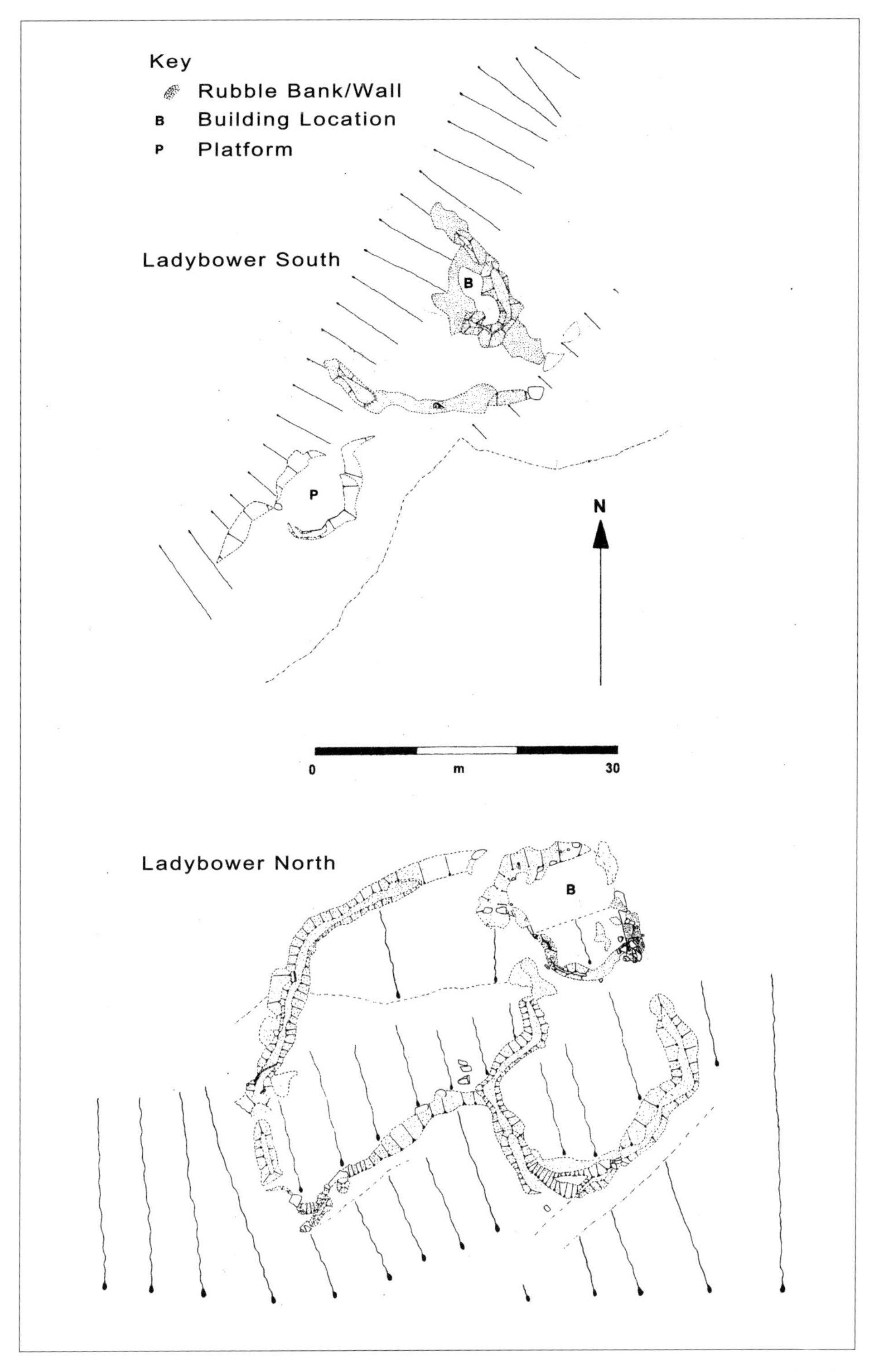

28 *Romano-British settlements above Ladybower Gorge survive as stone walls and rubble banks which define small enclosures*

terraces of level ground which face each other across Ladybower Gorge (**28**). This is more than coincidence – the settlements were positioned by people who wanted to be able to see each other. No other boundaries are visible to divide the surrounding land into fields suggesting that they occupied an unenclosed landscape and that whoever dwelt there did not grow crops. Each was built at the transition between the valley and the uplands, possibly where woodland on the steep valley-sides below gave way to peat-covered undulating moorland above. They are links between topographies, movement between landscapes apparent in their stations. The people who lived within these settlements may have been pastoralists who made their livings solely by raising sheep or cattle. More likely is that they lived here while tending livestock pastured on the extensive grazing of coarse grasses and heather. Cattle and sheep required close attention by day and corralling by night if they were to be protected from predators such as wolves and bears. While here, they would also have used the other resources afforded by the moors - stone, peat, bracken and game all being close by. In this interpretation, they were part-time occupants who shared their time between these and other houses elsewhere.

Romano-British pottery has been found elsewhere in the Upper Derwent, in small quantities at thirteen locations in the valley where the reservoirs again allow artefacts to be collected from eroded soils (**27**). Most are just a small handful of sherds lying in proximity to each other, traces where someone dropped a vessel or deposited the remains of an earlier breakage elsewhere. At six of the locations numbers of sherds are higher and may represent the locations of settlements or middens. These scatters are located near to the confluences of the River Derwent and six of its tributary streams. Spindle whorls for spinning wool, quern stones for grinding corn and fragments of first to second century AD glass vessels have also been found amongst the scatters. One of these locations is the same large area of flat land between Abbey Brook and the River Derwent where previous generations had made flint tools or buried the dead. Another location in the Woodlands Valley, where pottery, glass and a brooch have also been found, occupies an oval platform terraced into the valley-side and is likely to be the site of a building. These may be the other houses where the occupants of the settlements above the valleys also lived, moving between fields and open pastures with the seasons and their livestock. Some of the patterns of land-use seen in the millennia before were being reworked during the Roman period, perhaps by the descendants of those who lived here generations before, and all but one site were to be later re-occupied in the thirteenth century AD.

All of the pottery dates to between the second and fourth centuries AD. Most is a distinctive type known as Derbyshire Ware which was used to make jars, bowls and dishes – vessels used for storage and at the table. They were produced in the middle and south of the county, and large kilns have been excavated at Derby and Chesterfield. Their sherds are commonplace at rural settlements, towns and forts throughout Derbyshire, Nottinghamshire and South Yorkshire. This does not indicate the date these settlements were founded but the years when the pottery was produced and used by households. The environmental evidence for the Upper Derwent at this time does not show a dramatic decrease in tree cover that would accompany colonists. Instead, levels of woodland and open ground remained constant from the Iron Age until the eleventh century AD. This implies the presence of similar population levels throughout. What presence of pottery in the Upper Derwent may indicate is the increasing interaction of the occupants of the valley with the social and political context of this region through the markets they visited to sell agricultural produce and buy these ceramic vessels.

Further afield

If the Upper Derwent valleys had not been improved from the medieval period onwards or later flooded, we might have seen more settlements and fields surviving as earthworks similar to those found elsewhere in the Peak District. Numerous sites survive across the region, most occupying patches of land which have proved too rocky or impractical to cultivate since the Roman period (**29**). They vary greatly, from isolated buildings enclosed within palisades or earthen banks to individual houses dispersed amongst fields and small hamlets clustered within yards with fields located nearby (**30**). At some of the hamlets timber-built round, oval and rectangular buildings nestle side by side. These may not all be contemporary, but the result of a great time-depth of settlement where different types of houses were built over hundreds of years. Round houses were the ubiquitous accommodation of prehistoric Britain but after contact with Rome, oval and rectangular houses were also built. Both had double rows of timber posts to support the roof and often consisted of one, large room inside as most round houses had done. At Roystone Grange, Richard Hodges' excavations discovered oval houses that were built in the second century AD. Some rectangular buildings were divided into smaller rooms. The affluent and those with pretensions to Roman society incorporated painted plaster, bath houses, mosaic floors, underfloor heating, glazed windows and tiled roofs. Such grander houses have been excavated at Carsington and Haybrook, just to the south of the Peak District. The adoption of rectangular buildings and private rooms indicates changing attitudes to domestic architecture over time by people growing up within a world dominated by Roman rule. Where round houses continued to be built and occupied, we can see resistance by local communities to the new ideas and materials they encountered.

Fields are usually rectangular and where slopes are steep, they betray their arable use where ploughs have moved soil down slopes to form large lynchets along field boundaries. Deep Dale near Taddington is typical of dispersed settlement where buildings are found within small enclosures in the corners of large, rectangular fields which run up either side of the dale. This contrasts with Chee

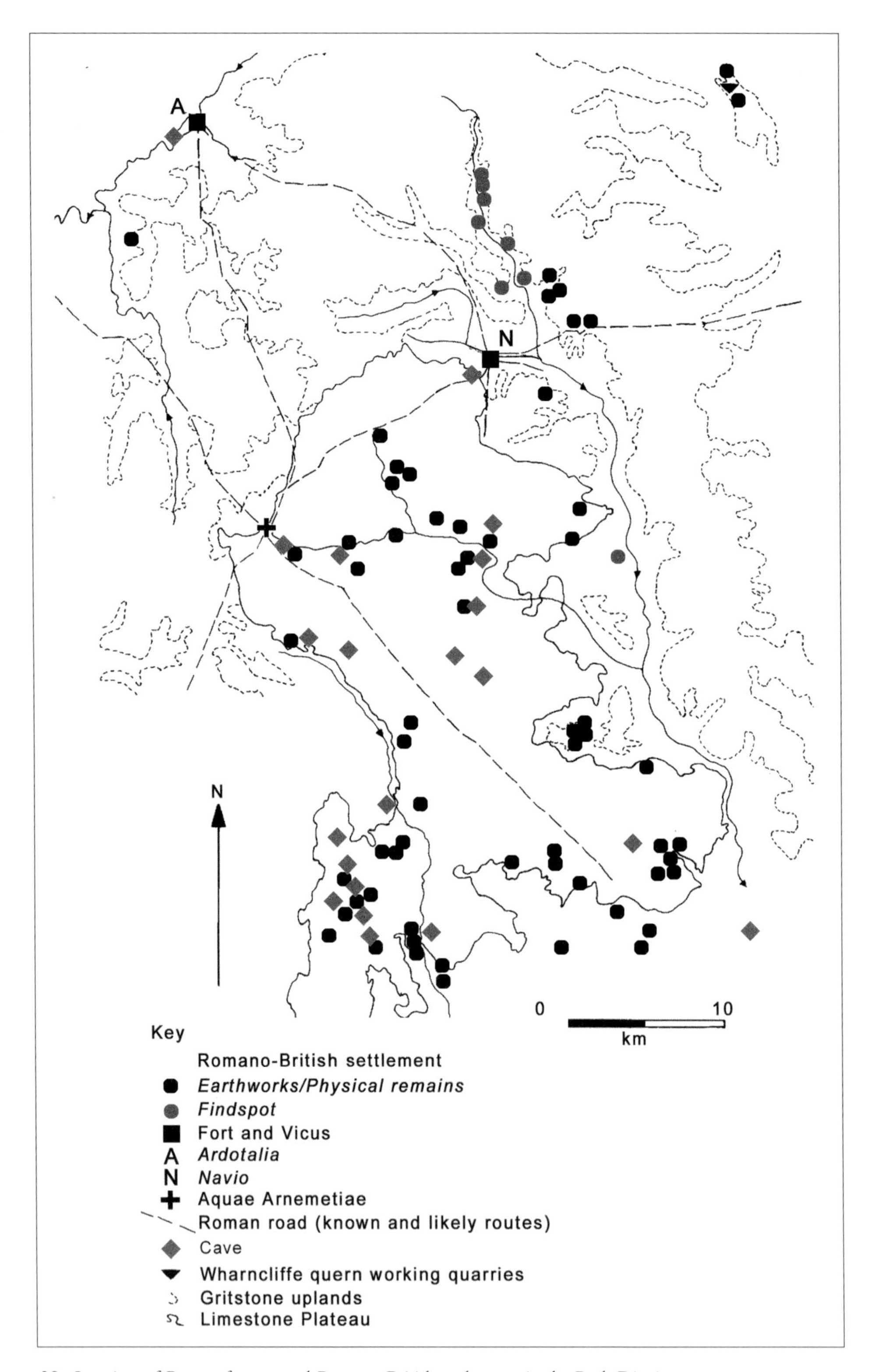

29 *Locations of Roman features and Romano-British settlements in the Peak District*

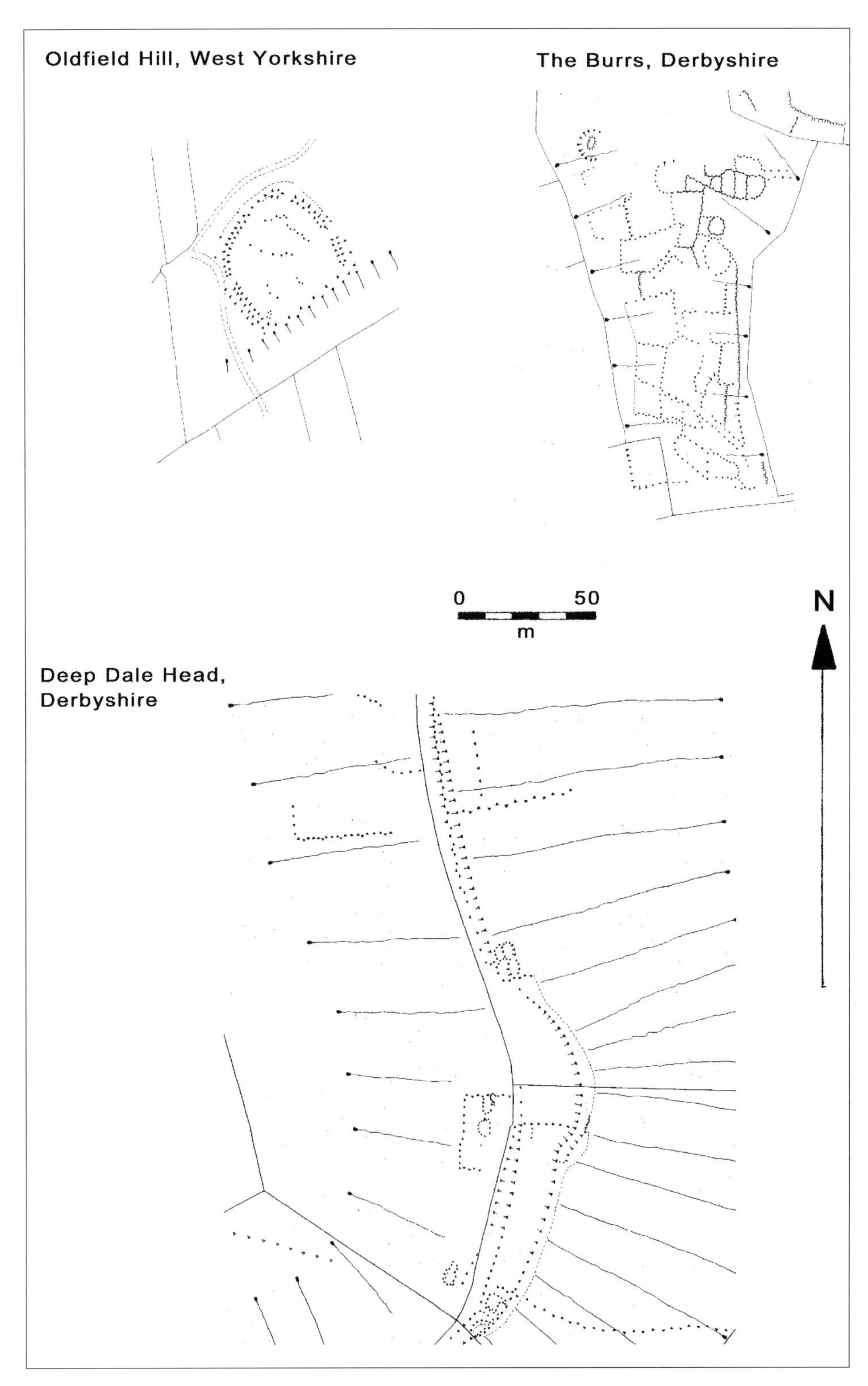
Oldfield Hill, West Yorkshire
The Burrs, Derbyshire
0
50
m
N
Deep Dale Head,
Derbyshire

31 *The valley sides of the Upper Derwent may have been enclosed with small, rectilinear fields like these at the Romano-British settlement of Chee Tor on the Limestone Plateau.* Photo by Ray Manley

Tor at Blackwell where a hamlet of rectangular buildings is clustered on a rocky promontory within small yards separated by stone and earth walls. Some of the square fields of the hamlet survive a short distance away as substantial lynchets on a steep valley side (**31**).

Earthwork sites similar to those in the Peak District have also been found further north in Pennine valleys such as Swaledale and Wharfedale. In Derbyshire, south of the Peak District, field boundaries are preserved not as earthworks but as deep ditches and other features cut into the ground which have been plotted from cropmarks. Cropmarks have also been identified in south and west Yorkshire and in north Nottinghamshire, where a brick-work pattern of fields dominate the Romano-British landscape.

The closest surviving Romano-British hamlet to the Upper Derwent is the Warren, near to North Lees, which occupies a tributary valley of the Derwent only 5km to the south (**29**). Rectangular buildings lie within a series of terraces carved out of a gritstone outcrop which descends a shallow slope. Many of the terraces are revetted with massive gritstone boulders and lie between patches of uncleared, stony ground. One enclosure stands out from the others. A substantial wall encloses a large, level circular area which probably accommodated a substantial round house. This may be the dwelling of the head of the hamlet. Traces of the boundaries of fields survive as low earthen lynchets in improved pasture adjacent to the outcrop. It is likely that people living in the Upper Derwent had contact with those from the Warren, perhaps while visiting the same market or sharing high pasture grounds. There may have been other settlements elsewhere in the vicinity of the Upper Derwent – there is a possible house near Mam Tor, a quern has been found north of the Hope Valley, and a Roman Diploma records the granting of land to an army veteran at Stannington, near Sheffield.

Settlements in the Upper Derwent are likely to have been isolated farmsteads with fields, separated from each other by woodland. As well as those sites discovered in the reservoirs, there are other favoured locations hidden from the fieldwalker such as Crookhill and gentle valley side slopes which may have been occupied. Again we are confronted by the enclosed pasture fields of more modern farms which hide much evidence below improved, permanent turf. The querns discovered by the road-building navvies near to Howden Dam were found in just such a place. Some dry-stone field walls of these pastures lying on gentler slopes to the north of Millbrook follow or cross large earthen lynchets forming rectangular enclosures similar to those seen in Romano-British fields elsewhere.

Back to the Romans

But what of that popular symbol of Rome, the well-drilled army which dominated its provinces from within imposing forts? The army probably first entered the Peak District around the beginning of Agricola's push north into land associated with a group of people known to the Romans as the *Brigantes* in the late 70s AD. The Romans had moved north up either side of the southern Pennines in the 50s AD, building forts at sites now known as Derby, Chesterfield, Rotherham and Trent Vale near Stoke-on-Trent. Forts were the command centres for the army as they entered new lands and made contact with the peoples who occupied them. They not only provided safe, defendable, bases for soldiers and administrators but were physical statements about the power and intent of Rome. By the 80s AD they had built forts at *Navio* near Brough in the Hope Valley, at *Ardotalia* near Glossop and possibly at Buxton where a spa town called *Aquae Arnemetiae* later became established (**29**). A thriving civilian settlement, known as a *vicus*, quickly developed adjacent to each fort for civilian camp followers and locals who saw the opportunities in providing services and amenities to the garrisons. *Navio* was briefly abandoned in the middle of the following century as the frontier was pushed north to the River Tyne but it was re-occupied around AD 158 as the result of an uprising against Roman rule to the north (**32**). Romans were not likely to maintain the expense of garrisoning a fort unless there was good reason. Its proximity to an access route, via Bradwell Dale, to the northern part of the lead ore field on the limestone plateau has been put forward as such a reason. It is located on the southern bank of the River Noe, so any perceived threat is likely to have been from the north.

Navio is little more than 3km away from the Upper Derwent and surely would have indirectly influenced the lives of those living in the valley. They would have been well aware of the fort and its *vicus*, where large numbers of people were concentrated in a small space and would require such local produce as grain and meat they had no time to farm themselves. Some enterprising local people may have moved there to make something of the new opportunities afforded by the presence of the Roman officials. The army and civilians based at the fort may have carried out administrative tasks for the Empire, travelling to the surrounding areas to collect taxes or impose the rule of law.

The forts and new towns were linked by a network of imperial roads (**29**). These Roman roads do not represent the full extent of communication routes in the Roman period but those which were deliberately planned and laid out by the Romans as instruments of imperial rule. They enabled soldiers, officials, goods and information to be transported quickly over long distances between important locations such as towns and forts. Roads were also another important symbol of Roman control over a province. Their construction would have caused major disruption to the lives of people living along either side of their course. When a route was decided upon, the ground had to be surveyed, cleared and made ready for the road constructors, with or without the agreement of the local population. The levelling or separating of settlements, fields and other important social or religious sites along and to either side of the routes would have had a major impact on the everyday lives of local communities, their perception of the world and of the Roman occupiers. Later, when a road was established, nearby communities may have been able to take opportunities for trade or provisioning travellers.

A route between *Navio* (Brough) and *Ardotalia* (Glossop) forts reputedly left *Navio's* northern gate to enter Edale, cross over the ridge into the Woodlands Valley and pass over the Snake Pass before it descended into Glossop. A series of hollow-ways, terraced trackways and, on Alport Moor, a section pitched in stone and flanked either side by narrow drains supposedly preserves the line of this road (**33**). Known as Doctor's Gate the route was a packhorse trail from the medieval period onwards but whether this did indeed follow the line of a Roman road is far from certain. There is no evidence to date this trackway to the Roman period beyond that it is a line which connects the two forts via the most direct route. If it is Roman then this routeway is the most direct influence the Romans had on the landscape of the Upper Derwent.

Classic endings

Excavations at Roystone Grange, in a remote valley in the south of the Peak District, have provided evidence which shows something of how the end of Roman rule influenced changes to the landscape. Towards the end of the Roman

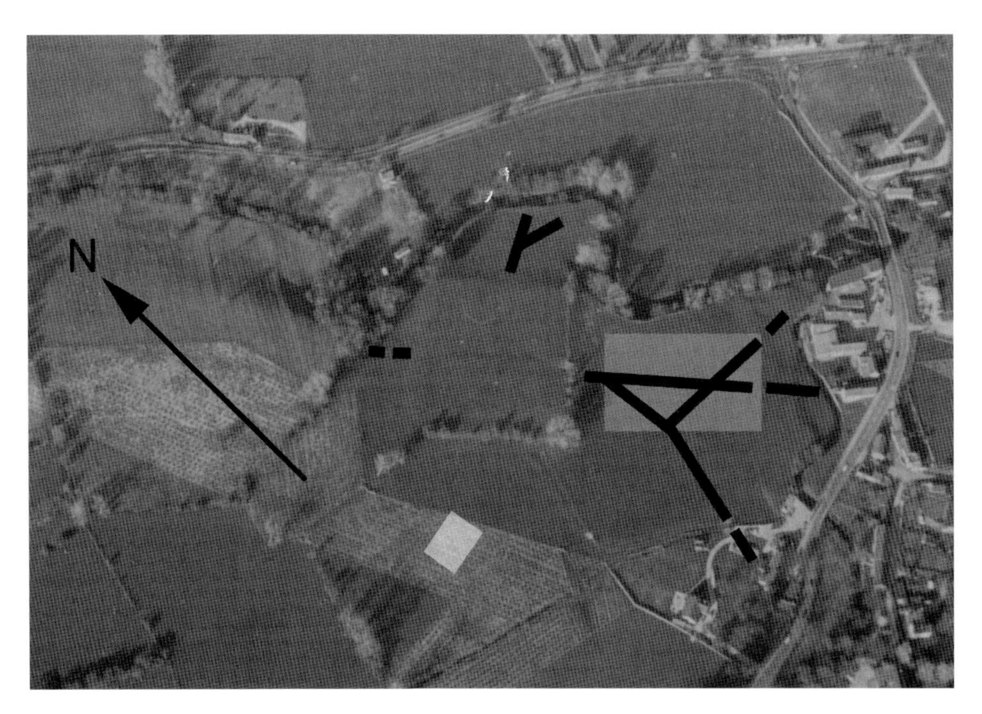

32 *The Roman fort of* Navio *in the Hope Valley was only 4km south of the Upper Derwent. It was a regional symbol of Roman rule and the adjacent vicus would have been an important local market for exchanging goods. Dark grey shading indicates the extent of excavated vicus buildings, black indicates roads and light grey shows unexcavated early vicus.* Photo by Ray Manley

period this settlement appears to contract, to become poorer in terms of material culture, and then is abandoned. This decline in rural prosperity and reduction in the intensity of farming occurs in many places in Britannia during the early fifth century AD. This could be the result of a collapse of the market economy and political upheavals caused by the retreat of the Romans. Interpreting changing use of the landscape after the Romans withdrew their Legions is made all the more difficult by the almost total collapse of pottery and coin production. The social conditions which had made clay the preferred material for vessels were changing and it quickly lost its popularity to be replaced with skins, baskets, wood and other organic materials throughout most of Britain. Any understanding of rural life between the fourth and sixth centuries is obscured in the darkness created by the abandonment of enduring material culture, a gloom which is only now being lifted by environmental data, radiocarbon dates and genetic studies of skeletal material in burials. Preserved pollen indicates that settlement and farming continued throughout much of Britannia cum Anglia with abandonment being localised. Rare sherds of fifth-century pottery are found on some Romano-British farmsteads, 'Anglo-Saxon' cemeteries contain both British and Saxon individuals as identified by genetic traits, and we find records of Saxon nobles with British names such as *Caedmon* or brothers called *Mul*, meaning 'half-breed'.

The wider political structures within which people lived and local society had developed were being removed while new ones were created. For many, these changes may have occurred around them with the only transformations being in the people they acknowledged as their rulers. However, people living in towns, vici or agriculturally marginal places such as the Upper Derwent would have faced increasing difficulties in sustaining existing livelihoods based on the market economy. They may have changed their lifestyles to carry on living where their ancestors had, or made the decision to move somewhere else – if possible. Whichever, there is no further archaeological evidence for settlement or land-use in the Upper Derwent until the thirteenth century AD. Should we write off these 800 or so years between the dates of observed archaeological remains as a time in which nothing happened? Or do we need to look at this period in the context of what is happening in the surrounding region?

33 *Doctor's Gate paved with gritstone cobbles where it crosses moorland near Snake Pass. Reputedly the line of a Roman road between forts at Brough and Glossop, no secure dating evidence has yet been found.* Photo by Bill Bevan

Mind the gap

Between the fifth and eleventh centuries it is pretty safe to say that the political and ethnic make-up of Britain was in a state of complex flux which we are largely made aware of through the various poems, sagas, chronicles, histories and treaties of the time. How different this was to prehistory is, therefore, unknown. The most striking cultural changes are the Anglicisation of language and place-names. Both large-scale population migrations and elite take-overs of existing populations have been used to explain the changes evident during this period. At different times and in different places either were likely to have happened. How this affected the average farmer in the paddock is unclear. If you take some accounts at face value, it would have been just as well for the farmer to give up trying to cultivate his fields and instead set-up a transport café for all the Anglians, Saxons, Britons, Mercians, Northumbrians, Vikings, Danes, Hiberno-Norse or Normans who might be passing through on their way to another heroic battle.

So, all very exciting but seemingly passing the Upper Derwent by. The area is at a significant location which came to lie on or near borders that were to be reworked and re-conceived from the fifth century AD until the Norman Conquest. At some point after the Roman period a large bank and ditch boundary, known as Grey Ditch, was built across Bradwell Dale to divide this easy access route on to the limestone plateau from the Hope Valley to the north (**34** & **35**). With its ditch facing northwards, the boundary was built by a group of people living on the plateau as a physical marker to differentiate them from others living in the valley. It is unclear whether this was a local border or had wider geographical and political significance. There is a similar linear earthwork, known as Bar Dike, 5km to the north-east of the Upper Derwent. Built on a ridge between valleys, it faces south-east and was probably built by a group occupying the high ground, though its date is unknown.

During the seventh century a series of Anglian burials in earthen round barrows were made across the region and all are on the limestone plateau (**35**). In some places the dead were buried in existing prehistoric barrows. Grave goods of everyday items, such as knives, were placed with some of the burials while much more elaborate or special objects, including swords, gold and jewellery with semi-precious stones, were deposited with others. Only certain individuals were selected for this sort of burial, possibly the landholders and heads of kin-groups who formed the local elite. By physically marking the graves of the dead these local communities were conducting explicit ancestor rites which both reinforced their group identity and claims to the places they inhabited. They were also making statements to associate them through their rulers with the wider social world now dominated by Anglian identities, whether or not they themselves were originally of Anglian or British descent. As such, actual genetic make-up was only important within the context of what people believed their ethnicity to be.

The people who buried these dead were the *Pecsaetna* who are recorded in the seventh century Tribal Hidage. This is a list of peoples owing tribute to the kingdom of Mercia, centred on the Trent Valley to the south, in terms of the amount of land they held. The Hidage counts the *Pecsaetna*, or Peak Dwellers, as numbering 1,200 families. Immediately to the north, occupying much of present day south Yorkshire, were the *Elmetsaetna*, who possibly identified themselves as British rather than Saxon, and the kingdom of Northumbria. The Upper Derwent lies between these three.

During the ninth and tenth centuries much of the North and Midlands was subject to some sort of 'Viking' settlement, whether Norse, Danish or Hiberno-Norse (Norse settlers in Ireland). This seems to have been most extensive in the north Midlands, Yorkshire and Cumbria, with military victories by Scandinavian elites over Saxons enabling more widespread settlement to follow. The Peaks were just within the western part of the Danelaw. The kingdom of Wessex conducted successful military campaigns to expand their dominance north in the early ninth century against Mercia and returned in the tenth century to confront the 'Vikings'. Dore village, now in Sheffield, is recorded on both occasions as on the border with Northumbria. At the same time around sixteen stone crosses were built across the region, most of which are still standing (**35**). Four at Hope, Alstonefield, Ilam and Ashbourne are typical of Mercian decoration and four at Eyam, Bakewell, Bradbourne and Wirksworth are stylistically similar to Northumbrian crosses. The remainder are comparable to examples found in the west of Britain which are associated with the Irish-Norse who settled marginal areas in the early tenth century AD. These can be found in a group south of Glossop, another group in the Derwent Valley and one at Bakewell. This mix of styles hints at the complex ethnic division of landowning interests in the region. A fragment of one of the Scandinavian crosses was found at the site of Derwent hamlet where it was excavated from within the nineteenth-century wall of a cottage (**35**). It could mean the presence of a Norse community, however, its presence in the wall could be the result of it being imported in building material during the nineteenth century.

During this period the border position of the Upper Derwent and surrounding moorlands would have made it both a central and marginal location. We should not think of borders as being the lines on maps of today but as wide areas of landscape where political dominion was contestable. Physical boundaries such as Offa's Dyke or the Grey Ditch were only built under certain conditions. Borders may have been perceived as important buffer zones where the threat from competing and neighbouring kingdoms needed to be prevented from continuing further. Settlement may not have been too safe if it was subject to raids from neighbouring kingdoms or, it may have been actively encouraged by lords to put 'bodies' in the way.

Contemporary with the ninth to eleventh century ethnic and political changes, was the nucleation of settlement on the limestone and in the major valleys into villages surrounded by common fields. Prior to this, rural settlement had been in individual farmsteads and small hamlets. The creation of villages with common fields was mostly concentrated in a belt of land running from north-east England through the Midlands to the south coast. The mitigating reasons for nucleation are complex and vary from place to place. Farmsteads may have coalesced over time into villages if populations expanded or people may have chosen to reorganise the way they lived into more communal settlements in relation to changing local economic and social conditions. The layouts of many villages suggest they were planned, probably by local landowners enforcing re-settlement for their own needs. In many areas of the limestone plateau villages completely replaced isolated farmsteads. At other places, such as the Hope and Derwent valleys, villages appeared alongside dispersed settlements, while they were completely absent from the Upper Derwent and elsewhere in the Dark

34 *Grey Ditch was built some time after the end of Roman rule to control access between the Limestone Plateau and Hope Valley along the Roman road.* Photo by Ray Manley

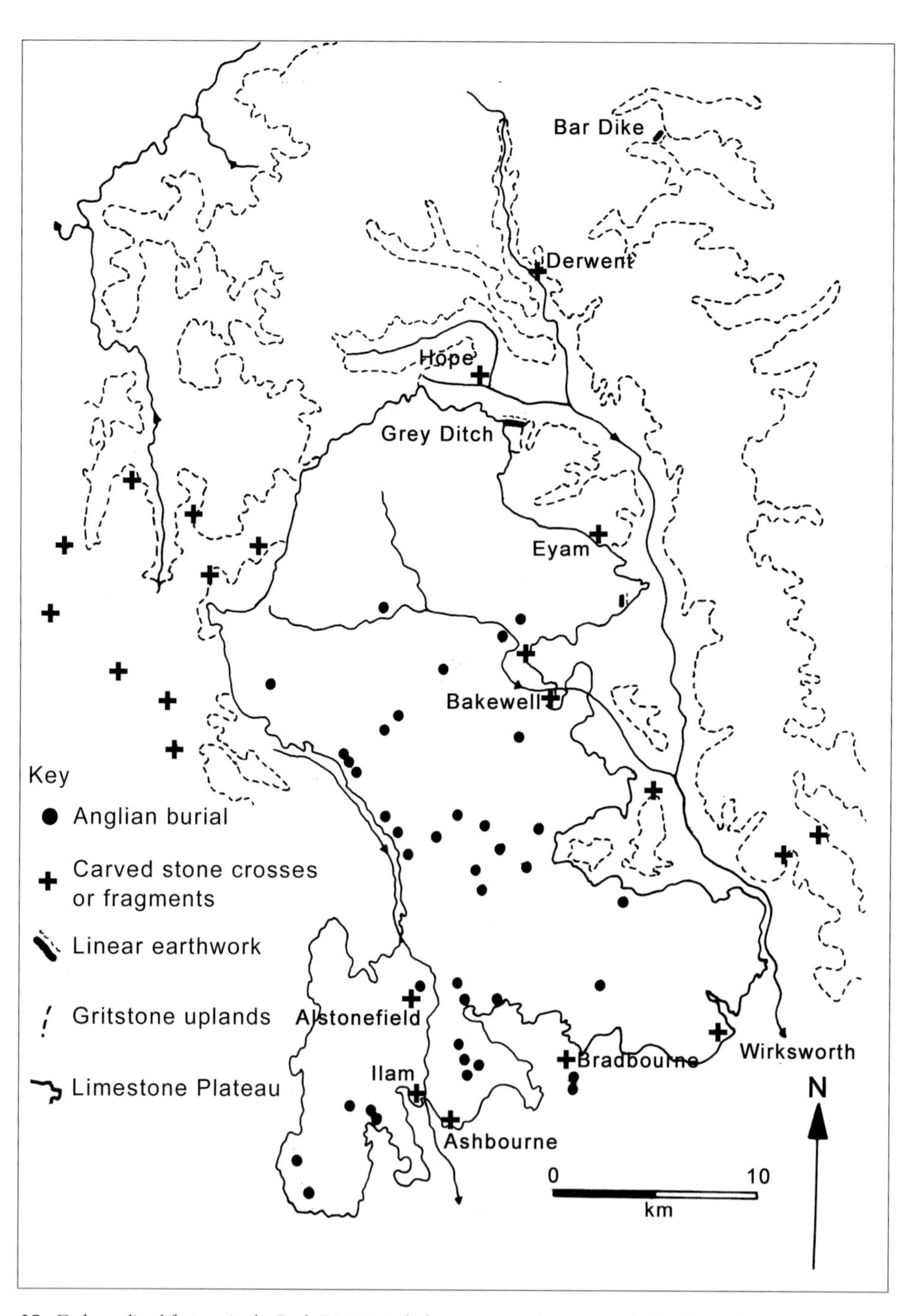

35 *Early medieval features in the Peak District, including nearest settlements recorded in Domesday*

Peak. The neighbouring settlements of Bamford and Thornhill, situated less than 5km apart and each with strip fields, are the most northerly villages in the Derwent valley. The lack of medieval village creation in the Upper Derwent may be the result of a very low population and unsuitable topography.

Domesday approaches

The Norman Conquest of 1066 was, in many ways, one more elite takeover in a long history of such takeovers. It was famously followed by the 'harrying of the North' as the newly proclaimed King William and his barons ruthlessly asserted their authority over Northumbria. This disrupted the livelihoods, if not the very lives, of thousands of people as the burning of property and destruction of livestock and crops made it difficult for large sections of society to feed themselves. Any potential settlements in the Upper Derwent which had been archaeologically invisible in previous centuries may have been affected by this harrying, either directly or by moving away to occupy recently vacated better land elsewhere. The continuation of villages and strip fields throughout much of the region and the descriptions of places in Domesday suggest that if harrying did affect many communities, it never wholly destroyed them.

Domesday of 1086 was compiled because of William's desire to audit the land which he now controlled. As the first extensive documented survey of England it has long provided a watershed in historical studies of how the landscape was used and organised. Many settlements in the Peak District are listed in Domesday, though many others are omitted. The effects of Norman destruction and intimidation are indicated at only a small number of places, such as Hope and Hathersage where land is described as reduced in value, or Derby where a reduced population and unoccupied houses are recorded. The Norman barons also built castles as strongholds from which to control the estates they had taken from Anglo-Saxon landowners. William Peveril was granted much of the land in the Peak and built his castle on a rocky promontory above the village of Peak's Arse, which was subsequently renamed after his fortification – Castleton (**37**).

The closest named places to the Upper Derwent are Edale and Aston as outliers of Hope, Bamford as an outlier of Hathersage, Glossop, Kinder, Sheffield and Hallam. The absence of a named settlement cannot be taken as its lack of existence at the time because the aim of Domesday was to list the names of estates and their administrative sub-divisions rather than all settlements. What is more telling is the lack of eleventh- and twelfth-century pottery sherds. Pottery vessels were now commonplace again and to be expected where there was settlement of this period. After all the archaeological uncertainties of the previous centuries we can be more confident that post-Conquest occupation in the Upper Derwent was non-existent, temporary or extremely sparse.

The hard work of clearing the ground of woodland to make fields and ploughing the earth is aided by the canons who pray for a good year and strong crops in Ashop and Derwent. I'd say to our cloaked landlords 'What use prayers without labour?' They'd answer 'what use labour in a Godless world?'

FIVE

MEDIEVAL FOREST AND MONASTIC ESTATES

The world in words

So far in this history there have been no written words to read about how the Upper Derwent landscape was used, no manuscripts to document the names of people and where they lived, no fragments of poetry or prose to conjure images of moors and vales. Nothing. Literally, not a jot. As we have seen already even the most comprehensive record of land use in medieval England, Domesday, omitted the Upper Derwent. Then, with an act of contrite generosity from a member of the royal family hoping to ease his entry into heaven, the print comes into focus in the medieval period. John, the Earl of Mortaigne, who would later come to rue the importance of written words, came up with this piece of forward planning. As John, King of England, he was forced to sign the Magna Carta by rebel barons who were sick of the heavy financial burden he imposed on them and the Church.

At the end of the twelfth century AD, about 100 years after Domesday, when he could find nothing to write about the area, John granted to Welbeck Abbey in Nottinghamshire a piece of land described as:

> the pasture of Crookhill, the woods of Ashop up to Lockerbrook and from Lockerbrook up the valley of the Derwent and ascending up to Derwenthead.

These are names which still occupy maps, names that are as recognisable to today's walkers as they were to the medieval canons who came to carve a farm out of their blessed wilderness over 900 years ago.

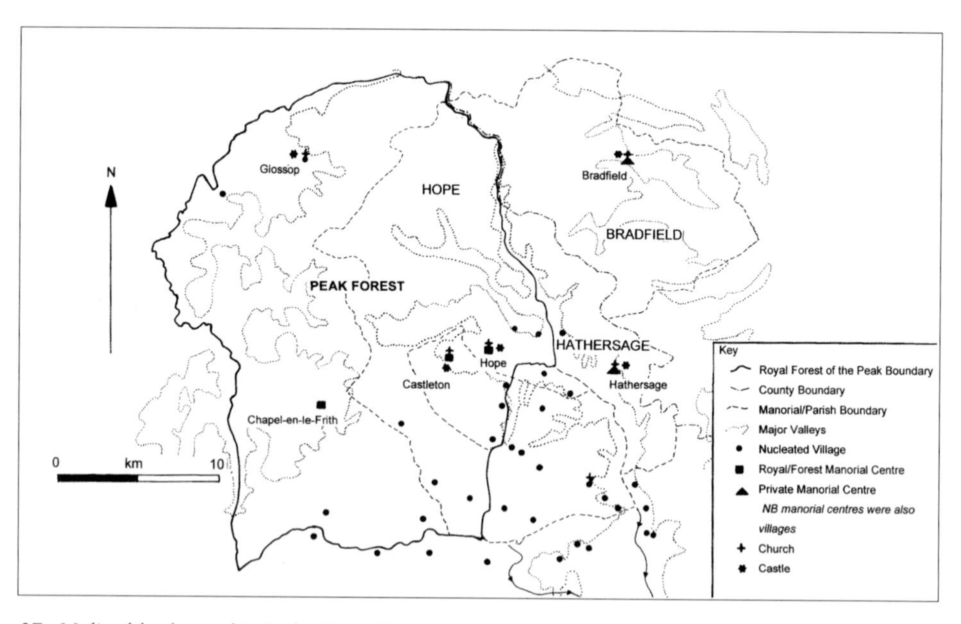

37 *Medieval landownership in the Upper Derwent*

From the medieval period onwards written documents become available alongside archaeological remains and artefacts as part of the evidence for interpreting use and perception of the landscape. Throughout the medieval period documents are very restricted, and are predisposed towards recording the activities of social elites. But, these elites provided the legal, landowning framework within which the landscape was lived and worked so their activities are not irrelevant. We just need to remember who is talking to us through the written word, and why. Documents become more common from the sixteenth century onwards, and tend to be written in English, recording more everyday activities. Until the nineteenth or twentieth centuries the vast majority of documents were still written at the behest of people in positions of power and all too often women, children and the poor are excluded. So, words contribute greatly as historical evidence but have their limitations. Documents need to be integrated into the act of archaeological interpretation, another vital piece of evidence but one not allowed to dominate.

Landownership and landscape

The twelfth-century landscape of the Upper Derwent appears to have been a mix of woodland and moorland within which people were active even if there was no settlement. The area was divided between three large manors and parishes (**37**). Hope lay to the west of the River Derwent, and included the west side of the valley, the Woodlands Valley and the moorlands in between. Hathersage stretched up the east side of the river as far as Abbey Brook and within which was the township of Derwent. Bradfield, in Yorkshire, ran eastwards from near Sheffield to drop into the Derwent Valley north of Hathersage and followed the river to its source. Each had a lord of the manor originally appointed by William the Conqueror and the majority of occupants were tenants of this lord.

All of Hope parish was within the Royal Forest of the Peak which was formalised by William the Conqueror in 1066 out of a tract of sparsely populated countryside. The term 'Forest' does not necessarily imply the existence of woodland but was a Norman-French term for lands dedicated to hunting. The amount of blood-sports carried out in Forests is open to question. Forests were as much about the newly proclaimed Royals and their supporters asserting status, grabbing land and imprinting their rule on the inhabitants of the English countryside. Few kings themselves hunted and professionals were employed to kill deer which would be consumed at royal feasts or given as gifts to favoured subjects.

The Royal Forest occupied much of the High Peak moorlands, the Edale and Hope valleys and the north-western corner of the limestone plateau. Its eastern boundary ran south along the River Derwent from its source to the confluence with the River Noe which it then followed up to Bradwell Brook where it turned south once more along Bradwell Dale. William granted the Forest, but not ownership of the deer, to William Peveril of Castleton in AD 1068. Peveril Castle, from which Castleton derived its name, was the administrative centre and the men who made sure that Forest Law was upheld, the Foresters, had a chamber at Peak Forest. The Forest was managed through courts at Chapel en le Frith, Tideswell and Castleton/Hope where offences against Forest Law were judged, fines imposed and inquisitions held. Offences included trespass, poaching deer and other game, damaging or grubbing up woods, enclosing land and constructing buildings.

In practice, Forest management also differed from the Law. Officially any change to the landscapes was prohibited but they could actually be susceptible to greater change than land outside their boundaries. The opportunities for new settlement and enclosure within Forests were greater than outside, because of the lower densities of existing settlement in large areas of Forests and the use of fines as a convenient mechanism for generating revenue for the Crown. Surviving accounts of Forest courts show this, with lists of illegal land enclosures and buildings; twenty-two cases of enclosing cultivated land in 1216 and 131 buildings erected in 1251. In most cases the enclosures and the buildings were allowed to remain, with the people concerned being fined and made to pay annual fees while their heirs had to pay double rent for the first year after inheriting the land.

Beyond the documented landownership of the area, we know little of what the landscape actually looked like or how it was specifically used in the Upper Derwent. The twelfth and thirteenth century grants to Welbeck Abbey refer to woodland which probably occupied much of the valleys while the higher lands were peat moorland. Extensive eleventh and twelfth century settlement was unlikely, though the grants record pastures and an enclosed meadow which were already in existence. While the pastures would have referred to areas of moorland grazing, the enclosed meadow required work to sustain it as open grassland within woodland and someone to build its boundary. These were probably temporary grazing areas, known as shielings, where people from further south in Hope and Hathersage manors came to pasture livestock in the summer.

Granges of Welbeck Abbey

It was into this landscape that canons and lay brothers of Welbeck Abbey came to found a grange farm on the land granted to them by John (**38**). Welbeck was founded in 1153 and was part of the Premonstratensian order of canons. This order was one of many set up in the twelfth century by those

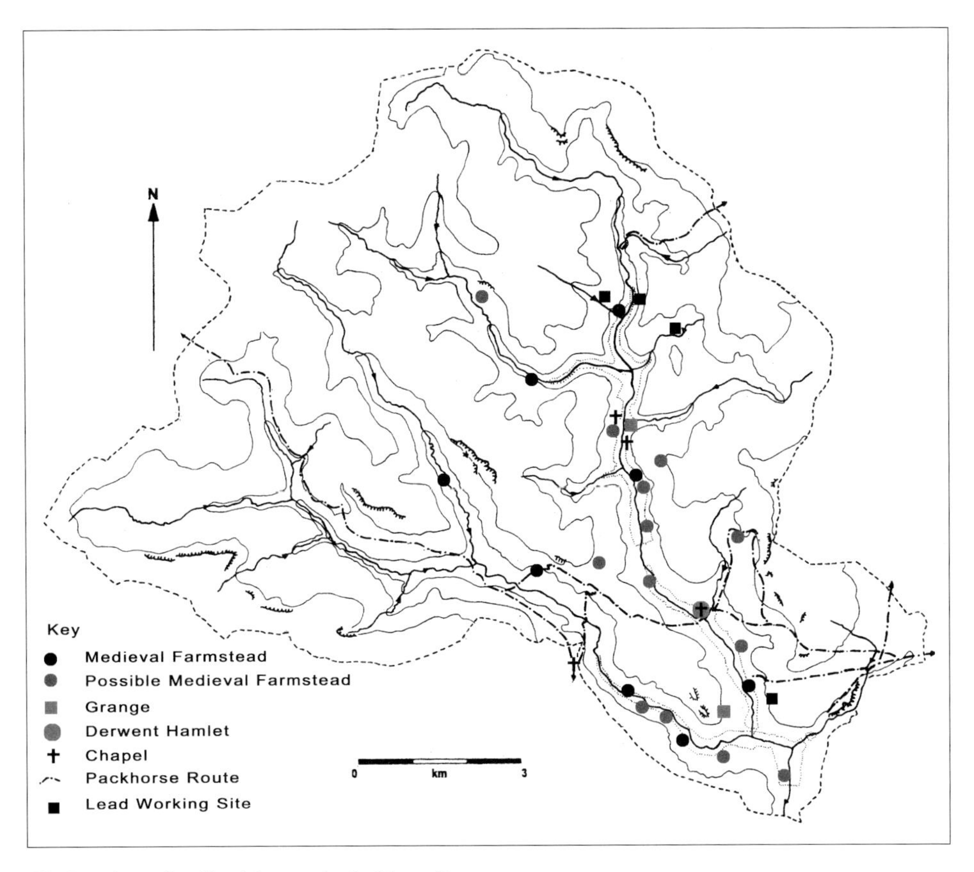

38 *Locations of medieval features in the Upper Derwent*

who felt that existing orders, such as the Benedictines, had lost their way from the monastic ideal by indulging in too many home comforts and acquiring wealth. The new orders looked to more remote locations to establish their monasteries, seeking the closest equivalents in western Europe to the desert wildernesses that attracted holy men soon after the death of Christ. Land was also acquired to grow produce to feed the canons and to sell at market to pay for monastic buildings. While the Benedictine estates were often integrated into the agrarian regimes of well-populated lowland areas, the later orders again preferred remote areas with low populations. Which was just as well, as by the twelfth century most wealthy landowners hoping to buy their way into heaven were reluctant to part with anything more than their more marginal land that was often uplands or marshes. Granges were built by another new order, the Cistercians, as a flexible and efficient means of running an agricultural estate to exploit such sparsely populated areas.

The original Crookhill endowment was for land that the Abbey could turn into a grange (**39**). As well as the pasture at Crookhill, this included

39 *Crookhill Farm from Derwent Edge. Crookhill is one of the oldest farmsteads in the Upper Derwent. It was founded as a grange by Welbeck Abbey after they were granted land here at the end of the twelfth century AD.* Photo by Bill Bevan

extensive tracts of moorland and land in the Derwent Valley, including woodland, to the north. The grant was confirmed in 1215, the year John signed the Magna Carta, but this time he reserved the wood and venison to himself. However, the wording is vague and it is likely they were allowed the land but not the timber and game living on it. Often brushwood (branches and twigs) and underwood (young saplings) could be taken while the timber was reserved by the lord or owner. Seventy years later the Forest courts of 1285 list damage to the woods by the Abbots of Welbeck who were described as both dead and present, suggesting that the damage had been occurring for a long time. The later extent of the Hope Woodlands township and estate as handed to a landowner after the Dissolution of the monasteries suggests the Abbey did own the land covered by woodland, or had at least persuaded subsequent officers of the Crown that this was the case.

As was typical for monasteries they set about consolidating and expanding their land. In 1251 Crookhill Grange had expanded to include buildings, 50 acres of pasture or farmland and an assart – an initial enclosure made out of common land or Forest which had the advantage of being exempt from paying tithes to the Church. A year later they added a horse-stud to their estate, possibly breeding horses for sale as well as for their own use. Crookhill was still expanding a century later as livestock levels were increased and the canons claimed exemption from payment of tithes for newly tilled lands which were planted with vegetables, gardens and orchards.

On the east side of the River Derwent they had acquired a common pasture for eighty cattle in Hathersage parish from the Lords of Hathersage. This was most likely the area of Derwent township. By the 1250s the Lord's descendant either wanted this back or wished to add to his grandfather's gift by endowing the monastery with an enclosed meadow called One Mans Field. This was situated on the southern side of the confluence between the River and Abbey Brook, on one of the few large level areas of light sandy soils which were regularly washed with alluvium from the nearby watercourses (**38**). It had regularly been a focus for activity throughout prehistory and the Roman period. The meadow may have been an isolated field of hay and grazing for a farmer from a village or farmstead further down the valley in Hathersage manor. It has also been suggested by the place-name scholar Kenneth Cameron, that it may have been a hermitage. Welbeck began developing their new land immediately by building another grange which they called One Man's House. The canons may have also identified with the Field's marginal location right on the border between Derbyshire and Yorkshire.

After the grant of One Mans Field, the Abbey then received grazing land in the part of the Yorkshire Bradfield manor situated in the Derwent Valley from Lord Furnival of Sheffield. This land bordered the earlier endowments and completed the expansion of its estates in the Upper Derwent.

Crookhill and One Man's House were two of many granges in the Pennines. There are at least fifty known in the Peak District, about half are Cistercian and the majority lie on the higher land of the southern half of the limestone plateau. There are four Cistercian granges in a 3km area near Pilsbury Castle alone. Basingwerk Abbey was granted land centred on Glossop with pastures on Kinder and other moors neighbouring the western and northern boundaries of Welbeck's estates. Welbeck ran its granges directly and employed lay brothers to take on much of the day to day work.

The impact of granges on the medieval landscape was immense. Throughout the thirteenth and early fourteenth centuries they were innovators of agricultural and industrial production. They had the extensive estates, long-term continuity of settlement, substantial capital, wide-ranging vision and centralised decision-making to advance technologies, improve soil conditions and develop new systems of working the land. These may have been important considerations where their estates were so often on poor land. As well as supplying the needs of the abbeys themselves they were also tuned into long-distance markets. Wool was one commodity they excelled in, exporting the fleeces of their own flocks as well as those of secular farmers across Europe. Some granges exploited fully the exemption of sheep from tithes, some tolls and Forest Law. This was a period of rising production.

Within 100 years the whole system had changed. By the early fifteenth century Welbeck had rented Crookhill to Thomas Eyre, and it became another tenanted farmstead like the others on their estate. The reason for this is complex and is related to slowly deteriorating economic conditions, political decisions taken within the Order and a combination of disastrous events during the fourteenth century. For a start, some Premonstratensian lay brothers protested against regulations forcing them to wear beards in the thirteenth century. The Order reduced their numbers and they disappeared entirely as agricultural workers by the fifteenth century. Wider afield, monasteries were finding it more difficult to sell wool across Europe and then came the Black Death, widespread cattle pestilence, and a worsening in the weather in the fourteenth century. The effect of the plague on the European countryside cannot be underestimated as whole communities were infected and tracts of land were depopulated. The Peak District seems to have escaped the worst of the plague but still it lost a lot of its population as people took up offers to resettle recently abandoned better land in the lowlands. This was a period of major change and political upheaval. Some landlords took the opportunity to remove the surviving tenants from their land and establish large sheep ranches, showing that there were still wool markets to sell to. Others, such as many of the monasteries, reacted by renting out their estates to save costs and reduce risks. This is how the Eyre family came to live at Crookhill until the nineteenth century.

Welbeck's influence beyond the granges

Whether or not Welbeck owned land in Derwent township apart from One Man's House, they did have a major impact on its landscape. The Abbey built a bridge to carry the packhorse route from Sheffield to Hope and Glossop across the River Derwent in the thirteenth century. In the early fourteenth century a charter specifically mentioned the Sheffield to Derwent section of these routes as a 'common way' between the two, suggesting that Derwent was an important destination in its own right as well as a stopping point (**38**). The canons built a chapel nearby in the thirteenth century which would have served the population of the area and travellers along the packhorse route, so forming a physical reminder of the place of Christianity in their world, and of Welbeck Abbey as its representative in the locality.

The canons of Welbeck built a chapel because they were canons rather than monks; they lived a monastic way of life but went outside the Abbey's confines to preach to lay communities. Premonstratensians combined this pastoral role with a desire for isolation. However, during its early years the order did not condone the building of chapels at its granges because of worries that this would dilute connections between the mother house and those canons commonly living at distant estates. It was also concerned that tithes could be diverted away from the local parish church if the chapels were open to laymen. In 1246 the order gained a general concession from the Pope to build chapels at granges for communion and to avoid any unnecessary contact with the lay public. This would appear to somewhat contradict the order's pastoral role, but it really indicates the prescriptions of medieval life, the circumstances in which classes of people in social power believed it appropriate to mix with commoners. Presumably Welbeck considered it acceptable to have religious contact with laymen only when leading them in mass or taking their confession, and consequently, in a position of ecclesiastical authority. But it was not proper for peasants to attend service alongside the brothers in anything seeming like equality. Therefore, the Abbey built two chapels to serve its social ideals, the one at Derwent hamlet where the canons conducted services for local laymen and one at One Man's House for their own private use. After the Dissolution, fabric from this second chapel was incorporated into later farm buildings while its bells and lead were excluded from the sale of the farmstead.

Reputedly, the Abbey built two further chapels in the Upper Derwent, one near to Birchinlee on the opposite side of the valley from One Man's House and another on the line of the Hope to Glossop packhorse route where it crossed the ridge between the Woodlands Valley and Edale. These would probably have been for public use. Neither of these latter sites has been dated definitely as medieval and the one at Birchinlee appears as the `New Chappel' on Saxton's county map of Derbyshire published in 1577.

The chapel was built close to the pond which took water from Millbrook to power a corn mill. This was the only mill in the Upper Derwent and indicates that there were enough cereals being grown to justify the cost of its construction. It was probably built here because it lay just outside the Royal Forest and the Hathersage lord of the manor saw an opportunity to make money from those living in the Forest. Lords of the manor usually built corn mills and demanded that their tenants' cereals were processed at them. Such a restrictive practice was common as landowners attempted to control the activities of their tenants and to maximise their income from the produce of the land. The lay brothers and later tenants of the granges, along with other farmers living in the surrounding area are also likely to have paid to have their cereals milled here.

With a mill, chapel and river crossing point in close proximity to each other, a small centre of population and social activity was growing beside the river. Its location on a major long-distance packhorse route would have made it an important place for news and contact with people from further afield. From the evidence of artefacts this activity may be the earliest occupation of what was to become the small hamlet of Derwent (**38**). Pottery found in the vicinity dates to no earlier than the thirteenth century, though as we have already seen the hamlet may have earlier origins if the fragment of tenth-century AD cross-shaft found within the build of a cottage is near its original location. If this piece of cross is a true indicator of tenth-century occupation then the lack of eleventh- and twelfth-century pottery in its vicinity suggests that the settlement was later abandoned, perhaps shortly after the Norman Conquest.

Farmsteads scattered amongst the waste and forest

Who were the people whose souls were being saved by Welbeck's canons and corn ground in the mill? In addition to mentioning the Abbots of Welbeck, the Forest courts of 1285 state that occupants of Derwent and Ashop were damaging woodland. By this date settlers were establishing farms in both valleys, as indicated by sherds of medieval pottery that have been discovered by fieldwalking at eleven other farmsteads and at Derwent hamlet (**38**). The earliest pottery dates from the mid-thirteenth century – the same time that Welbeck was expanding its estate and the Forest court were fining those responsible for 131 new buildings and twenty-two enclosures throughout the Royal Forest. It is not possible to fieldwalk at the sites of all the known farmsteads because many are situated within permanent pasture higher up valley sides or along the upper reaches of the Woodlands Valley. Some of these farmsteads may also be as old as the thirteenth century.

Where were these settlers coming from? The most likely answer is that they were opportunists from villages to the south looking to have a go at improving their lot away from the constraints of more heavily populated townships. Perhaps they were from families who already took their livestock to graze on any other pastures and meadows that may have existed. They may have been chancing their luck with the forest officers and landowners, squatters hoping not to be evicted. Or they may have been invited by officers and Welbeck Abbey looking for people to improve land which would increase income from fines or rents. Recolonisation of the waste would be a trend which the Abbey could manage from the granges.

As people settled in the two valleys from the thirteenth century onwards, the choices they made or had available to them about where they would found their farmsteads set the pattern of settlement which would characterise the area until the twentieth century. The thirteenth-century settlers appear to have sought out comparatively good agricultural land at locations some distance from each other. Their farms are all located on small terraces of relatively level ground on the valley sides, many lying just above the narrow valley bottoms and the flood levels of the rivers, with good access to the pastures above and nearly always within 100m of a watercourse. As there were many more good locations available than the number of early farms it shows that they were not simply constrained by land quality. Depending on how active the forest officers or Welbeck's granges were in directing new settlement, this separation was either decided for settlers or came from their desire to create distance between each other. Whichever, this isolation from neighbours encourages and, over time, reinforces quite an independent mind-set.

This pattern of dispersed settlement is typical of much of Britain in the medieval period, especially the uplands including the Pennines. In many other places it does pre-date the Norman Conquest, and there is the likelihood that some farmstead sites have been occupied since the Roman period. Early medieval nucleation of settlement into villages, the quintessential image of the English landscape, is really the oddity rather than the norm. Over time more farmsteads come into focus as they were recorded by name in land management documents. A charter of the late fourteenth to early fifteenth century lists a number of farmsteads, including places such as Rowlee and Alport in the Woodlands Valley, which are located away from the reservoirs and other areas suitable for fieldwalking. Some of these may also date to the thirteenth century for the earliest record is just that, the earliest date from when a document survives rather than the record of the farmstead's earliest date of occupation. Nevertheless, new settlement would

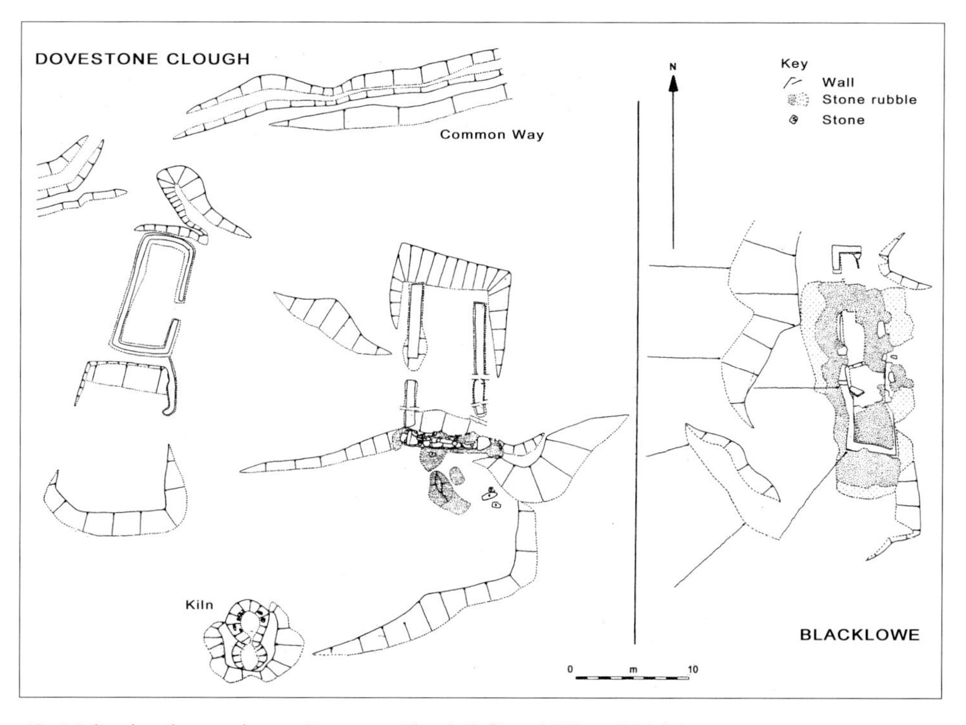

40 *Medieval settlement plans at Dovestone Clough* (left) *and Westend* (right)

41 *Medieval longhouse at Westend, looking south along the building. The upright slab is approximately midway and probably on the line of an internal wall.* Photo by Bill Bevan

have continued throughout the medieval period as prospective occupants came to try and exploit the other expanses of unenclosed land or as existing families divided their farms between their heirs.

We have found pottery dating from throughout the medieval period at all the farmsteads now under or adjacent to the reservoirs. The majority are locally produced, everyday storage and serving vessels. Five farmsteads, One Man's House, Ronksley, Shireowlers, Tinkershouse and Nether Ashop, stand out from the rest in respect of numbers of sherds and range of vessels represented (**38**). Fine and decorated wares, such as elaborately glazed Cistercian ware from Yorkshire, are present – indicating the desire to signal their own ideas about their social standing by using crockery which looked good on the table. The recipients of these signals are equally as likely to be the family themselves, in a sense bolstering their own self-image, as guests to dinner. While this may go hand-in-hand with economic prosperity, the discovery that fine tablewares at Nether Ashop are cheaper 'seconds' shows that actively giving the appearance of style and civil respectability may outweigh financial reality.

Structural evidence for medieval buildings is rare. Most of the medieval sites were occupied until the early twentieth century and buildings were periodically rebuilt so removing or masking external evidence for earlier building phases. Buildings survive near the River Westend and Dovestone Clough which appear to have been abandoned during the medieval period and so their original structures and layouts can be seen (**40**). At both, platforms were terraced into sloping ground to construct longhouses with narrow doorways in the long sides. One building is evident at Westend (**41**) while there are three at Dovestone associated with a yard and kiln adjacent to the Sheffield to Derwent 'common way'. Stone was gathered from the ground surface or from small, shallow quarries to build the lower dry-stone walls. Timber from nearby trees was taken to build timber-frame walls or high-gabled roofs on these walls. The roofs were then made from thatch, turves or bracken cut from fields or common. Both sites are remote and at only one is a yard visible while larger enclosures are not identifiable. They are settlements that were not as successful as others in the Upper Derwent. The reason why cannot simply be laid at the door of one external influence, such as climatic deterioration or the economy, as is often the case for such upland landscapes. There are farmsteads in the area in similar remote locations that were continually occupied until the twentieth century. The complexity of local landholding patterns and farm inheritance is also significant. A marriage or death without heirs can be as equally important in shaping settlement as climate or economics.

Enclosed fields and open commons

The nature of new 'fields' enclosed out of the Forest and waste from the thirteenth century onwards can be pieced together from documentary references and from the pattern of fields depicted on later maps or which survive today. Farmers sought out better land and so created ribbons of enclosures on the valley bottom and sides characterised by small, irregular fields with mainly walled boundaries. The walled fields became intermixed with surviving woodland, and enclosure would have given way on higher ground to common moorland pasture.

Surviving field patterns adjacent to the other known thirteenth-century farmsteads can be taken to reflect something of medieval enclosure. Maps of Hope Woodlands township over the last 300 years show the more recent layout of fields to be stable in many places and in those locations where there has been new enclosure it has been undertaken within the context of existing fields. This argues for progressive enclosure, building on what exists at any one time rather than any large-scale re-ordering of fields. Within the overall arrangement of small, irregular enclosures there is local variation. Those west of the river in the Derwent Valley appear to have one or two oval enclosures looping out along the contour to one or both sides of the farmsteads beyond which are numerous smaller and more rectangular fields. The remote Ronksley House is the exception to this. Here a group of large enclosures quickly gives way to moorland grazing. East of the river, farmsteads on the steeper slopes are mainly surrounded by small fields which tend to radiate out from the farm buildings before giving way to a more irregular pattern of enclosures. Rectangular fields that follow the contours in broad lines occupy broader terraces of gently sloping land to either side of Millbrook (**colour plate 10**). More rectangular fields, arranged in blocks, surround thirteenth century-farmsteads in the south of the Woodlands Valley.

Three distinctive oval walled fields near to Ashopton seem from their shape and apparent later incorporation into the wider surrounding enclosure pattern to represent the earliest enclosures in that locality. Two are likely to be assarts while one was built to keep livestock out of a heavily boulder-strewn area resistant to clearance, either to prevent injury or to protect woodland.

Over time, more ground was enclosed in this piecemeal fashion with farmers progressively taking in more land from open moorland and woodland. This work was especially heavy in woodlands where dense vegetation and thick roots had to be cleared. It was also liable to attract attention and therefore fines, so tenants may, in part, have been motivated to enclose small areas at a time to reduce detection, to 'get away' with as much as they could. This may have been an effective strategy at a time when land use was described in vague terms and detail was reliant on memory. A substantial amount of stone also had to be cleared from some areas, stone that lay on the surface and which was turned up by the first ploughings.

As a claim to 'ownership', the boundaries and the improved nature of the ground, can cause or reduce contention over competing claims to land. There may have been friction points where different farmers saw the same area of land as being theirs to enclose next. Adjudicating over such arguments may have been the role of the landowners and sometimes 'getting there first' might have been enough. Over time the lines of the boundaries would become more and more accepted as permanent parts of the landscape. The farming landscape was being set in stone.

Rights of way were defined as walled lanes between fields to form a network of routes along the valley connected to individual farmsteads into which came the established long-distance packhorse routes. Moving along these routes would take you through a wooded landscape that was being progressively broken into smaller compartments by the open areas of improved grasslands and arable.

Agriculture gave a geographic and temporal pattern to the occupation of the landscape. The year was structured by the seasonal demands of birth and sowing in the spring, pasturing and growing over summer, harvesting and culling in autumn, and overwintering and dormancy in winter. Other activities were worked around these, such as the provision of winter fodder by collecting hay or browse from trees. There is no evidence for the development of wood pasture and it seems that livestock were meant to be excluded from the woodlands of Royal Forest. People lived close to their livestock, which had to be protected from predators by corralling in the enclosures and close herding when on the moorland pastures. Wolves were a danger, but hunting through the medieval period reduced this risk as their numbers diminished until their extinction in England. Hunting of wild animals, including the poaching of the King's deer, should not be overlooked as an

42 *This deeply incised hollow-way is part of a well-used route linking Derwent hamlet with the moorland common above. The hollowing is caused by repeated use where its line is limited to a walled lane.* Photo by Bill Bevan

important activity, providing further sources of food and controlling the perceived threat of predators to both livestock and crops.

The extensive moorlands were more than just unimproved lands lying beyond the farmsteads waiting to be enclosed and worked. They were a fundamental part of the farm in providing numerous 'wild' and actively managed resources which tenants could use by common right. They also reinforced the social separation between individual farmers by forming wide boundaries between each other's enclosed land. Rights included some that are obvious to us today such as pasturing livestock, cutting peat for fuel (turbary) and quarrying building stone. Rights to cut peat and pasture livestock on commons within the Royal Forest date to at least the thirteenth century. This may also be the time when peat erosion began due to grazing. We know there were pastures in Ashop and Derwent because they were recorded in the land grants to Welbeck Abbey. Less obvious are the various plants which were collected, bracken for thatch, cattle bedding and potash, bilberries for food, coarse grasses for hay and heather for fuel and thatch. The routes that farmers took to go up onto the commons are still visible as eroded hollow-ways on the steep valley sides which radiate out from individual farmsteads (**42** & **colour plate 11**).

Many long-distance routes also crossed the moorlands that separated settlements and villages, the difficult terrain proving no hindrance to transport by pack animal and foot traffic. They were used by right, similar in effect to common land, and their routes developed over time through regular use. Where they passed through enclosed farmland they were bounded lanes, their lines tightly demarcated on the ground to prevent trespassing on to private land and trampling of crops by livestock. On open commons the routes often spread out as wide bands of hollow-ways created by the repetitive use over generations of the same approximate line. They often follow the most suitable topography situated in relatively straight lines between places in common communication. As well as the Sheffield to Derwent 'common way', Cut Gate ran across the high moors to Penistone market and Doctor's Gate ran along the Woodlands Valley between Hope and Glossop (**38**). Both are clearly defined as a series of braided hollow-ways taking the gentlest gradient where possible by climbing diagonally across the valley sides then forming zigzags where forced to ascend more steeply.

Leading industries

So far I have painted something of a rural scene of woodland, moorland and walled fields, of remote grange, tenant farmer and landowner, of people making new settlements out of forest and waste. There was also an important industrial side, of smelting metals and noxious fumes.

Lead ore was mined in the limestone plateau where extensive deposits of galena were first exploited in prehistory. During the medieval period it was smelted on the gritstone moors to the east of the River Derwent where the sites of numerous bonfire furnaces, known as 'boles', are recognised from place-names or finds of slags. These were powered by the natural updraughts coming up the south-west-facing valley slopes and fuel was provided by extensive woodlands in the valley itself. Many areas of the medieval upland countryside had the resources necessary for industry, water for power and wood or peat for fuel. Only much later did extensive urban areas grow as centres of industrial production. Some of the earlier manufacturing sites were the basis for the towns and cities, others became abandoned as new factors became important for siting industries.

A bole was built above the confluence of the Derwent and Ashop Rivers on a south-western facing slope, which came to be called Lead Hill as a result. Wood and lead ore were stacked in a large bonfire and set alight when the prevailing winds were in the right direction. This was a somewhat precarious operation because the winds had to last the length of the smelt, two or three days, and if they dropped too soon the ore would not be properly smelted so wasting the money spent on the raw materials. A good knowledge of local weather patterns was essential for success.

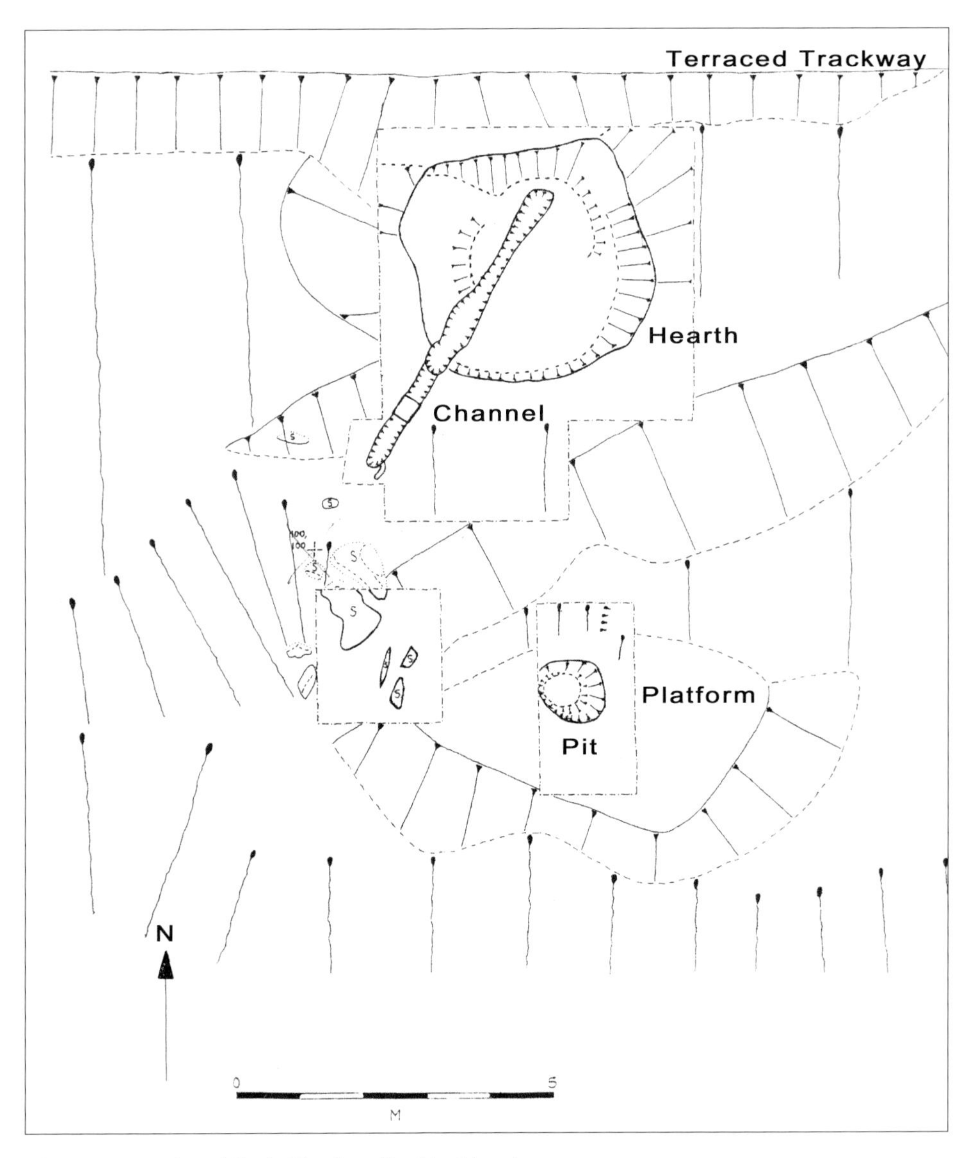

43 *Excavation plan of Linch Clough medieval lead hearth*

One way to overcome the vagaries of weather was to control the air going into the hearth with a set of bellows. This method was used at a small lead hearth built low down in Linch Clough (**43** & **colour plate 9**). Here a shallow scoop was made into the ground and gritstone blocks were used to make a rudimentary structure. A narrow channel ran under the hearth to allow air to be forced under the furnace from foot bellows. It appears that fairly wide oak stems and branches were used to make charcoal to fuel the hearth, possibly on charcoal-burning platforms terraced into the opposite

44 *In Howden Clough lead objects were melted in a rudimentary hearth on a remote natural landslip during the thirteenth century.* Photo by Bill Bevan

side of the clough. It is unclear whether they were smelting lead ore or resmelting lead-heavy slags from previous smelts. The hearth was last used sometime between 1430 and 1470 presumably by tenants of nearby Ronksley House or under the supervision of Welbeck Abbey.

A complex of charcoal production platforms, hearths, a quarry pit and a leat all enclosed within a boundary and situated next to a watercourse survives on the other side of the Derwent River on the lower valley side. This appears to be a similar but much larger operation to that in Linch Clough. Other concentrations of lead slag are found in similar locations suggesting that lead was smelted throughout the Valley. Some may represent the locations of substantial hearths, others may be smaller one-off operations such as that found on a small, natural platform-like landslip far along Howden Clough. Situated on the landslip was a simple, makeshift hearth where lead was *melted* in the thirteenth century (**44**). It was only used once either to produce useable objects from lead ingots, known as pigs, or more likely to recycle broken/unwanted objects. Branches were cut from oak, birch, hazel, hawthorn and cherry growing in the surrounding clough-side for fuel. Two pottery vessels, a cooking pot and a jug, were smashed into the fire and partly covered in molten lead towards the end of the melt. The remote location and hasty appearance of the operation suggests an opportunistic melt by shepherds or perhaps something more clandestine.

These medieval valley-bottom lead hearths of the Upper Derwent are not found elsewhere in the Peak District. The wide scale nature of the industry down in the valleys and the single find of an upland site suggests that those behind it were working with slightly different ideas to the bole smelters of the gritstone moors further south. However, there is always the chance this is the product of archaeological visibility and more valley hearths may currently lie hidden elsewhere in the region. The most likely influence for lead working in the Upper Derwent was the Abbey which had a large need for lead for roofs, plumbing, cisterns and sometimes for the coffins of select members of the order. They also appear to have smelted iron in a bloomery near to One Man's House. Palls of toxic smoke may have commonly drifted up the valley sides to cloud the pastoral idyll.

Disafforestation and dissolution

As more settlers moved into the Royal Forest where they cleared land and pastured their herds and flocks, the conflicts between the interests of maintaining the Royal deer herd and grazing livestock became more widespread and intense. This reached a climax in 1526 when a Royal Commission was set up to investigate the matter including the dangers to deer posed by the overgrazing of grass by cattle and sheep. Tenants also made depositions to the Crown claiming that Forest officers were stealing sheep. The same officers were variously accused of damaging the King's woods, murder, releasing prisoners for bribes and even of stealing furniture from Peveril Castle. Counter complaints were made that farmers were damaging the woods and poaching deer. During the reign of Elizabeth I disputes over the respective rights of deer and livestock intensified. Encroachment throughout the forest led to the building of a wall in 1579 to finally demarcate an area which was to be the exclusive deer preserve where they were protected from livestock. This area equated to that of the present Peak Forest parish and was much smaller than the original extent of the forest. The remainder of the forest, including the Upper Derwent west of the river, was still under Forest Law so deer were allowed to compete with cattle and sheep. This untenable position was resolved in 1674 when the forest was finally legally disafforested.

The sixteenth century was also a time of major change for Welbeck Abbey. By this time Crookhill grange had been let out to a tenant, the up and coming Eyre family, and the other farmsteads continued in rental. It is possible that the Abbey was landlord over all of Derwent township (though this still remained in the manor of Hathersage) as well as Hope Woodlands. When Henry VIII became desperate to divorce one wife for another he thought more likely to bear him a son, he approached the Pope for a divorce. The Pope refused, largely because Charles V of Spain, nephew of Henry's current wife Catherine, surrounded Rome at the time. On refusal Henry broke with the Roman Catholic Church in 1533 and set in train a series of events which would lead to the Reformation and England becoming a Protestant nation, though Henry never saw himself as a Protestant.

It was an opportunity that Thomas Cromwell, the King's chief minister and very much a Protestant, took quickly. To claim the monastic wealth and prevent Catholicism from returning he was responsible for dissolving all the monasteries and abbeys of England by 1540. Their land was first controlled by the Crown before being turned over to private ownership in a complex rush of grants, rewards, land claims and intermarriages. In Derbyshire and South Yorkshire, the latter was greatly influenced by Bess of Hardwick who went through four husbands in quick succession. The distribution of monastic lands to important families was, in practice, to buy their services and support for the Protestant Crown. Much of the region's monastic land was acquired by Talbots and Howards, who were established aristocracy, and the Cavendishes who were up and coming nouveau riche.

By 1554 Sir William Cavendish, a Dissolution Commissioner, had married Bess and acquired the townships of Derwent, Bradfield and Hope Woodlands – as Welbeck's estate in the Royal Forest was coming to be called. His two sons were bequeathed much of his landholding so that in the early seventeenth century the Earl of Devonshire owned Hope Woodlands while the Earl of Newcastle owned at least part of Derwent. By this time the Earl of Arundel, a Howard, had gained the Cavendishes' estates in Glossop and Bradfield as a dowry for marrying a daughter of one of Bess's later husbands.

The medieval landowning structure of Royal Forest and monastic estate greatly influenced the landscape that the new lords acquired. These structures determined the conditions within which people settled and used the land. Tenants, laybrothers and Forest officers pushed for what they could get, so developing a richly worked landscape of dispersed farmsteads, woodlands and moorland commons. Pottery found at the sites of reservoir-level farmsteads suggests something of the impact of Dissolution on the Abbey's tenants. Numbers of sherds drop significantly at all of the farms in the sixteenth century before steadily increasing again in the following century. Pottery all but disappears from the grange at One Man's House where large amounts of medieval pottery have been found. At a time when tablewares were beginning to become more fashionable and packaged as desirable items they seem not to be reaching the farmsteads in the area in any significant numbers. The patterns of people's lives in the farming community were obviously disrupted in some way. Established markets with the Abbey were removed so curtailing profits that could be spent on other goods. The pattern of ceramics associated with Ronksley House is more complex. Sherd numbers also fall dramatically but at the same time fine glassware from the Rhine and the Netherlands is being used. This shows that, at this one farm, at least, the tenants were still able to be economically successful to some extent and so partly satisfy their social pretensions. It is likely that those farmers who were mainly keyed in to growing produce for the Abbey's markets were most affected while others either already had greater access to markets in nearby towns or were able to switch more quickly.

Local folk memory has preserved some local links to the Abbey in the names chosen for places. One Man's House became Abbey Farm and two local routes in the valley were known as Chapel Lane and, erroneously given that they were canons, Friar's Walk.

The packhorseman often asks 'is it meat or muck that keeps us alive?' Manure feeds the fields and peat stokes our fires so it all comes down to what we can return from our own earth. A broken milk jug disappears into the muck heap, to be spread this winter onto the paddock where the cows are kept. Although it is farmers who mark out the land in stone, the landlord's ownership of the walls is underlined when they are drawn on his maps.

SIX

TENANT AND LANDOWNER

LATE SIXTEENTH TO MID-EIGHTEENTH CENTURIES

Mapping the landscape

Frequently we come to know landscapes from above, through the stylised, two-dimensional representation of the map with hedges, buildings and pylons rendered as lines, colours and symbols. They are so commonplace that we accept the map-based view of the world as being an objective and accurate way of pictorially representing land based on survey, measurement and scale. But behind every map are the reasons for its production and the aims of the organisation or person who commissioned it. The first comprehensive national mapping programme in the world, Britain's nineteenth-century Ordnance Survey, betrays in its name its origin as a tool for military defence of the nation, yet it has become the mainstay for recreational use of the countryside. This is in part seen in the changes made in how features are represented between the mid-nineteenth century and today. Decisions are made by the mapmaker about which features to survey, how to depict them and the level of accuracy that is required. The result is a representation of the world created within set conventions. Coats of arms, cartouches, the size and character of lettering, icons, colours and borders all contribute to the political and social meaning of maps, for cartography 'maps' relations of power as much as it records natural and built features.

William Senior was the Earl of Devonshire's mapmaker in the early seventeenth century when he conducted cartographical surveys of the Earl's Peak District estates. In 1627 he produced the first detailed map of the township of Hope Woodlands. Divided into six sheets, each one with a decorated border, the map depicts and names farmsteads, fields and their boundaries, woodlands, cloughside scrub, enclosed moorland and pasture. Colours are used to highlight each of these different landscapes, with the farmland being the most visually striking. Buildings are more stylised than precisely represented. Typical of its time, it is a map of land-use, a visual description of the productive value of the Devonshire's estate, acquired over seventy years previously. Attached to it is a written catalogue known as a terrier which lists all the parcels of land on the estate and what they were used for. The colourfully decorated borders, gold leaf and dedication panels which re-iterate ownership leave no doubt that it is also more than just a management tool, it is an expression of local landed authority, of power over place. Estate surveying was also part of the trend from traditional manorial community towards a more modern landscape of market enterprise.

Senior's survey was the first detailed map of anywhere in the Upper Derwent, in effect it is the local Domesday of our history of Hope Woodlands (**46**). It shows that the landscape of the township was highly organised. The isolated farmsteads continued to be the main focus for daily life, not only in 1627 but throughout the following centuries, surrounded by walled fields interspersed with woodland and associated with specifically designated areas of pasture on the adjacent moorland (**47**). Not all farmsteads lay in neat blocks of fields. There were four farmsteads huddled together at the head of Alport Dale and their fields

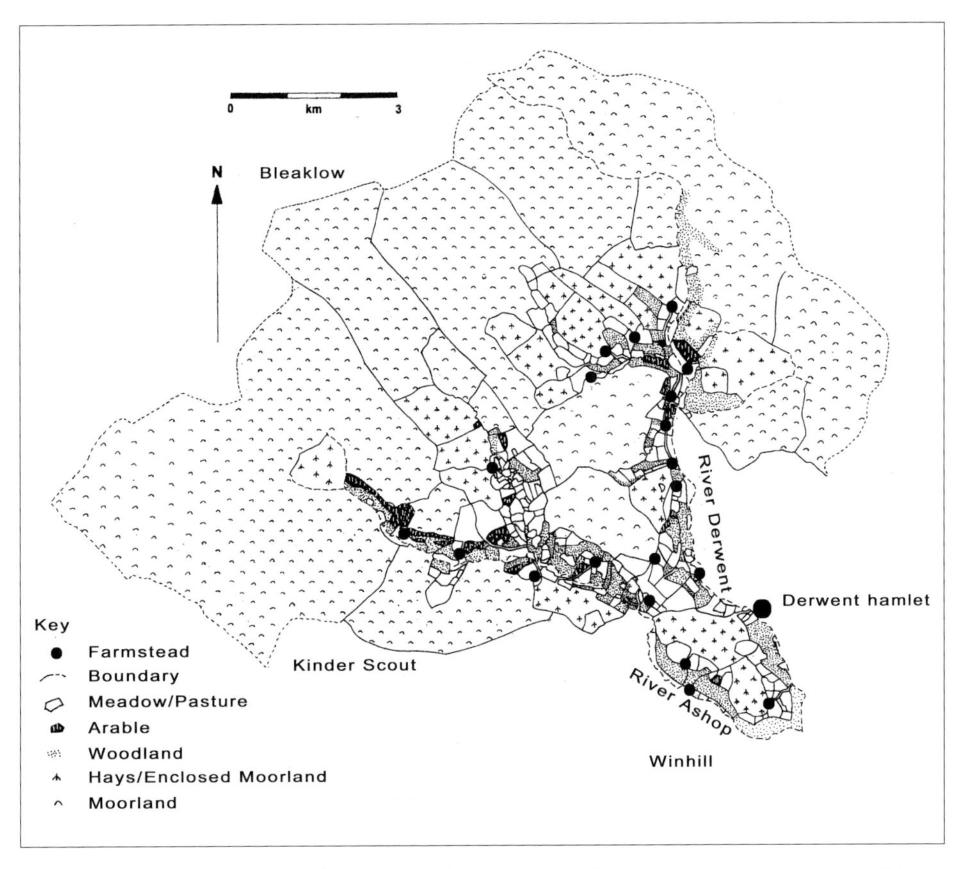

46 *Hope Woodlands township and Howden farmholding in the early seventeenth century, reconstructed from estate surveys*

were intermingled with each others. Some farms, such as Grimbocar and Crookhill, had only limited or no moorland pasture next to them so were allotted grazing on distant moors in the north-west of the township. This suggests that these were later settlements created when the moorland was already apportioned, a hint of chronology in the otherwise snapshot picture that the map provides.

Senior depicts twenty-two farmsteads in Hope Woodlands, while surviving written documents for Derwent township and Bradfield refer to some farms, though their mention is reliant on the more ad-hoc nature of these records. Howden House was the only farmstead of Bradfield parish in the Upper Derwent, lying close to neighbours in Hope Woodlands but miles from any of the other Yorkshire township's settlements. It may have been strange to be subject to completely different manorial regulations to these neighbours and to be the only Yorkshire household in an otherwise Derbyshire valley. Our knowledge of the number of farms in seventeenth-century Derwent is hazier. In the sixteenth century, various plots of land in Hathersage manor, including

Derwent, were bought by the Fitzherbert family to form a consolidated estate. Derwent was then sold to a number of purchasers in the seventeenth century with some, but not all, of the Derwent properties leaving the family. Two things could explain the lack of a map. The complex purchase and sale of different premises meant there was no stable, central estate management for any length of time. The family were also swept up in the religious conflicts of the time and were regularly imprisoned, had lands confiscated by the Crown or tried to avoid some confiscation by letting out other properties. There was simply little time for map-making. Piecing together the picture from finds of pottery, building fabric and various documents, we know that there were at least ten farmsteads

47 *Woodlands Valley. Farmers from the medieval period onwards created this landscape of walled fields and small woodlands with moorland common above.* Photo by Ray Manley

48 *The seventeenth-century stone packhorse bridge from Derwent Village was moved further up the River Derwent to Slippery Stones when Ladybower Reservoir was flooded.* Photo by Ray Manley

and sixteen tenants in the seventeenth century. Farms included Abbey Farm, Ashes Farm, Bamford House, Dingbank, Grainfoot Farm, Hollin Clough, Lanehead, Shireowlers, Tinker's House and Walker's Farm (**colour plate 12**). Some of the tenants lived in the hamlet which continued to provide a central focus for the farmsteads of the township and the whole of the valley.

Derwent hamlet

In the seventeenth century, Derwent hamlet continued to thrive on the east bank of the river of the same name and alongside the line of the packhorse route between Sheffield, Hope and Glossop. The mill and chapel built in the thirteenth century still served the wider local community, as did a blacksmith who forged agricultural tools, door and window fittings and shod horses. The hamlet was also well-served with drinking establishments, as would be expected in a settlement on a long-distance trade route, with four ale houses recorded in 1577. This was the main stopping off point for anyone making the long journey between Sheffield and Glossop. In the seventeenth century the medieval wooden packhorse bridge was replaced by a more substantial stone structure (**48**). Bridge-End farmstead was built in 1673 at the southern end of this bridge. Though it was situated over the river in Hope Woodlands township, socially it was part of the Derwent hamlet.

In 1672 a major change to the hamlet's built and social landscapes was made when the Balguy family bought a plot of land to the west. The three existing cottages were cleared to make way for Derwent Hall, a small manor house with a walled formal garden. The Hall was an H-shaped two-storey house with mullion and transom windows constructed of dressed Millstone Grit quarried from local outcrops. It was by far the grandest and most imposing building in the hamlet or elsewhere in the surrounding Derwent and Woodlands valleys. It can be imagined that its construction attracted a lot of interest amongst inhabitants of the area and travellers passing on the packhorse route, not least because the Balguys were a locally prominent yeoman family. Balguys lived at Hope and Aston Halls, and the family who built Derwent Hall had been living at Hagg Farm, Hope Woodlands, in 1627 and with relatives at neighbouring Rowlee in the latter part of the century. Their elevation to such a high status house, architect-designed and with a walled garden, would have no doubt been discussed with some passion by their neighbours. To reinforce to visitors and, on a more daily basis, to themselves how real their social standing was, they displayed their coat of arms above the Hall's main door.

They patronised the chapel, endowing it with a stone font in the year of building the Hall then applied in 1713 to Queen Anne's Bounty to augment the income of the priest. But by 1757 the chapel's medieval fabric was so dilapidated it was pulled down and replaced by a much smaller building. Ten years later the Hall became a farmhouse as the Balguys moved on to Swanwick Hall in eastern Derbyshire. The presence of resident 'lords of the manor' at Derwent had lasted only 100 years, but they had left a Hall that would attract the attention of another Lord a further 100 years later.

Around the farmsteads

Dispersion

The seventeenth century distribution of farmsteads across the landscape followed that laid down in the medieval period and was finely attuned to local topography (**49**). Most are not only on shelves of more level ground along the lower valley sides, but tend to form loose clusters along those parts of the valleys where extensive sections of the slopes are gentler. Moving north-west from its confluence with the Derwent, the Woodlands Valley starts with a gentle north-facing slope until it narrows at Hagg then the south-east facing slope becomes the

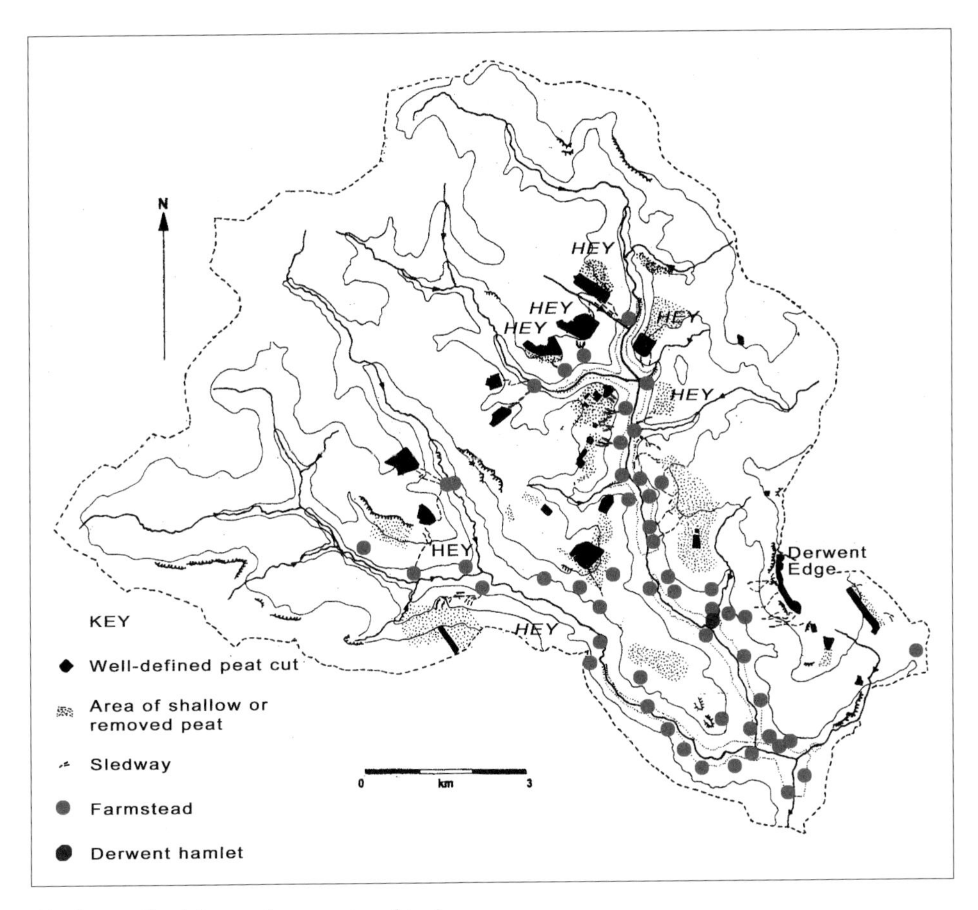

49 *Post-medieval farmsteads, peat cuts and trackways*

gentlest. Numerous farmsteads are strung out along the gentler slopes while they appear only intermittently on the steeper ground opposite. So where we find Hagg, Rowlee, Wood House and Upper Farm distributed along 4km on one side of the valley, there is only Upper Ashop farm opposite (**colour plate 13**). Other farmsteads followed Crookhill's lead and were built higher up the valley sides, at the break of slope with moorland plateau. Ridge, Bank Top, Lockerbrook and Two Thorn Fields are all found at elevated altitudes. These were probably located where valley woodland gave way to open ground so the farms had immediate access to extensive grazing.

Farmers kept a physical distance between their homes with individual farmsteads rarely being less than 500m apart. The only exception in Hope Woodlands is Alport where we find a small hamlet more akin to the Booths of Edale. Here, four farms were clustered together at the head of the valley in 1627. Six tenants shared these farmsteads, four of them with the surname Hall, one Eyre and a Harrison. The preponderance of Halls suggests that an original, single medieval farmstead was divided over time through inheritance and sale. Alternatively, a group may have built the hamlet as they occupied the valley, rather than settling in isolated farmsteads as elsewhere in the Upper Derwent. The settlement location is intriguing. It occupies a roughly oval area of ground raised above the River Alport at its confluence with Swint Clough. This area is enclosed within a wall and sub-divided like the spokes of a wheel. We will return to Alport later, to discuss its fields, and search for ideas about its difference.

There is also a variation in the pattern of dispersed farmsteads in Derwent township. Eight farmsteads appear to be paired together through being built close to each other. Shireowlers and Walker's Farm, Hancock Farm and Hollin Clough, Old House Farm and Hill House, and Grainfoot Farm and Riding House form four pairs where the respective farmsteads are separated by no more than 300m. Shireowlers, Walker's, Hollin Clough and Grainfoot all appear to be thirteenth-century settlements while we cannot be sure when the others were founded except to say they were all built by the nineteenth century. This pairing may be the result of a desire for sociability or that each of these farms was divided in two with new farmbuildings built for the second holding. Some new settlements may have been created by the inheritance of tenancies by two sons while others, such as we have seen at Bridge-End Farm, were the result of the deliberate re-organisation of farms by the landowners. The only other new farmstead to be built before the middle of the eighteenth century was Townrowhag which appears in an area that was being enclosed and cleared of woodland at this time. During the seventeenth and early eighteenth centuries there was no other expansion of settlement outside of Derwent hamlet. The occupation of the landscape appears to have stabilised sometime between the later medieval period and the early seventeenth century.

Pottery

Pottery finds from fieldwalking at the locations of farmsteads and Derwent hamlet begin to increase between the late sixteenth and the early eighteenth centuries. There are differences between farms with some using more pottery than others throughout the seventeenth century. This was a time when urban households were acquiring more goods, pottery was beginning to replace metal and wooden vessels while porcelain was increasingly used for the consumption of hot drinks. These tablewares were produced to meet the desires of a rising urban mercantile elite who thought crockery more civilised and befitting for people of status. It may be that pottery producers and salesmen were slowly beginning to market their wares in large numbers to the rural populations of the area. As in the medieval period some farmsteads stand out from the others in regards of the numbers and variety of vessels being used. The occupants of Ronksley were buying a wide range and large number of pottery vessels compared to other farmsteads. Unfortunately, we cannot be clear about the use of such material culture at Derwent Hall because the house only surfaces above the waters of Ladybower Reservoir during exceptionally dry years and when it does is covered in deep layers of silts – conditions not conducive to fieldwalking. There are many other farms, such as Crookhill, Rowlee and others in the Woodlands Valley, where no fieldwalking has been undertaken. They are located far from the exposed soils of the reservoirs and surrounded by fields of permanent pasture. Nearly all the pottery and glassware, from the thirteenth to early twentieth centuries, is found in specific locations directly on the sites of ruined farmsteads and in the closest neighbouring fields. This suggests that once broken, vessels were being thrown onto nearby midden heaps with manure and fire ashes. In the early eighteenth century one document even mentions 'manure around the house' at Rowlee. The middens were discarded across nearby fields, possibly those containing crops which were often closest to the farmsteads.

Rooms

From the sixteenth century, radical changes in building styles were seen across much of Britain. Vernacular architecture was reworked to such an extent that houses were effectively transformed internally from medieval to more modern. Much of the population in medieval Britain lived in longhouses. These generally comprised a single room with a central hearth or inglenook for accommodation in one half of the building and an animal byre in the other half. The more prosperous Yeoman farmer might live in a 'hall house' where the main room was a large hall with a hearth. One or two bedrooms, storerooms and a scullery were attached. In the sixteenth and seventeenth centuries, domestic architecture changed as greater comfort and privacy were desired. Window glass and chimneyed fireplaces were introduced, the internal space was divided into small rooms on two storeys and entrance lobbies allowed movement into the house to be better controlled.

Some of the seventeenth-century layout of rooms and their contents can be seen in inventories of wills made on the death of the head of a household. There are a number which survive for families in the Upper Derwent and provide useful information. They were relatively common in England between the middle of the sixteenth and middle of the eighteenth centuries, though they were rarely produced for women and the poor. Descriptions of objects and rooms also vary greatly in detail. Caution is therefore required in using inventories to widely interpret the nature of households and the objects they owned because of who and what they may exclude. The inventories allow us to see in through the windows on some aspects of domestic life but not to complete the scene.

Taking Rowlee as an example, we can see the layout of the house and the changes in range of material objects between the deaths of Henry Balguy in 1686 and William Greaves in 1719. Henry was a yeoman farmer, someone of modest wealth who today might be labelled middle class. In that year the farmhouse at Rowlee comprised a large number of public and private rooms according to the tastes of the time. The ground floor was divided into a hall, dining room, study, great parlour, pantry, lesser parlour, kitchen and dairy. Above these were a new chamber, bed chamber, parlour chamber, kitchen chamber, stable chamber and the husbandman's chamber. The hall and dining rooms appear to be the public rooms with tables, a sideboard, soft furnishings and objects for display – swords, a hunting horn and clock. The study was arranged for one person, having a single table and chair as well as books. Presumably this was Henry's private room. The kitchen, dining room and new chamber contained the most things, ranging from the newly fashionable consumable items such as a looking glass and cushions to those essential for the upkeep of the house – the pans and fire irons. The locations of the irons suggests that the kitchen and dining room had the only two fireplaces in the whole house which probably stood back-to-back against a shared wall. The bedchamber was presumably the bedroom of Henry and his wife for it contained only one bed while the other chambers and the parlours contained two or more, including in one room a pull-out wheeled truckle bed which stowed away under the other bed. There were a total of twelve beds in the house. These would have accommodated the family, 'husbandmen' who worked on the farm and possibly household servants. Pottery and glass vessels are only specifically listed in one of the upstairs rooms and pewter appears in the kitchen. However, the presence of a sideboard in the dining room and two dressers in the kitchen hints at tablewares.

Forty-three years later, on the death of William Greaves, the list of objects and number of rooms were greater. At least two upstairs chambers had been added which presumably corresponded with rooms downstairs, however a number of ground floor rooms had been simply grouped as 'house'. In addition to most of the items listed before it appears as if the acquisition of material objects had increased and become more important to the rural yeoman. Soft furnishings proliferated in the form of cushions, table cloths, napkins and window curtains, as did the accoutrements for entertaining guests at dinner – brass candle sticks, a set of twenty-four knives and forks, two silver cups, two silver salts, six silver spoons, two glass decanters with eight drinking glasses and 'other wares'. The range of display objects had expanded to include pictures, brass furniture for a range and three pairs of stag horns. William also had a silver watch with a chain.

Similar lists of rooms and their contents can be found for Ronksley and Crookhill, though the listing of rooms is much more inconsistent than at Rowlee. Again soft furnishings are itemised, including table cloths and napkins which imply table settings for dining, but pewter or ceramic tablewares are not, even though Ronksley is one of the few locations in the Upper Derwent where substantial numbers and a wide variety of seventeenth-century pot sherds are found. This, and the inconsistent listing of rooms, suggests omissions on the part of the people who drew up these inventories unless tablewares were owned by someone else in the households.

Clustered around each of the farmhouses were one or more outbuildings. Again the inventories of wills indicate something about farming in the seventeenth and early eighteenth centuries. Cattle, sheep, horses and hens make regular appearances but not pigs. Products from their own farms and those bought at market are listed: salt beef, bacon, dripping, cheese, butter, malt, wool and cloth. Hay and oats are common while wheat, hemp and flax are occasionally mentioned in small quantities. There are ploughs and harrows, saddles and yokes, sleds and carts, looms and spinning wheels. Manure was also deemed important enough to will in one case. Sleds were commonly used to carry peat down from the moorlands to the farmhouses. These are the materials of agriculture, the routines of which radiated out from the farmstead into the landscape of fields and moorlands where time was spent in relation to the seasonal cycle of tasks.

Of fields and walls

Through clearance and enclosure of woodland and rough ground, the landscape was becoming more obviously and visually managed. The flatter surfaces of fields supplanted the more three-dimensional woodlands and the hand of human construction spread along the network of newly built walls. This was a process being enacted over a long period of time, beginning in the thirteenth century and carried out by generation after generation of tenant farmers living in the area. Nearest to the farmstead were the fields forming a pattern of enclosure continuing from the medieval period. Those farmhouses on the lower valley sides were surrounded by walled fields, while those near the break of slope between valley and moorland plateau were located on the junction between enclosed land and open. In 1627, Senior shows that most of the farmsteads in Hope Woodlands were associated with a small number of fields surrounded by woodland (**46**).

There is no overall plan or regular order to the field layout in the Upper Derwent, it was not planned by a centralising landowner nor the shared product of communal farming. Rather it was created over time by successive generations of occupants at individual farmsteads who built on what already existed and added to it. More and more of the favourable areas of land were taken into cultivation by clearing woodland or improving rough grassland and making fields which were bounded within dry-stone walls. Farmers worked with local topography, seeking out the better soils, the more level ground or the least boulder-strewn areas available to them at the time. Boundaries were built in relation to watercourses, changes in slope, the needs of livestock and crop management, and where neighbours had already enclosed land.

Much of the early enclosure is likely to have been near to each farmer's house but it was not always a simple case of progressively working further and further outwards (**50**). In 1627 Rowlee farm comprised six adjacent fields surrounding the farmhouse and two isolated enclosures nearby which were separated from each other by woodland. By the beginning of the nineteenth century all of this woodland was cleared and divided with walls into small fields, the individual patches of agricultural land becoming a cohesive block. It appears that the earlier fields occupied the better drained land while later enclosure may have been undertaken with the development of better drainage techniques in the seventeenth or eighteenth centuries. More striking is the development at Two Thorn Fields to the west of Crookhill. The farmstead is first documented in 1623, four years before Senior surveyed Hope Woodlands and referred to the farm buildings as being 'ancient'. Situated just above the steep side of the Woodlands Valley, the farmstead was located in between two large oval enclosures with woodland below and moorland pasture on the ridge above described as heath and turf moss. Most of the farm's fields were situated on the other side of this ridge in Derwent Valley. By the early nineteenth century the oval enclosures were sub-divided into smaller fields, the woodland was cleared and the open land walled to make small enclosures, and the moorland was split into three blocks by two straight walls. Here the dynamism of clearing and enclosing the land for agriculture is very evident and was mostly carried out after 1627.

The expansion of enclosed farmland which the farmers at Rowlee and Two Thorn Fields were undertaking is seen throughout Hope Woodlands township. At least half the woodland present in the early seventeenth century was replaced with pasture and arable. Areas of moorland common pasture were also enclosed as fields spread up the valley sides or existing large walled blocks were subdivided with new boundaries so that they could be used more effectively. Because this expansion was undertaken within a context of estate organisation, the landowner would have influenced where it could take place. The division of the estate into single landholdings attached to each farmstead constrained each farmer's enclosure within set bounds. The rapid reduction of woodland gives the impression that landowners were keen to see the amount of farmland expand which would increase the value and therefore the rents of each farm. Clearance of individual areas may have been discussed with the landowner or the tenant given a free rein within the farm. Woodland did have potential uses to tenants, providing fuel for fires and fodder for livestock. Holly is a particularly good animal feed, when cut the leaves become soft and are very nutritious, and the name 'hollen' – for a holly grove – appears in a number of places in the valleys, most notably as the name of a farmstead and watercourse as 'Hollin Clough'.

Again, Alport is the exception to much of this. The hamlet is located at one end of the most extensive stretch of enclosed farmland in the township and woodland was restricted to two areas beyond the fields (**46** & **colour plate 14**). The six tenants in 1627 did not have a single, distinct, block of land each. Instead their fields were complexly intermingled with each other along the whole of the valley. A group of enclosures here, another over there separated by a neighbour's fields. The locally unique nature of Alport, with a group of farmsteads within a sub-circular enclosure and the intermixing of farmland, raises questions about

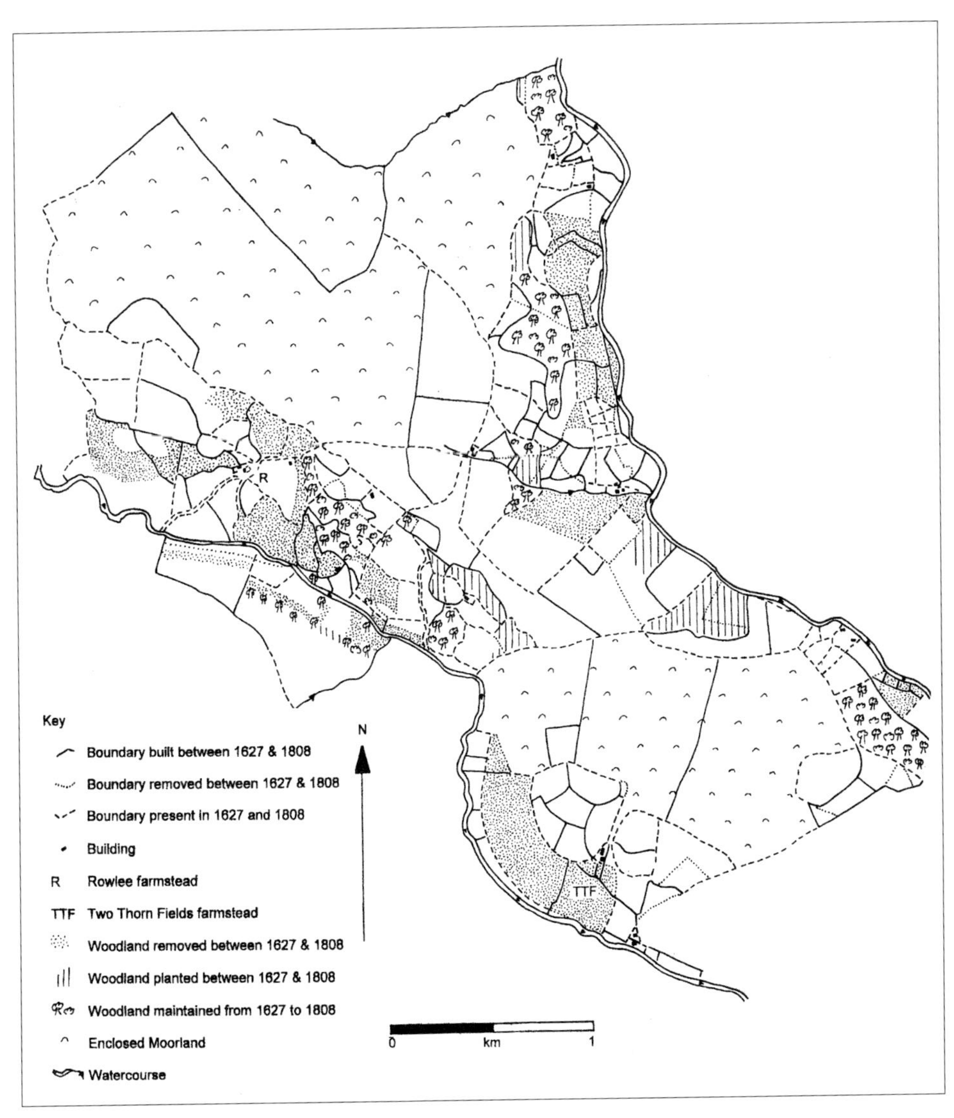

50 *Post-medieval expansion of enclosure at Rowlee and Two Thorn Fields was not a simple case of working progressively further out from the farmsteads*

local variability of landscapes. Here we have a place where the organisation of farmland is superficially similar to that practised in villages with open fields but appears different to its nearest neighbours. Was it because a different approach to medieval settlement was taken or was there an older pattern of land-use already established that influenced later occupation? Was woodland already absent by the medieval period or did medieval farmers have more opportunities to clear trees in this separate valley? The earliest dating evidence is a fourteenth- to fifteenth-century charter. No opportunities for fieldwalking or environmental sampling have yet been forthcoming to open up its chronology through artefacts or radio-

51 Above: *Wall junctions such as these can be clues to the boundary between different farmers' responsibilities for maintaining a field wall.*
Below: *A blocked gateway preserves the line of an abandoned routeway.* Photo by Bill Bevan

carbon dated pollen. So, unfortunately no answers yet, but we have identified a set of questions and methods of investigation.

The pattern of fields and walls is deeply connected with the social relations and practices of people living, working and travelling in the area. Enclosures were the places where farming families spent most time in their daily routines of tending livestock, crops and hay. The majority of fields in the Upper Derwent were used to pasture livestock with some fields being reserved to produce hay during early summer or arable crops in autumn. Returning to the inventories of wills also gives an idea of numbers of livestock in the seventeenth century, a century earlier than surviving estate records of animal numbers. In 1679 Edward Barber of Ronksley owned 218 sheep, ten cattle and a mare, while in 1686 Henry Balguy of Rowlee left 700 sheep after his death. The inventories are not so good for indicating arable production. They regularly mention the machinery of cultivation, such as ploughs, and crops in store but rarely quantify amounts.

The personal and family connections to the farmstead were reinforced through the regular toil needed to manage the land and to build and repair the physical field boundaries. Sometimes a junction was built into the wall to mark where two farmers' responsibilities for maintenance met (**51**). Work by John Roberts, analysing walls at Hagg in the Woodlands Valley, shows many to have one face constructed to a much neater appearance. The better finished sides formed the external boundary of the farm, the outside face presented to others, at the time the walls were built. This care suggests that walls were more than just the tools of farm management or convenient ways to clear stone. Each stone would be selected by eye and hand judging its size, weight and structural presence within the overall wall. Walls were statements of 'ownership' and farming pride, the line on the ground between neighbours or between private and public land. They signalled to others the hard work required to take land into husbandry; to the landowner, to other farmers and to younger members of the family who might be hoping to take on the tenancy of the farm in the future. They spoke silently about the craft of wall building, the neater side showing to others in the valleys the quality of work put into the wall and, by association, into the rest of the farm.

The compartmentalisation of the land created by such enclosure also enables and constrains movement along certain directions. Specific areas are blocked so forcing or encouraging people to move along restricted pathways to avoid trespass. Rights of way develop hand-in-hand with the creation of the enclosed landscape, at some locations boundaries may follow existing trackways while at others routes will develop in relation to boundaries. Patterns of movement around the landscape can be seen in the locations of the walled lanes which connect the farmsteads with the wider world. Most farmsteads were set back from the public rights of way which they were connected to via an access lane, though some were on the lines of these longer-distance trackways. Anyone approaching a farmhouse would know they were entering restricted land when they stepped from the public road into private lane. The spatial separation of farmhouse and public space also helped to keep strangers, from outside the local community, at what was perceived to be a safe distance. This 'isolation' also worked on a more local level, because farmsteads were rarely connected to each other by direct routes. This emphasised the separation between families that was already established through the dispersed pattern of settlement. Privacy in the landscape of the Upper Derwent may have preceded notions of privacy within the household.

Movement within the farm, around the fields and onto the moorland commons, was nearly always made through fields. Barns, livestock folds, gateways and sheep creeps were constructed throughout the fields to facilitate management (**51** & **52**). Moving to the edge of the enclosed land, at the boundaries between field and moorland common were gathering folds and sheep washes (**53**). Folds were small pens that allowed sheep to be corralled while pasturing them on the commons, perhaps when small groups needed to be separated from the remainder of the flock or when sheep from different flocks needed sorting. Sheep were washed in rivers to remove skin parasites before the introduction of chemical dips in the twentieth century. The remains of multi-compartment folds are found at suitably slow-moving and deep stretches of watercourses where sheep could be dipped in the water and the clean ones separated from the dirty.

Onto the common

Beyond the fields the farmer would move on to the common, most often through gates in the top wall and sometimes via walled lanes where these facilitated gathering or where farmers living in the valley bottom had to pass through the higher fields of neighbours. At the end of such shared routes trackways might branch out in different directions when they reached the moorland, the regular return of people, sleds and animals to specific areas eroding fanlike patterns of hollow-ways (**colour plate 11**). In Hope Woodlands the common was strictly regulated by the landowner from at least the seventeenth century. Most farms had a well-defined area of moorland which often comprised an enclosed area called a hey just beyond the farmland and outpastures or sheepwalks further out (**46**). Both were used for sheep grazing.

Many outpastures were immediately above the farm they belonged to and the numbers of sheep allowed on each were agreed with the estate. Each of the individual outpastures were divided from others by earthen banks or dry-stone walls. Some of these were stockproof and aided livestock management but others were built to physically mark the pastures' boundaries. Farms with limited moorland nearby, such as Two Thorn Fields, Rowlee and Crookhill, also shared grazing rights on the remote moorlands of Kinder and Bleaklow to the north-west.

52 *Grindle barns is a group of typical seventeenth-century two-storey field barns, one is dated 1647 above the door. They are located on a branch of the Derwent to Sheffield packhorse route.* Photo by Bill Bevan

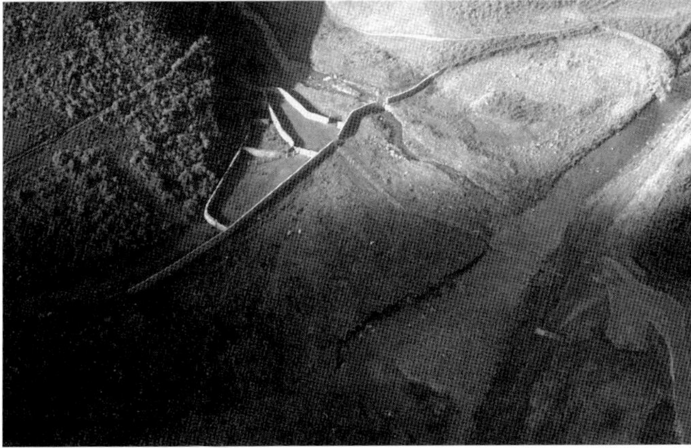

53 *A multi-compartment sheepfold located on the boundary between enclosed land and moorland, and next to a watercourse. This may have been used to sort different farmers' sheep when brought from the moor and for sheepwashing.* Courtesy of the National Trust

Farmers had a wider range of rights in the heys, and in other unenclosed moorland areas at similar locations. Here, peat could be cut, stone quarried and cattle grazed. Extensive areas of shallow peat ending at vertical sections in the deeper, uncut peat can still be seen in each of these heys. Peat was brought down from the cuts on wooden sleds to be stored and dried at the farmstead (**49** & **colour plate 14**). The sleds were led or ridden down to farmsteads via sledways gouged into the sloping valley-sides akin to rocky bobsleigh runs, the farmer using his feet to steer and brake. The heys were divided from the outpastures by banks, ditches or walls and their legal status was somewhat blurred as technically they were part of the common but in practice they were an extension of the tenanted land.

On the east side of the Derwent Valley the moorland pastures of Bradfield and Derwent townships were not legally assigned to individual farms. Numbers of sheep were set by the manor court and those of any tenant in each township could theoretically be grazed anywhere on their respective commons. In practice, sheep were pastured on favoured areas so that specific areas of the common became associated with individual farms even though different flocks were free to mix. Derwent and Bradfield commons were also subject to agreements allowing tenants of each township to pasture their livestock on the moors of the other, an activity known as inter-commoning. These commons were adjacent to each other with no physical boundary to prevent the livestock of one from wandering on to the other. Derwent tenants had been using commons in Bradfield since before 1574 for which they paid an annual sum of sixteen pence.

In Bradfield, Howden House concentrated peat cutting in two enclosed heys which were reached via hollow-ways. Farmsteads in Derwent also had peat cuts on moorland nearest to the top of the valley but these were not enclosed. Again, routine practice identified places on the common with individuals even where this was not legally designated. The occupants of Derwent hamlet could not so easily have their own extensive peat cuts because each household could not be geographically linked to a different part of the moorland. Instead, their turbary rights were organised very differently. Three sledways lead up the valley side from the hamlet and as they approach Derwent Edge they divide into numerous branches (**49**). Above the Edge the branches lead to a series of narrow, long peat cuts lying adjacent to each other and separated by baulks of free-standing peat. Nucleation in settlement required nucleation in peat cuts, neighbours at home being neighbours on the moor.

Who actually owned commons was not devoid of controversy and argument. A legal battle began in 1574 over the boundary between Hallamshire and Hathersage manors, between Yorkshire and Derbyshire, and to which manor the commons at Moscar on Derwent Moors belonged. The details of the case not only tell us something about the importance of commons but also how disputes were settled through memory and recourse to local elders. Counsels for both lords met with 'diverse old and ancient men' of the two manors who were called as witnesses. The men of Derbyshire brought with them a man of 'five score years or thereabouts' who recalled that a cottage was built at Moscar and when the tenant fell into arrears on his rent he gave a black horse as equity to the Lord of Hallamshire. Another witness, aged sixty, remembered his father saying that Hallamshire tenants had torn down walls built on the common by the Lord of Hathersage. In 1656 the bounds of Hathersage were ridden and written down as following a line which clearly placed Moscar in Derbyshire, and a note was made that these bounds had been ridden many times before 'without disturbance or contradiction'. Forty-nine years later 'men of Bradfield' drew up a petition demanding all right of common on Derwent Moors from which they were being excluded. Witnesses were again called, men aged in their sixties and seventies, who stated that they tended sheep and cattle for farmers in Hathersage from their earliest memories. A decision was finally made in 1724 after further witnesses gave their testimony. In this year the oldest was John Trout who was eighty-five years old and could remember assisting in driving Bradfield sheep on to Derwent Moors sixty years ago and on another occasion ten years before that. Another newly built cottage at Moscar was referred to. The dispute had dragged on for over 150 years, the memories of increasingly older men had been tested, walls had been built and removed, boundaries had been ridden to confirm their lines and the small matter of a Civil War had been fought. In the end the decision went to Hathersage.

Connecting with the world

Throughout the dispute, Moscar was traversed by the packhorse route from Sheffield to Derwent and Hope. The status of packhorse routes was much like the commons in that they were rights of way. People had, in effect, common rights to travel along them. But where common grazing rights were restricted to the occupants of an outpasture's township, rights of passage were universal. These were the communication routes that connected the Upper Derwent with the outside world, everyone and everything passing into, out of and across the area used them (**37**). Landowners and their agents used them to travel to their estates and hawkers would appear at each farmstead to sell all manner of wares and services. Their names are varied, the route to Sheffield being known by its destinations at either end – Derwent to Sheffield, while that to Glossop and Hope was named Doctor's Gate after a local landowner, Doctor Talbot. The route to Penistone was known as Cut or Cart Gate, though the latter is most likely a corruption of the former. The tough terrain it traverses would break up or bog down any cart taken along it and 'cut' may refer to the excavation of an artificial route through the peat and down to the mineral soil below.

Maintenance of packhorse routes and the provision of waymarkers were variable. Doctor Talbot acquired responsibility for the maintenance of the Hope to Glossop route between 1491 and 1550. The Talbot family owned land throughout Derbyshire, including Glossop and Sheffield, so the route was important for connecting their estates. Sections of cobbling on the moorlands above the Snake Pass may be the work of the Talbots or the Romans (**33**). The Derwent to Sheffield route was also paved across a number of boggy places below Derwent Edge, and above the Edge, a guidestone was erected in 1737 to point the way to Sheffield, Hope and Penistone (**54**). In 1697, an Act of Parliament formalised the erection of guide posts to facilitate trade which had been expanding since the sixteenth century. The Act called for county justices of the peace to erect guide posts, where cross-roads were remote from villages. It was not until 1709 that Derbyshire began its programme of waymarking.

The packhorse routes took people first to the neighbouring towns of Sheffield, Penistone, Stannington, Hope and Glossop where there were markets. The networks that they formed with other routes spread their reach further afield to cities, ports and other countries. Markets were some of the main places for the occupants of the Upper Derwent to interact with this wider world. Sheep, cattle and other agricultural produce were taken to market for sale where prices were determined by both local and more distant demands. News of such major events as Drake's voyage, the Spanish Armada, Civil War or Great Plague, could be heard, debated and argued over. Everyday provisions not grown in the valleys would be bought. The changing fashions of society may have been evident in

54 *Guidestone on the Derwent to Sheffield packhorse route. The stone was erected in 1737 and points the way to Sheffield, Hope and Penistone.* Photo by Bill Bevan

the new tablewares, furniture and clothes which were available to buy, not forgetting those bizarre and recently discovered plants from the Americas. The find of a late sixteenth-/early seventeenth-clay pipe bowl at Hollin Clough Farm shows that tobacco smoking had not taken too long to reach the Upper Derwent.

During the seventeenth and early eighteenth centuries existing towns began to grow considerably and completely new ones were founded. Sheffield was home to 2,207 individuals in 1616 and 120 years later it had grown by fourfold to 10,121. England was one of the most urbanised countries in Europe at the time and was rapidly becoming more so. The towns played a major role in determining prices for agricultural produce and in spreading consumer objects throughout the country. As urban populations grew during the early seventeenth century the increasing demand for food pushed up prices. The wealth evident in the wills of the occupants of Rowlee was probably made on the back of this inflation. In the second half of the century supply continued to increase but the population did not and the value of wool and grain slumped. Livestock prices, on the other hand, still rose due to meat being eaten in greater quantities, another consumer good of the times. In the early eighteenth century, urban populations again expanded but prices fell or remained steady. Over this period small farmers were beginning to link into the capitalist commerce afforded by the size of the landless population and wider trade. The Upper Derwent farmers would be able to take livestock to any of a number of regional markets, many animals ending up on the tables in nearby towns of Sheffield and Manchester as joints and stews of lamb, mutton and beef.

The commercial profits from selling goods helped the towns grow. The larger and better trade networked towns had the greater range and more fashionable items. Sheffield grew throughout the seventeenth and early eighteenth centuries, building on its medieval metalworking base by utilising the plentiful resources of wood and water for fuel and power. Forges, cutlers and other workshops spread along its many valleys and the Company of Cutlers was formed in 1624 to regulate the local industry. Its reach had already stretched as far as the Upper Derwent along a packhorse route since the medieval period. In 1693 the large Attercliffe Forge bought charcoal from a Widow Aaron of Derwent for 6d. This was a sign of things to come. In the next centuries Sheffield's rapidly growing forges and population would have a significant influence on the landscape of the Upper Derwent. The maps were about to be redrawn.

As the city comes closer, farmers' lives are drawn further into urban streets and houses they have never visited. Lime improves the pasture to fatten the sheep that feed the ironworkers, the commons are privatised and divided by grids of stone, and tradesmen hurry from one city to another on Telford's toll road.

SEVEN

IMPROVING THE LANDSCAPE

MID-EIGHTEENTH TO LATE NINETEENTH CENTURIES

The upper reaches of rationality

Anyone coming to Derwent from Sheffield in the mid-nineteenth century might have travelled along a very different road to that taken over the previous 600 years. For generations travellers had crossed the extensive moors which lay between the two areas by packhorse route and descended into the valley from above Derwent hamlet. In the 1820s a new well-engineered road was built between Sheffield and Manchester by Thomas Telford. It took a shorter route across moorland and ran through the narrow Ladybower Gorge where branches of the oaks that clung onto the precipitous cliffs either side pressed against the coach. There was a toll to pay for using the road but the journey promised to be quicker and smoother. If you stopped off at the toll booth near Ashopton, perhaps to refresh at the new coaching inn, you could join the walled lane that ran part way up the east side of the Derwent valley. Walking past small fields of sheep and hay intermingled with woodlands you would come across one or two farmhouses but most were set well-back from the lane, their grey-brown gritstone walls giving out an air of dour privacy. After a short distance the hamlet would be spied in the distance, nestled in the slight dip of Millbrook and almost completely camouflaged in woodland. Only the chapel bell tower and roofs of the higher buildings would be visible above the trees made hazy by smoke from the hidden chimneys. After fording the brook a left turn leads into the settlement which was strung along its 'high street', the packhorse route of medieval origin. Passing a house and stable, the chapel, further houses – one of which had recently been converted from dog kennels – a workshop and the corn mill you would come to the River Derwent with an inn set on its bank. Circumnavigating the walled garden of the Hall would bring you to the seventeenth-century stone packhorse bridge and then across the river to Bridge-End Farm. The valley sides tower upwards on either side and the mix of fields and woods give way to the heather moorland above where, until recently, peat was cut for fuel. Now a cart brought coal from the mines in Yorkshire and soon some of the miners would come too, as ramblers escaping into the clean air and open spaces.

The wider world beyond the Upper Derwent and Woodlands valleys was changing dramatically. Industrialisation, urbanisation, the market economy and agricultural improvement were fast increasing in scale and pace of change. Manufacturing towns and cities developed in the eighteenth century with the invention of steam power and the factory system. Sheffield and Manchester were the nearest of these to the Upper Derwent. Sheffield's cutlers were the most specialised work-force in England and came to dominate the world's cutlery trade by 1800. Metalworking expanded in the city during the eighteenth century to the extent that it dominated the world steel trade by 1900. 'Steel city's' population of 10,121 in 1736 had grown impressively to 130,000 in 1851. Changes were not just happening over the hills and far away. In the lower Derwent Valley, the river's waters had been harnessed to power mills since the end of the seventeenth century. But, during the eighteenth century, mill building proliferated along the River Derwent and its tributaries with over twenty mills working by the beginning of the nineteenth century. Throughout Britain, the countryside also became a supplier of resources such as food, stone, coal and timber. New roads were being built across the country to reduce travel times and costs for trade over longer distances. As industry grew, labourers were also attracted to the cities from rural areas in search of sustained employment. In the late eighteenth century a quarter of cutlers' apprentices came from more than 8km outside of town and the majority of migrants originated in Derbyshire and Yorkshire.

Landowning classes not only continued to be the dominating influence on the rural landscape but also increased their control through more prescriptive estate management. The landed gentry held influential positions in town as well as country and supported their urban and industrial enterprises with the economic resources and political power of their country estates. The biggest landowners in the region, the Dukes of Devonshire, were intimately involved in politics and the 4th Duke was Prime Minister from 1756 to 1757. Ruling classes symbolised their right to govern the nation by the way they managed their estates. To increase production, and profits, land was subject to agricultural improvement which was seen as progressive, rational and scientifically testable. Handbooks appeared advising on land management and estate maps proliferated to describe, catalogue and quantify the land they owned, how it was used, its value and productive potential. New breeds of livestock and strains of cereal were developed to maximise output in a new farming system which relied on high inputs of raw materials such as fertilisers from outside the farm. New farm buildings were constructed and common land was privatised under Parliamentary Enclosure Acts. The Upper Derwent was very much caught up in these trends as the estates took a more active role in the everyday aspects of farming.

Farmsteads and designer patterns

One of the more lasting impacts of the improving zeal of landowners has been the construction and remodelling of farmbuildings in the nineteenth century. Every building was altered to some degree. Some existing buildings were extended, others were demolished and replaced, and at others completely new buildings were added. Rebuilding was undertaken as and when old buildings became dilapidated and, in Hope Woodlands township, was the financial responsibility of the tenants. Such an apparently piecemeal process should have thrown up a variety of building types based on traditional vernacular styles. However, observing the surviving farmsteads today, what is striking is their similarity and the architectural embellishments which seem somewhat out of place on what are otherwise utilitarian buildings. This is because the landowners required that buildings were constructed to their own cohesive estate styles with standard

56 *Pattern book farmhouses. Blackden View* (left) *and Rowlee* (right) *farmhouses were both rebuilt in almost identical style by the Devonshire estate in the mid-nineteenth century.* Photos courtesy of the PDNPA

building layouts and architectural adornments such as circular pitching windows, flat kneelers and round gable finials. Rowlee and Blackden View farmhouses were rebuilt in 1849 and 1854 respectively to identical designs which must have been chosen from the same architectural pattern book (**56**). Adornments can be clearly seen on barns at Rowlee Bridge and Upper House or farmhouses such as at Ashes and Alport. Embellishments are not part of the vernacular tradition of the region, nor do they contribute to the agricultural functioning of the buildings. Instead, they are designed with two powerful ideals in mind; they demonstrated the ruling classes' beliefs on how buildings should contribute to the scenery of the rural landscape and they reminded farmers of their place as tenants of the landlord through their day-to-day living and working with the buildings. They are another expression of landowners' authority over place, as are the estate maps, though the symbolism in the buildings is much more apparent locally.

Buildings also incorporated new ideas on how farms should be organised to increase their efficiency. Many farmbuildings throughout England were rebuilt during the late eighteenth and nineteenth centuries along model lines aimed at increasing farm efficiency as a part of the general movement for agricultural improvement. In the Upper Derwent this can be seen mostly in new and altered barns which were often laid out along lines of rationalised working practices rather than in traditional styles. The small and simple rectangular layout of seventeenth-century barns, such as a group of three at Grindle Clough, can be compared to the much larger nineteenth-century Low Barn built as a cohesive unit comprising three ranges situated around a courtyard (**colour plate 15**). New barns incorporated large entrances so that carts could drive straight in to unload.

The current farmhouse at Rowlee was built in 1849 to replace two buildings. The larger of the two, to the north-east, was a house, as indicated by a surviving undated drawing. It was stone-built and had two storeys and five bays. The central door had a Georgian pediment. The small building to the south-west was presumably an outbuilding and is illustrated as stone-built with two storeys and windows in the gable end that may have been mullioned. The new house was a large, two-storey, double-pile dwelling with a decorated gable to the front bearing a carved stone shield inscribed 1849 (**56**). The farmyard was completed with two large barns constructed during the mid-nineteenth century, replacing existing barns, while a further two, smaller, barns were built about the same time or soon after.

As well as the remodelling of existing farmsteads a series of new ones was built following what had been a period of relative settlement stability in the seventeenth and early eighteenth centuries. The landowners re-organised elements of the agricultural landscape by carving these new farms out of existing landholdings. These new farmsteads appear regularly; Hayridge between 1754 and 1808, Gillott Hey *c.*1810, Blackden View *c.*1854, Lee End between 1822 and 1847, Wood End in the 1840s and Wood's Farm sometime between 1840 and 1880. The Trustees of Birley's Charity, Sheffield, who held land at the mouth of the Woodlands Valley, concluded in 1818 that a new farm could be created out of Ashop Farm's land north of the River Ashop, on the basis of current beliefs about ideal farm sizes and efficient land use. It was not until the building of Wood End almost thirty years later that this was finally carried out. The estate was held to provide income to the charity, which funded a Free School for writing and arithmetic, a church minister and retired tradesmen or their widows.

We also see farmers in the Upper Derwent buying greater amounts of crockery from the eighteenth century onwards. During the later eighteenth century tablewares became mass-produced, mould-made and relatively more affordable by a wider range of households. Cheaper prices and better transport links opened up crockery ownership to more people and motivated its greater commercial sale. Ceramics totally replaced pewter and wooden tablewares by the end of the eighteenth century. Whereas earlier pottery found in the Upper Derwent had been mostly locally produced on the Derbyshire and Yorkshire coal measures, later ceramics were being made further afield. Local wares were still common but there were also vessels from the Staffordshire Potteries, Nottingham and London. Pottery was more available at market towns and from travelling salesmen who had more incentive to take wares into rural areas than in the seventeenth century. Its wide scale ownership was intertwined with the other strands of industrial consumer capitalism that characterised the changing landscape of the Upper Derwent in the later eighteenth and the nineteenth centuries: agricultural improvement, building of toll roads and exploitation of the woodlands for charcoal. Yet the new styles and forms still ended up in the same place when broken – thrown onto middens and distributed across fields near to farmhouses during manuring.

Grass is greener

By the late eighteenth century most of the enclosure of land into fields had already taken place in the Upper Derwent. Attention was now turned to ways to improve those fields. Again, landowners were instrumental in this and applied their improving ideals to how both the farmland and the commons could be made more efficient. This desire began during the later-eighteenth century and, as with the farmbuildings, it was the tenants who were expected and encouraged to carry out this improvement. Accounts of farms in the Duke of Devonshire's Woodlands estate in the 1770s give an idea of how they were managed. They stipulate the improvements tenants were required to make. Tenants were to fertilise their fields and drain boggy ground, using covered drains that had recently been invented as a replacement to open ditches or ridge and furrow. The number of stock held by each farmer was counted and approved, with the comment that '2 acres of pasture or common is supposed to be enough for a sheep'. Each tenant was also required to improve the heys which lay between the farmland and moorland by digging and burning the turf before adding forty horse loads of burnt lime to each acre. The documents do not record the tenants' view of these prescriptions, whether they were as enthusiastic to improve as the estate or felt this was an imposition by their landlords.

The relative importance of livestock compared to crops in the mid-nineteenth century is highlighted in a number of farm surveys. The 1847 tithe survey of Hope Woodlands parish lists 3,688 acres of enclosed titheable agricultural land of which 3,523 acres were pasture or meadow, 165 acres were arable, and another 16,000 acres were described as 'uncultivateable moor' for rough grazing. Similar proportions of pasture and meadow are mapped by Fairbank for Derwent in 1810. The Upper Derwent, like much of the upland countryside, had become a large-scale commercial meat supplier to urban markets and national trade. The nearest regular livestock markets were held at Hope, Glossop, Buxton, Bakewell, Tideswell, Penistone and Sheffield. In 1784 an Act of Parliament 'For enlarging the Market Place, and regulating the Markets in the Town of Sheffield' was passed specifically because of the growth in trade associated with the town's expansion. The self-sufficient farming of the medieval period, where produce was grown both for home consumption and sale, had largely disappeared. Foodstuffs no longer produced by the household were now bought using profits from livestock sales.

Enclosure movement

Both open fields and commons were subject to enclosure as part of the ideology of agricultural improvement. Enclosure was sometimes conducted by application by the landowners of a given parish to Parliament for an Act. In other cases landowners of large estates undertook private enclosure or agreed amongst themselves to enclose common land across a parish without recourse to Parliament. Enclosure removed common rights and apportioned the land amongst a select number of landowners and their tenants. Resistance to enclosure was strong but largely unsuccessful. Enclosure movement boundaries are usually distinctively straight, dividing the land into regular blocks, as a result of being initially laid out by surveyors on a map rather than constructed in relation to local topography. Such boundaries are common on the White Peak where huge tracts of commons were enclosed.

In the Upper Derwent, it was to the east of the river that Parliamentary Enclosure impinged on the landscape. Derwent and Little Howden Moors were enclosed in Derwent parish as a result of the Hathersage, Outseats and Derwent Enclosure Act of 1808, Howden Moors by the Bradfield Enclosure Act of 1811 and Bamford Moor by the Bamford Common Enclosure Act of 1855. While all three allowed for the privatisation of the commons, only the first two led to the construction of walled boundaries.

The Bamford Enclosure Act was responsible for new, large, regular, valley-side fields on the east side of the Derwent Valley below Bamford Edge which were farmed by the newly created Wood Farm. The Act of Enclosure for Hathersage, Outseats and Derwent lists nineteen different landowners in Derwent township, most of whom were described as copyholder tenants except Thomas Furniss who was a freeholder owning Riding House and other land parcels, and the Duke of Devonshire. All but five of these owners rented out their properties to tenants. The desire to enclose Derwent led to a survey and assessment of the three parishes. A survey of Derwent was made in 1810 which produced a plan of existing enclosures and open commons, listing of tenants and description of individual fields. As well as open common, land which had been enclosed since 1778 was liable to Enclosure and allotment to a farm of the landowner's choice, though in the end the existing ownership of those fields was simply confirmed. This information then went into the Enclosure Award, produced in 1830, which finally defined and legally ratified enclosure so allowing it to take place.

Those boundaries created by Act of Enclosure consist of the ruler-straight walls defining a block of moorland immediately above the valley-side and the more irregular wall below Derwent Edge (**57** & **colour plate 11**). The stone for the walls came from large quarries which can be seen from the footpath above Lane Head. The main motivation behind their construction was to create more land for improvement. Wide roads built to standard specifications improved access to the newly-enclosed moorland. Today only the lower slopes within these enclosures are observably more improved than the open moorland outside. A clue as to why most of the ground remains as 'uncultivateable moor' is a unique example of an experiment in moorland improvement. This is a heap of lime, now grassed-over, situated within a rectangular bank and ditch enclosure measuring 150m by 80m. It is beyond the Parliamentary Enclosure walls at 390m above sea level, but on land still allotted to a private owner in the Award. Little could grow at this exposed position and altitude, though improved pasture may have been thought viable. The enclosure is first mapped by the Ordnance Survey of 1880, but is likely to be earlier than this date. It appears to be an exploratory attempt to 'rationally' test the improvability of the ground associated with the Parliamentary Enclosure Act.

Grouse shooting

Another motivation for Enclosure of the moorlands in the Upper Derwent was grouse shooting. It became popular across Britain during the eighteenth century, alongside the landed classes' increasing enthusiasm for wild, upland scenery. The hunting and consumption of game was one of the main ways in which the elite defined themselves in the eighteenth and nineteenth centuries. Better transport provided by turnpikes and railways and improved gun technology increased its popularity further in the mid-nineteenth century. By this time grouse shooting came to be seen by many landowners in Derbyshire as a more important and profitable use of the moors than livestock pasturing.

In Bradfield, the 1811 Act was used for a specific purpose by the Duke of Norfolk. The Duke, who had owned Howden since the 1780s, used Enclosure to evict the tenant farmer at Howden House and replace him with a gamekeeper. Over the following years the Duke added to Howden by buying properties in Derwent to create a remote and 'wild' shooting retreat for himself, family and friends centred on Derwent Hall. He rebuilt farmsteads in a cohesive estate style and added new buildings solely for his use, including a shooting lodge and a chapel in the nineteenth century. Across the moorlands he had also constructed cabins, lines of shooting butts and even a small duck pond with artificial nesting islands to add variety to the shoot.

This was mirrored throughout the Upper Derwent by other landowners. Gamekeepers' accommodation was provided at farmsteads or purpose-built houses. Shooting butts and cabins are found across all the moorlands. Beating of grouse over prepared positions was introduced during the mid-nineteenth century leading to the construction of lines of grouse-shooting butts. This may have been related to the building of Parliamentary Enclosure walls across moorlands which blocked traditional stalking walks and provided shooting lines into which butts were often built. On Little Howden Moor there is a line of them built into an earthen bank forming the outermost boundary of the block of enclosures built as a result of the 1808 Derwent Enclosure Act. Elsewhere, lines of butts came to be used across moorlands whether they were sub-divided by Enclosure walls or not so, even if initially influenced by Enclosure walls, this method became the appropriate way to shoot.

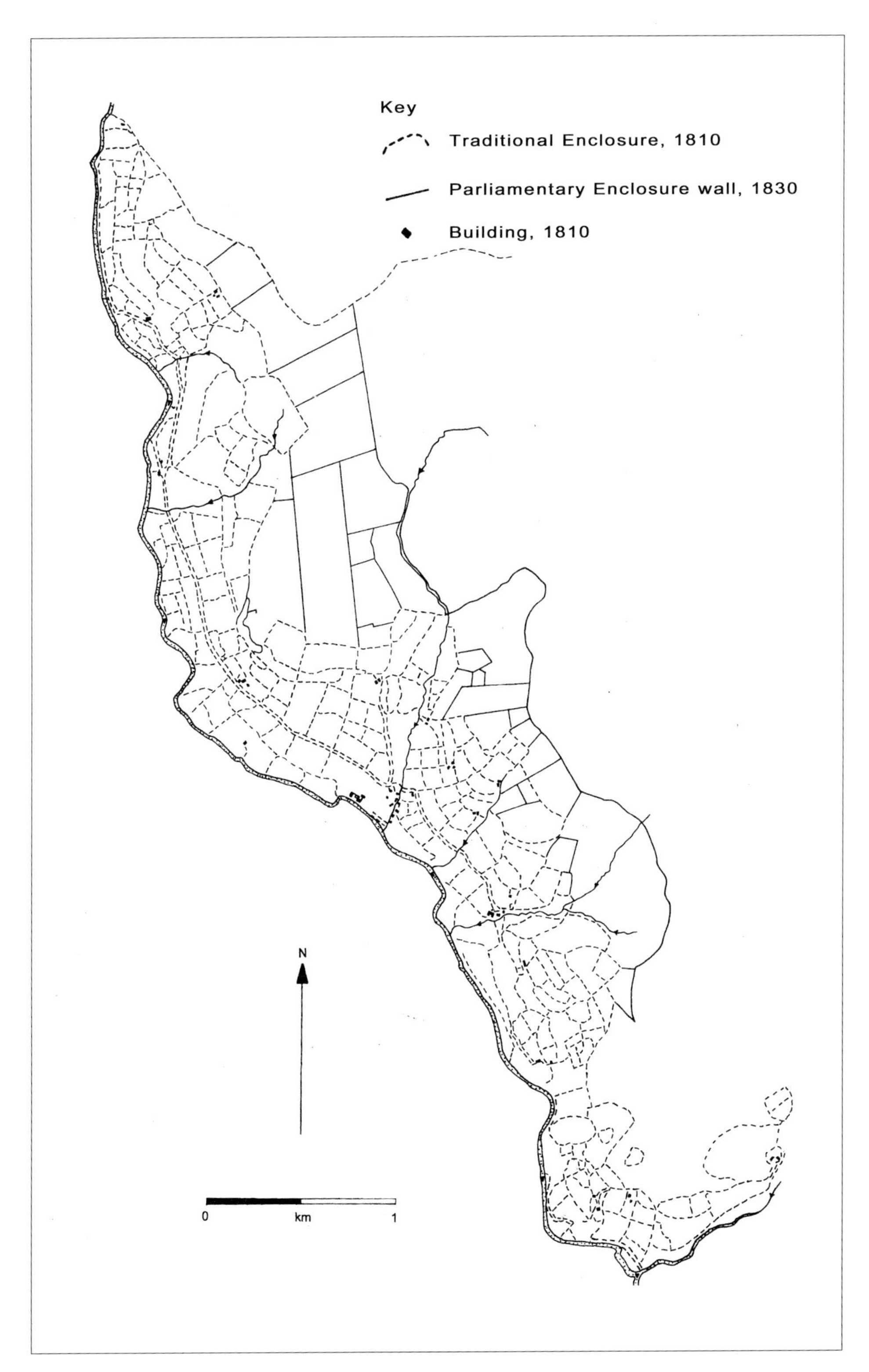

57 *Traditional fields and nineteenth-century Parliamentary Enclosure in Derwent*

58 *Social hierarchy of grouse shooting cabins. These two cabins were built as shelter for shooting parties on Ronksley Moor. The left-hand cabin has a door, window and benches for the shooting guests while the other cabin, for beaters, is open and contains no furniture.* Courtesy of the National Trust

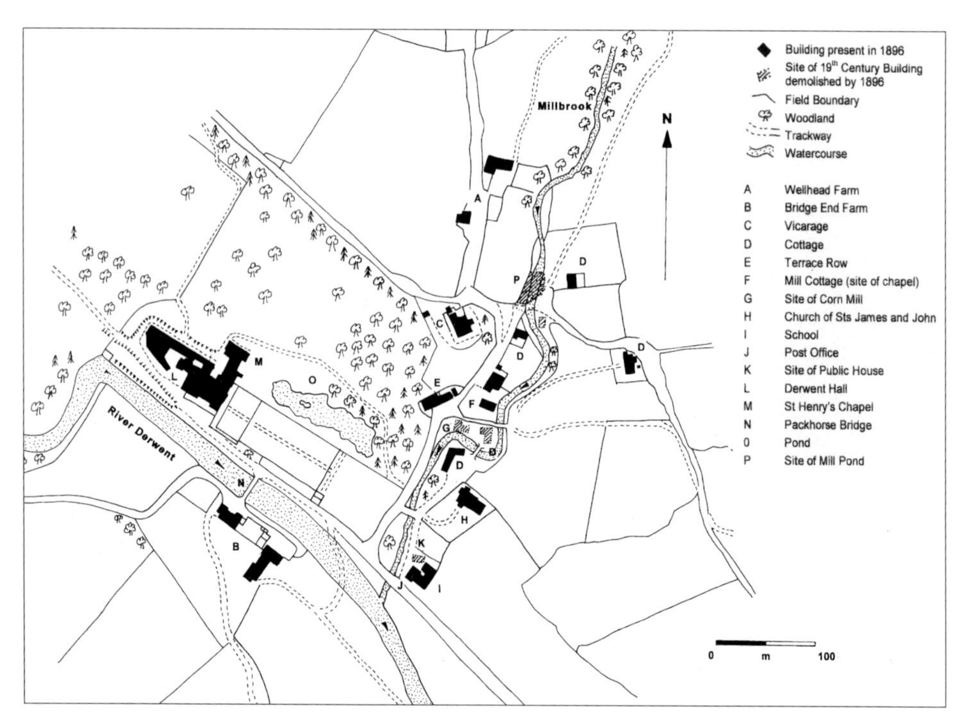

59 *Derwent village in the late nineteenth century*

1 *The Upper Derwent looking north. This photograph shows all the elements of the landscape: reservoirs, plantation woodlands, enclosed pasture and open moorland.* Photo by Ray Manley

2 *The Woodlands Valley. Farmers from the medieval period onwards have shaped this landscape of small, walled fields and woodlands with moorland common above.* Photo by Ray Manley

3 *Salt Cellar is one of a number of prominent tors on the ridge of Derwent Edge given names based on their distinctive shapes. They may have been important landscape features in prehistory, possibly places to watch for game and imbued with spiritual significance. The surrounding moorlands were covered in scrub during the mesolithic.* Photo by Ray Manley

4 *The different elements that characterise the Upper Derwent landscape: reservoir, woodland, enclosed farmland and moorland.* Photo by Bill Bevan

5 *Crookhill Crags form a distinctive and prominent local landmark. People buried their dead here in later prehistory, possibly near to settlement. Welbeck Abbey founded a grange here in the medieval period, the site of which has since been continuously occupied by a farmstead.* Photo by Ray Manley

6 *Mam Tor and Crookhill from Derwent Edge. Mam Tor hill and later prehistoric enclosure is caught by the sun in the background. Crookhill is in the foreground, and between the two is Losehill, presented to G.H.B. Ward in the 1940s for his service to rambling and access to moorlands.* Photo by Bill Bevan

7 *A pit filled with sand cuts an earlier pit containing burnt stones and charcoal, radiocarbon dated to 2500 BC. They were found on a level terrace near the River Derwent. The pit fills may have been from fires for cooking or sweat lodges.* Photo by Bill Bevan

8 *Howden barrow, built between 2500 and 1500 BC, is usually under the waters of Howden Reservoir. It is next to a scatter of contemporary stone tools suggesting settlement.* Photo by Bill Bevan

9 *A fifteenth-century lead working hearth being excavated in Linch Clough. The hearth occupied the simple scoop in the ground which has been turned pink from scorching. Foot bellows may have been used to pump air into the fire via the narrow channel.* Photo by Bill Bevan

10 *Enclosed farmland comprising small, irregular fields occupies the valley side between the reservoir below and the open moorland common above. This type of enclosure characterises the Upper Derwent and originated in the medieval period.* Photo by Ray Manley

11 *A route from Derwent hamlet onto moorland common follows a walled lane through valley side fields. This lane begins in the woodland in the bottom left-hand corner of the photo and runs diagonally upwards to the centre of the image. Here, the trackway reaches what was once open moor and branches out into numerous lines. These can be seen as the sinuous 'tracks' in the snow. After nineteenth-century Parliamentary Enclosure, walls were built across this traditional right of way.* Photo by Bill Bevan

12 *Bamford House was situated high above Derwent Valley, adjacent to the line of a hollow-way that ran along the top of the valley side. The farmstead had peat grounds on moorland above that were reached by a deeply incised sledway.* Photo by Bill Bevan

13 *The farmland of Upper House Farm sits on more level ground in between extensive areas of rough grazing. The fields existed before 1627 while the grazing was created from cleared woodland in the seventeenth and eighteenth centuries.* Courtesy of the National Trust

14 *Alport farmsteads. Alport is unusual because the farmsteads are nucleated in a group rather than being isolated. A peat sledway runs downslope from the top right corner of the photograph.* Courtesy of the National Trust

15 *Low Barn was built in the nineteenth century along 'modern' ideas of farm efficiency and adorned with architectural embellishments to symbolise estate ownership.* Photo by Bill Bevan

16 *Water roars over the top of Howden dam when the reservoir is full. The dam is partly hidden by a massive spoil heap created during the dam's construction. In front of the dam is the site of Abbey Farm, one of the locations repeatedly occupied since the mesolithic.* Photo by Ray Manley

17 *Moss-covered Elmin Pitts farmbuildings are lost in the forest. The remains of many of the farmsteads abandoned in the twentieth century survive either under the reservoirs or in the adjacent conifer plantations.* Photo by Bill Bevan

Shooting cabins provided shelter and storage for shooting parties. They were simple one-room, single-storey, stone buildings associated with lines of butts. At one shooting spot on Ronksley Moor social differentiation between the landed classes and the beaters, most likely employed from amongst the landowner's tenants, is physically represented in two adjacent cabins (**58**). One cabin is very basic having one wall open and no furniture, while the other has a wooden door, window, benches and a table.

Derwent: from hamlet to village

To chart the growth of the hamlet through the nineteenth century to its flooding under Ladybower in the mid-twentieth century, we can use a series of maps beginning with Fairbank's township survey of 1810 and ending with the Ordnance Survey of 1922 (**59**). The layout of the hamlet was irregular, with buildings seemingly placed without formal relation to each other. The riverside inn was replaced with a school and a post office which served the growing demand for letter post within forty years of the introduction of the Penny Black in 1840. New houses were built to the north-east and a more town-like terrace row was built to the north-west to which the post office later relocated (**60**). An important building, which had been important to the hamlets' medieval origins, was becoming less relevant during the nineteenth century. The corn mill had fallen into disrepair and lost its water wheel by the 1860s then was demolished within twenty years. Presumably this indicates the decreasing amount of arable grown in the valleys in the nineteenth century. As agriculture became more commercial, areas with low crop yields such as the Upper Derwent specialised more in livestock. Buying flour was preferred over milling one's own. Not only were there large corn growing areas nearby, such as Yorkshire and Nottinghamshire, but improved sea, rail and road transport had decimated the British market through cheap imports from North America.

As the fortunes of the mill declined, those of the chapel were transformed when in 1867 the eighteenth-century chapel was replaced with a church dedicated to Saints John and James. It was built on a new site east of Millbrook in Victorian Gothic style and a tower with a spire was added in 1873. The seventeenth-century font and masonry from the eighteenth-century chapel, some of which dated to the fourteenth century, were incorporated in the building. With the construction of the church came the right to bury in Derwent, so ending the dead's traditional trek to Hathersage Church and the last links to the medieval landholding patterns of the township. An imposing vicarage was built a little distance away on the west of the brook and the vicar could metaphorically baptise himself every day by crossing over water to church. About this time the joint parish of Derwent and Hope Woodlands was created by separating it from the larger parishes of Hope and Hathersage.

60 *The centre of Derwent Village at the turn of the twentieth century. Many of the villagers had obviously come out in their best clothes for the photographer. The Post Office is at the far end of the terrace and the main village street was on the line of the medieval packhorse route to Sheffield.* PDNPA Collection

Derwent Hall continued to be the largest building in the hamlet and was acquired by the Newdigate family in the mid-nineteenth century. After its life solely as a farmstead for 100 years, they re-constituted its grand past by enlarging it twice, adding St Henry's Roman Catholic Chapel and redesigning the gardens. The mullioned windows of the seventeenth-century Hall were copied in the mid nineteenth-century extension. Three different garden spaces were created which changed from formal to naturalistic when walked through from the Hall. To the north of the garden a pond provided a focus for a wilder, if romanticised, space. The walled garden was on a scale of privacy and design much grander than any other house in the Upper Derwent. This, in combination with the architectural splendour of the Hall, signified to guests and neighbours the social pretensions of the owners. The Duke of Norfolk acquired the Hall in 1886 and installed his younger son, who later became Viscount FitzAlan of Derwent. The Duke had acquired various properties in Derwent between the mid and late-nineteenth century to create a consolidated estate comprising the Hall, seven farms, three cottages and numerous other parcels of land neighbouring the Bradfield estate, which the family had bought in the 1780s. This became the Duke's shooting retreat.

Norfolk replaced the school in 1877 with St Henry's Schoolroom and built a shooting lodge next door at about the same time. Both are built in the architectural style common to all new buildings on the Duke of Norfolk's estate with coursed gritstone blocks and stone coped gables containing moulded kneelers. It was adorned with a Tudor-arched doorway, mullioned windows, a round-arched niche containing a statue of the Virgin Mary and a cupola bell-cote. These are the only buildings of the village to have survived the flooding of the valley behind Ladybower Dam, the tip of an historical iceberg that can still be seen today above the waters of the reservoir.

Charcoal and industrialisation

As demand for wood for industrial fuel increased in the eighteenth century, woodlands came to be seen as a valuable resource. Where previously woodland was perceived as occupying ground to be cleared and walled for inbye, now landowners rediscovered the commercial importance of trees. The relative value of woodland and farmland was weighed up by landowners who could direct the estate and their tenants to follow the most profitable land-use. Coppicing was increasingly used to sustainably produce the sorts of woodland products – such as charcoal – required by the market. Tenants had to maintain boundaries to prevent their livestock from grazing regenerating coppices, and could be fined if they failed or if they grubbed up trees that the landowners had reserved for their own use. Tenants carried a large responsibility for knowing which woods were those the estate wanted and for maintaining the boundaries around them to exclude their stock. Again boundaries play a fundamental part in defining social relations within the landscape. The purely economic basis for making decisions about land use is highlighted in an inspection of a woodland undertaken in 1769 which valued the land at four shillings an acre if maintained as woodland, plus it also needed the expense of building a stock-proof wall, while it was worth seven shillings an acre as pasture.

Wood had a wide variety of commercial uses. A distinction needs to be made here between timber which was the trunk and large branches used for buildings and ships, and underwood which was the smaller branches of standards and the coppice poles. Underwood had an almost inexhaustible number of uses including fences, clogs, charcoal, barrels, kitchen and dairy implements, domestic bowls and dishes, agricultural tools and tool handles. Bark was also in demand primarily for leather tanning and the production of birdlime. Few of these leave archaeological remains of their production, the common exceptions being saw pits, charcoal burning platforms and foresters' shelters. In the Upper Derwent the remains of charcoal burning platforms form an extensive and important element of the historic landscape (**61** & **62**).

Charcoal has been used as a fuel in a number of industries from the medieval period to the mid-twentieth century. It has been traditionally produced by slowly burning wood under controlled conditions in a turf-covered stack. Iron and lead smelting were the main large-scale industries in the region which required

61 *A charcoal-burning platform is revetted into the steep valley side. Charcoal was produced throughout the Upper Derwent and was at its height in eighteenth century when iron working forges in South Yorkshire bought the rights to charcoal in many of the woodlands.* Photo by Bill Bevan

charcoal and it was used in a variety of processes. It had been the main iron smelting fuel until the introduction of coke in the eighteenth century. After that date it still had its uses; for the production of blister steel in the new cementation furnaces, the blacking of moulds in iron foundries and gunpowder manufacture. In lead production, charcoal was used to resmelt slag that still contained high levels of ore until the late eighteenth century when new coal and coke hearths were introduced.

The survival of charcoal burning platforms throughout the two valleys and references to charcoal in the estate accounts of Hope Woodlands and Howden show that it was produced throughout the area during the eighteenth century. Over 250 oval earthen platforms up to 10m long have been terraced into sloping ground. They are distributed across the valley and clough sides singly, in small groups and in large, dense concentrations. The group in Hagg Side are also notable in that some of them each have a small mound of charcoal and soil deposited in the centre of the surface. This appears to be the product of scraping the platform surface clean after the last burn and may be a way of marking that each platform was still in use.

Historical maps for Hope Woodlands parish show changes in woodlands and can sometimes be equated with specific charcoal production events. Charcoal was produced in woodlands planted after 1627 at Hagg Farm, Hagg Side and

Ridges Coppice, parts of Grimbocar and Rough Wood most of which survived through the nineteenth century. A number of woodlands associated with charcoal platforms were felled between 1627 and 1808. There are also three woods in Hope Woodlands that contain a small number of charcoal burning platforms which do not appear on historical maps, suggesting the possibility of pre-1627 charcoal production. One of these areas was in Linch Clough, adjacent to the mid-fifteenth century lead smelting hearth which used charcoal as fuel.

Ironworking forges acquired charcoal by purchasing the right to fell woods from the landowner. In the mid-eighteenth century, the Duke of Devonshire sold rights to woods in Hope Woodlands to Attercliffe Forge, Sheffield, Wortley Top Forge, near Stocksbridge, and Mousehole Forge, Malin Bridge. The Hope Woodlands farm leases also allowed the Duke and his agents access to farms to build charcoal burning platforms, known as 'charcoal pitts'. Also that century, the Duke of Norfolk paid for charcoal platforms to be constructed on his Howden estate in Bradfield parish. There is a comparatively tiny number of platforms situated away from these identified areas suggesting that the majority of charcoal production in the area was undertaken for iron forges in South Yorkshire.

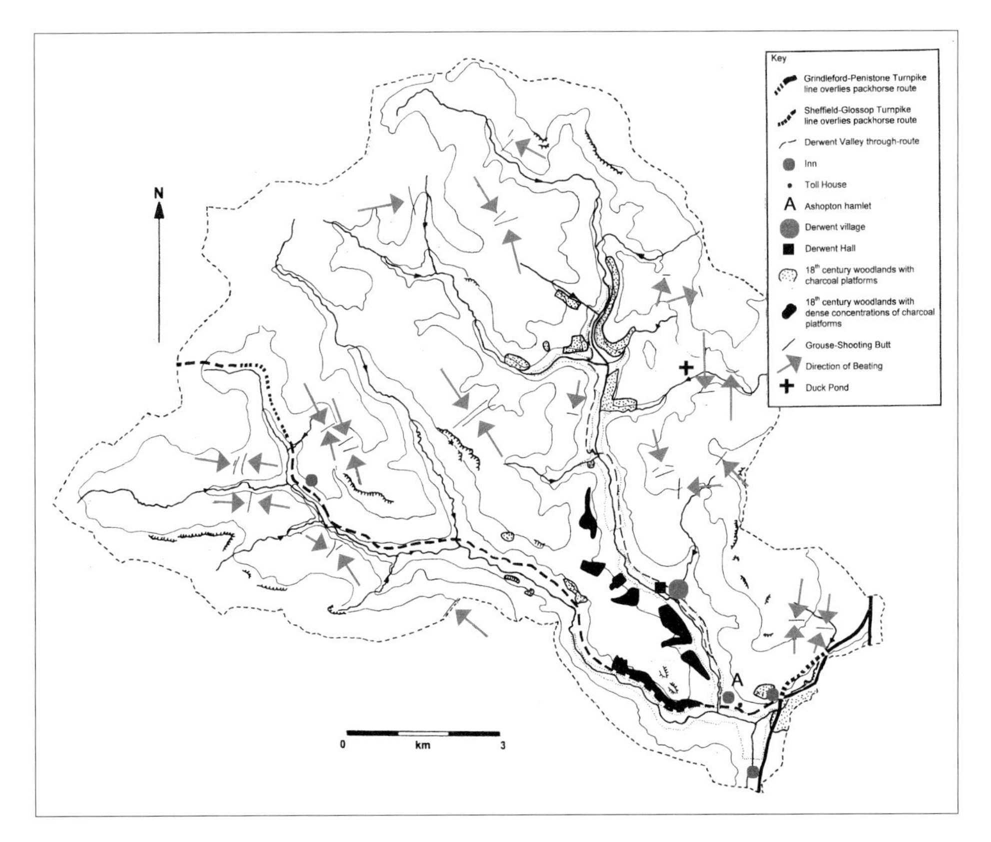

62 *Post-medieval features in the Upper Derwent*

The three forges which acquired charcoal from woods in Hope Woodlands during the mid-eighteenth century were all on the lines of packhorse routes traversing rough ground and situated at distances of 16km or more from the Upper Derwent. They all also had closer wood supplies at hand which they exploited. This confounds the received wisdom that charcoal was never transported further than 8km because it was easily damaged during transport. It shows that other influences, such as commercial concerns, were as important as practical technological needs in influencing where charcoal was acquired. Charcoal was sieved before use in iron working because only large lumps could be used. A certain amount of wastage from damage to the charcoal on such a journey could be expected, and transport of charcoal by sea from Galloway to ironworks at Furness, in Cumbria, was expected to 'lose' 25 per cent of the cargo.

The attitude of local farmers to intensive charcoal production in the eighteenth century is demonstrated by a petition made to landowners for better roads to enable coal to be cheaply imported into the valley. The petition refers to summer sometimes being too wet to dry peat and that wood is taken away for charcoal. In this one document the trajectories of three historical aspects of land-use and perception of the landscape come together. Farmers had been using a combination of wood and peat for fuel, collecting it according to common rights and traditions which had originated with the occupation of the Upper Derwent from the medieval period onwards. Woodlands had become a less important element of the local landscape following the disestablishment of the Royal Forest. With the rise of industrial production in the eighteenth century, trees became economically important as a fuel source and specifically because of the needs of three forges situated in South Yorkshire and lying on packhorse routes leading to the Upper Derwent. The rising economic-based perception of the landscape by landowners, incorporating the commodification of land and ideals of improvement, resulted in the re-evaluation of woodlands not as barriers to cultivation but as a financial resource to be reserved for their own use. Other elements of the industrialisation of Britain, coal mining and better roads connected to the turnpike network, were then called for as the answers to the local fuel problem. The petition also highlights the relationship of enforcement and dependency created between landlord and tenant by greater estate control over the landscape.

Turnpikes: rerouting the world

Progressive ideals also had an impact on communication routes because the traditional system of packhorse routes and other roads was seen to be failing with increased use. Since at least the medieval period the packhorse routes had provided the axes of long-distance communication between the Upper Derwent and the wider world. During the sixteenth, seventeenth and eighteenth centuries waymarking and maintenance had been increased as government saw a need to speed up the movement of goods and people to meet the growing demands of trade and industry. Government also encouraged trusts to be founded to pay for road building and upkeep with the charging of tolls to recoup costs. The first Turnpike Act was passed in 1663 and by 1830 3,783 trusts had been set up in England and Wales creating a dense network of turnpikes which form the basis of our non-motorway road network today. It was up to local people to form trusts to build specific stretches of road rather than these being determined or planned by national government.

Derwent's toll

Two turnpikes were built through the Upper Derwent and Woodlands valleys during the late eighteenth and early nineteenth centuries: Grindleford to Penistone and Sheffield to Glossop (**62**).

MORTIMER'S ROAD

The Grindleford to Penistone turnpike was built in 1771 after a Parliamentary Act of 1770. The route ran south from Penistone via Strines and Moscar House then turned south-west to cross Derwent Moors crossing Highshaw Clough via Cutthroat Bridge, a stone construction which appears to have been built for the turnpike to replace a ford approximately 50m to the north. The name Cutthroat was derived from local folk memory of an incident in the late-sixteenth/early-seventeenth century when a man was discovered near this site with his throat cut.

South-west of Moscar House the turnpike reputedly descended into Ladybower Gorge via the site of a later quarry. However the landlord of Ladybower Inn, who was also the Parish Surveyor, diverted the road in the 1770s to run adjacent to the Inn to boost his business. The enterprising landlord even charged 2d from travellers to offset the cost of the road. The informal diversion, which is still visible to the north of the present road, was eventually abandoned sometime before 1840 after years of argument with the county authority over its ownership. The new route joined with the Sheffield to Glossop turnpike to follow the latter through Ladybower Gorge. The turnpike's crossing point of the River Derwent south of the inn was improved in 1827 with the building of Ladybower bridge.

TELFORD'S ROAD

The Sheffield to Glossop turnpike was built between 1818 and 1821 by the engineer Thomas Telford as a direct route to connect those growing neighbours either side of the Pennines. It crossed moorland south-west of Sheffield, then descended into Derwent Valley via Ladybower Gorge where it crossed the River Derwent via Ashopton hamlet. West of the Derwent, it ran along the northern side of the Woodlands Valley to cross the moors near Bleaklow and start the long drop to Glossop. A series of bridges and revetments were built to carry the road across the numerous cloughs and support it along the steep-sided valley. Distances from both Sheffield and Manchester were marked on three-faced mile-stones set along the side of the road. Five of these survive along the southern edge of the road as it runs through the Woodlands Valley. It is now the line of the A57 Snake Pass, named after the Snake Inn which, in turn, took its name from the Duke of Devonshire's family crest.

Previous to the building of the turnpikes a network of packhorse routes connected Glossop, Hope, Derwent, Penistone, Bradfield, Sheffield and Manchester. The turnpikes improved communications for packhorse trains, which were the usual means of transport in this area until the mid-nineteenth century, and allowed access by wheeled vehicles such as stage coaches and carts. An idea of how much quicker travel times were along turnpikes can be gained by looking at the 373 mile journey between Edinburgh and London. In the mid-eighteenth century the mail coach took ten to twelve days to complete the journey. By 1837 this was reduced to just under four days. The flipside of better roads was that construction and maintenance costs were borne by travellers. Payment for the use of the roads was collected at strategically placed toll cottages, one of which was built at Ashopton.

Local access was also improved, allowing coal to be brought in, making it easier for grouse shooting parties to reach the shooting estates and enabling agricultural produce to be more cheaply transported to the neighbouring cities. In 1824 a new road between Derwent and Ashopton was built by the occupant of Derwent Hall to take advantage of the turnpikes. Many of the farmsteads founded or rebuilt in new locations in the late eighteenth and nineteenth centuries were located near to turnpikes, unlike their precursors which were usually built at some distance from through-routes. The most extreme example of positioning was at Bellhag where the farmyard fronted on to the Sheffield to Glossop turnpike.

A number of new inns were built to take advantage of the turnpikes, suggesting that the new roads had increased the numbers of people travelling. In addition to existing inns at Grimbocar and Ladybower, inns were built at Ashopton, Yorkshire Bridge and the Snake Pass to cater for the passing custom. Derwent hamlet was also effectively sidelined by the rerouting of the communication network. Whilst the hamlet had been on the line of the main packhorse route connecting the Upper Derwent with Sheffield and Glossop it was now over 2km from the Snake Road. This did not prevent Derwent expanding with the late nineteenth-century church, post office and school, but a lack of passing trade is the most likely reason why Derwent's only inn was closed between 1859 and 1880. It also directly led to the founding of a new hamlet in the area – Ashopton.

Turnpikes can be seen as part of the movement for improvement which spread through the landowning classes during the eighteenth century and greatly affected agriculture and commons. They spread rapidly across the country because of a perceived national need to improve road transport. In contrast to the development of packhorse tracks as rights of way, they were planned and travel was turned into a commodity which could be given a value and charged for. Packhorse routes could have remained in use by people who wanted to avoid payment, but often measures were taken to prevent this. In places along Doctor's Gate, access was denied by the construction of field walls across its line. In Derwent and Howden the Parliamentary Enclosure extinguished rights of way across the moorlands, along with other common rights, so that travelling the lines of the old routes became trespass. The Derwent to Sheffield 'commonway' was blocked by Enclosure walls between 1810 and 1840.

Ashopton

The new hamlet of Ashopton was situated on low-lying ground within Derwent parish at the confluence of the rivers Ashop, Derwent and the Ladybower Brook (**62**). There were no buildings at this location previous to the construction of the Snake Road in 1821. However, the name 'Ashopten' dates back at least as far as 1650. What this actually refers to is unclear but it could simply be the Woodlands Valley, which was commonly called Ashop. Located at the junctions between the Snake Pass and local roads to Derwent and Bamford, Ashopton was essentially a ribbon development of services for travellers that also catered for locals.

Focal to the settlement was the Toll House which was erected on the turnpike road during or shortly after the road's construction. The toll house was re-sited to another position further to the east in 1835 and used until the last toll was taken in 1875. After their demise as toll houses both buildings were re-used as houses. Ashopton Inn was built by 1824 as a coaching inn close by the site of the first Toll House. A large Methodist chapel was erected in 1840 and used as a Sunday school and meeting room. To the east of the hamlet there was also a smithy south of the road. Between 1880 and 1922 a post office was added to the west of the chapel.

Moving on

The landscape of the Upper Derwent was subtly changing during the eighteenth and nineteenth centuries. There were few of the dramatic changes seen in earlier periods. Few new settlements were founded, no wholesale enclosure of land was undertaken or large expanses of woodland cleared. Enclosure of commons and the building of new roads are the largest alterations we see on historical maps. On the whole, the existing pattern of land-use which had developed from the thirteenth century onwards was maintained. The biggest change was in how the land was perceived and used. In Hope Woodlands, tenants were being asked to improve land, landholdings were manipulated to create 'ideal' farm sizes and greater inputs of resources such as lime were used to gain higher yields. The

63 Above: *Townrowhag is situated high above the Woodlands Valley. It is now a barn but before the 1821 Sheffield to Glossop turnpike was built in the valley below, it was a farmstead next to the busy packhorse route visible in the foreground.* Photo by Ray Manley
Below: *The Hope Woodlands estate built the rationally laid out Bellhag farmstead to replace Townrowhag in the mid nineteenth century to take advantage of the new Sheffield to Glossop turnpike along the Woodlands Valley.* Photo by Bill Bevan

impact of improvement as an ideal of land management can be highlighted by looking at one farmstead in the Woodlands Valley (**63**).

A farm called Hags is shown on a map in 1767 high up on the side of the Woodlands Valley between enclosed inbye and open moorland. It was adjacent to the line of a long-distance packhorse route which crossed over high ground between the Derwent and Woodland Valleys. A tiny shelf of level ground provided just enough space between rocky outcrops and scarps for the farmstead, but not a level farmyard. The tenant had rights to pasture 106 sheep on the moors above Alport to the north. By the mid-nineteenth century it had become known as Townrowhag, probably because it comprised two semi-detached cottages, one occupied by a farmer and the other by a farm labourer. By this time, the Glossop to Sheffield turnpike road had been built along the lower valley side and by-passed the farmstead which could only be reached by a 1km-long walled lane. What had once been a significant location next to a packhorse route had now become a marginal one. Sometime in the 1860s the Devonshire estate took action to improve the farmstead. It was relocated adjacent to the turnpike to take advantage of the new transport opportunities for exporting livestock and was renamed Bellhag. Completely new buildings were built and incorporated gable kneelers typical of the Chatsworth estate style. The barns were much bigger than at the old farmstead and were arranged to form an 'L'-shape around two sides of a level courtyard with access for wheeled vehicles provided by a wide cart door.

Bellhag was better placed to supply the late nineteenth-century cities with agricultural produce. Urbanisation had heightened the difference between town and country with rural areas largely being seen in relation to cities – either as suppliers of food or places to escape into. Overall, improvement, industrialisation and the market economy combined to simplify the agricultural land-use of England into an arable-dominated south and east, and a pastoral north and west. The most productive agricultural lands were mostly in the lowlands and more amenable uplands such as the Peak District's limestone plateau. The Upper Derwent clearly fell into the pastoral zone. Its high moorlands and narrow valleys provided sheep and wood to nearby cities, and transport was facilitated by the turnpike network. In many ways the combination of progressive and improving trends resulted in the marginalisation of the Upper Derwent and by the later nineteenth century it was beginning to be perceived as more of a wilderness area. This became one of its major attractions for landowners who exercised their rights as members of the ruling classes by visiting the area periodically for grouse shooting. Rural areas became the 'countryside' in opposition to cities and were defined by the likes of John Ruskin as places of scenic beauty imbued with a natural way of life. Where cities were dirty, busy, over-crowded, fast-changing and dangerous, countryside represented peace, unchanging values and simple virtue. At the beginning of the twentieth century, the largest impacts of these changes were still to come and would be locally manifested in ways which define our perception of the Upper Derwent today.

OUR FIRST EXPERIENCE

What follows is an extract from *The Story of Birchinlee*: a memento of twelve years in the workmen's village, Derwent Valley Waterworks, Derbyshire by George Sutton, Missioner, 1914.

As one's memory goes back to the early days of Birchinlee's history, pleasant and difficult times flit across the mind. Up to the boot tops in mud, and with a tremendous shower bath coming from above, as it only can come in these mountainous districts, such was our first experience at this new village. Having traveled from Yorkshire, and having reached Bamford at 9a.m., we made our way to the Water Board's Office in Bamford village, and asked for Mr Edward Sandeman, chief engineer. After a little waiting, he came in and took us into his private room, and for nearly an hour we talked of the future prospects of the workmen and their families who would live in the village. Whilst we talked, sunshine gave place to heavy rain, and as we had promised to meet the Vicar of Derwent at Birchinlee, Mr Sandeman kindly ordered his carriage to convey us to Derwent. The kindness shown at that first meeting lasted right through the years he was here, till he left in September, 1912, after the opening of the Howden Reservoir, when he was succeeded as Chief Engineer by the Deputy engineer, Mr Sidney B. Winser, who has also been exceedingly kind.

On arriving at Birchinlee with the Vicar, who had promised to introduce the writer to the navvies, we came to a gang of about a dozen men, and eight of them dropped their tools and came across to meet us, some with tears in their eyes at seeing an old friend, and shook hands. The good parson at once saw that the introduction was not needed, as one fellow greeted the Missioner with 'Hello, old chum, what brings you in this hole?' Of course the village was only just being made, and 'holes' would have been more precise, so plentiful were they.

And what a difference between things around the place then and now can hardly be described. The work was only just being begun at the Howden Dam, chiefly excavation work. Only about forty huts had been erected. The school, hospitals and recreation hall were not in existence. The railway was only partly made, and not so far up the valley as the village, so that the materials for village and dam building had, so far, been conveyed by traction engines and carts, which cut up the roads very badly. But though the access to the place was very bad for a time, yet in those days the surroundings of the new village was most beautiful. Away up the valley, beyond the site of the Howden Dam, stood Howden House, buried amongst trees, but decidedly pretty on closer inspection, whilst lower down were the Abbey House and Abbey Grange at the foot of Abbey Clough, which, with its wooded sides, is a choice place for picnics. Birchinlee House at the northern end of the village, was picturesque, and on the opposite side of the valley stood Shire Owlers, covered with ivy from eaves to earth, backed by a pretty wood. The River, Derwent was 'a sight for the gods' in those days, for all along its banks were avenues of trees. Now the trees are all cut down, the soil and turf from the meadows removed, and the houses which were once the pride of the valley, are raised to the ground. A new road has been made with the many tons of soil and earth which had to be removed, but these tips are now being soiled and planted, so that very soon they will compensate for the spoilt beauty of olden days. In the distance stands the massive dam, which, after a heavy rain, has an overflow of 500 feet width, a sight worth seeing, especially when a high wind is blowing up valley, for then the spray is blown back from the crest of the dam, and rises to a tremendous height. Yes, the changes are many and varied, but all for the welfare of the people.

EIGHT

THE DAM BUILDERS

Flood

> A chapter devoted to the labourer may be regarded as intrusive by some, and as gossipy by others: by a third class it may be considered repulsive. But the 'navigator' is necessary…
>
> *Francis writing in 1851*

Archaeologists often think they see dramatic changes in past landscapes. Farming and fields were thought to have spread throughout Britain about 6,000 years ago, burial in small barrows multiplied some 4,000 years ago and ironworking was introduced no more than 3,000 years ago. In reality, these seemingly dramatic events were long-drawn-out affairs occurring over hundreds if not thousands of years. It was only by the later Neolithic that the majority of communities in Britain produced most of their food by farming, a period covering 2,000 years or more. We no longer talk about 'event horizons' where new ways of living appear at a single moment in time but realise that many changes in society are usually complex and lengthy. There are some events that do stand out for how short a time they took, a few happening even within the lifetime of a single generation or two. The arrival of the Romans was relatively rapid; within fifty years they had occupied Britannia as far north as the future line of Hadrian's Wall, introducing new forms of government. At the beginning of the twentieth century, the largest impact on the Upper Derwent landscape was about to begin and it too would be finished within fifty years. By the time it was complete, someone born into the family occupying Bridge-End Farm in 1900 was living in a new terrace house just north of Bamford. By then their farmhouse was demolished, fields and carefully maintained dry-stone walls were lost, Derwent Hall was a pile of rubble and the dead who had been buried in Derwent churchyard since the 1870s were settling into the graveyard at Bamford. The heart of the community had moved en masse.

The reason for this was the need for water in the growing cities and towns of South Yorkshire and the East Midlands. Three Acts of Parliament were passed between 1899 and 1904 enabling Sheffield, Derby, Nottingham and Leicester to improve their water supplies by flooding the valleys. Town planners in northern England looked to the valleys of the Pennines and other uplands as potential reservoirs. This flooding of the valleys necessitated the removal of much of the existing dispersed farming population and associated patterns of land-use while leaving the grouse moors relatively undisturbed. For a temporary period, a new society was implanted into the area comprising the navvy dam builders themselves who were housed in the purpose-built village of Birchinlee, also known as Tin Town. By the time the reservoirs were finished the valley landscape was transformed under large bodies of water which covered farms, fields, Derwent Village and Ashopton. For anyone living in the valleys at this time, the impact must have been incredible.

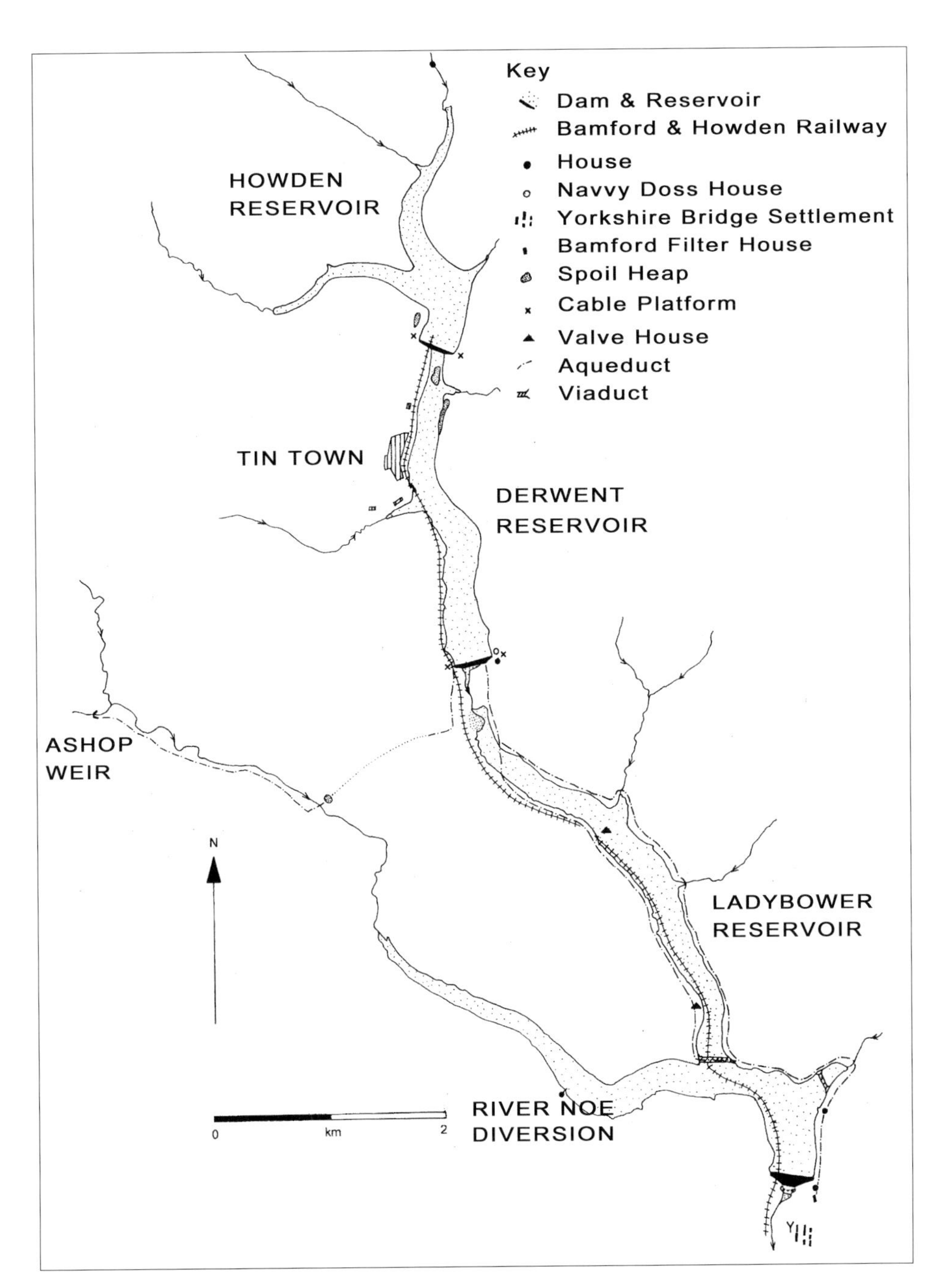

65 *Dams, reservoirs and related features in the Upper Derwent*

Gothic towers and massive walls

The building of the three dams which dominate the Upper Derwent today was the result of a lengthy process of negotiation and consultation between the interested cities during the late-nineteenth century. Each city had drawn up separate plans for damming the River Derwent and presented competing bills to Parliament. These were refused in favour of a joint bill which resulted in the 1899 Derwent Valley Water Act – at the time this was the largest reservoir scheme in Britain. A series of dams was proposed to be built in two stages, beginning with Howden and Derwent dams in July 1901 and February 1902 respectively (**65**).

The two dams were built of huge Millstone Grit blocks quarried from Bole Hill Quarry near Grindleford and transported to the Upper Derwent along a purpose-built railway – the Bamford and Howden Railway. This railway ran up the west side of the Derwent valley to just north of Howden Dam and was mainly used to transport building stone, other materials and navvies. The most visible surviving sections of the line are its route south of Ladybower, where it is currently used as the Thornhill Trail, and the stone, concrete or wooden piers which carried wooden bridges across the deep valley side cloughs. They are often submerged below Derwent reservoir but reappear whenever water levels drop. Rising above each of the dams are two towers built in Victorian Gothic

66 *Howden Dam rising above the valley during construction. The reservoirs transformed the Upper Derwent in the early twentieth century. Founded in the thirteenth century as 'One Man's House' it was demolished when the valley was flooded in 1915.* PDNPA Collection

style which included castle-like crenellations, arched windows and buttresses (**6, 10, 66** & **colour plate 16**). The towers contained water pumping equipment and plumb lines of fine steel wire to measure for subsidence. A huge tunnel was excavated under Ladybower Gorge to take water to the Rivelin reservoir near Sheffield. The remaining water was piped down the Derwent Valley for use by the other cities. If you walk along the sides of Ladybower Reservoir today you can follow the lines of these pipes and see the black, domed housings for valves that regulate the flow of water. When full, both reservoirs were designed to allow water to flow over the tops of the dams between the towers.

Stone-laying ceremonies were carried out at both dams on 21 June 1907. Large Millstone Grit record stones were placed over the doorways of the dams' west towers bearing identical inscriptions except for the name of the reservoir:

Glory To God In The Highest
IN THE YEARS OF OUR LORD
1902-
THIS DERWENT RESERVOIR
was built by the
DERWENT VALLEY WATER BOARD
for the use of the people of
DERBY LEICESTER NOTTINGHAM SHEFFIELD
and DERBYSHIRE

Both stones were laid with great formality by the chairman of the Derwent Valley Water Board and blessed by a clergyman. Howden dam was officially opened on 5 September 1912 in front of 2,000 officials, invited guests, workmen and families. In contrast the opening of Derwent dam in 1916 was undertaken without any ceremony, hence the date stone was not completed, which may have been because of the First World War.

Dam building involved a very different way of perceiving the landscape to that of any previous generations who had lived or worked in the Upper Derwent. The reservoir engineers were not interested in the pattern of fields and trackways on the surface of the land; instead they saw a huge water collecting 'bowl' with a surrounding catchment area. The only decisions to be taken about farmsteads were which should be demolished and which kept to accommodate Board employees. Farmsteads were thought to pose a risk of pollution to the reservoirs so most of those nearby, as well as those under it, were demolished.

The tramp of the navigator

The workforce employed to create Derwent and Howden reservoirs was composed of itinerant navvies, so-named after the navigators who built the canals during the eighteenth and early nineteenth centuries. Large numbers of navvies moved around the country working on such large engineering projects as canals, railways and dams. By the mid-nineteenth century they had developed a distinctive identity with its own form of language, dress, and social codes. Navvies were often treated with suspicion by local communities because of their socially peripheral conditions, 'strange' behaviour and unusual accents. They were outsiders. General opinion characterised them as being violent, drunken and immoral, spiritually destitute, revolutionary and that they formed gangs to terrorise local communities at will.

Navvy accommodation had often been communal barracks on eighteenth-century canal sites. By the mid-nineteenth century most contractors left accommodation provision to market forces and overall working/living conditions were generally deplorable. In remote areas accommodation, provisions and medical care either had to be acquired by the navvies themselves or from the contractors and gang foremen – at a price. On some projects living conditions were so atrocious that epidemics of cholera and diarrhoea were commonplace. Navvies were restricted to building their own makeshift shelters, bedding-down in barns, or renting accommodation from contractors. Huts were packed tightly with bunk beds each occupied by more than one individual, either at the same time or alternating when there were different shifts. On the construction of the Caledonian Canal in the mid-nineteenth century thirty men were lodged in a house intended for the lock keeper. Clean water, sewage systems and accident hospitals were non-existent. Provisions had to be bought from contractors' stores using tokens issued in lieu of wages – a system known as truck. The navvy was often sold food that was off, beer that was watered, given short-measures and to round it all off would have a commission deducted from the value of his ticket for the privilege. Contractors often made more profits from their provision stores, or from the 'bowels of their navvies' as one contemporary commentator noted in 1846, than from the contractual work itself.

One notable example of exploitation and squalid conditions was on the construction of the two Woodhead railway tunnels built below the Pennine moors between Sheffield and Manchester from 1839 to 1862. Contractors provided only forty shacks for a workforce of over 1,000 men and many navvies had to build their own makeshift huts on the moors. These were congregated in irregular groups around the airshafts and tunnel entrances that were the access points to the construction sites. Provisions and beer were provided through the token-based truck system at rates 20 to 50 per cent above Manchester prices and clean water was so scarce that dirty water was often drunk, causing epidemics of diarrhoea, while the damp working and living conditions also led to widespread bronchial problems. The navvies had to seek their own medical attention from a surgeon living over eight miles away. Most navvies were left with little of their wages once the contractors had made deductions for truck tokens, beer tickets and medical contributions. Working conditions were far from safe. Over thirty deaths and 650 injuries were suffered which brought a contemporary comparison with a severe battle.

Conditions were so bad at Woodhead that the plight of navvies was discussed in Parliament in the 1840s and recommendations were passed to improve social and moral conditions, to prevent depravity, immorality and violence, and to incorporate navvies into civilised culture. It recommended that the truck system be halted, wages should be paid weekly in money, proper accommodation and services for the sick and injured should be provided, special constables should be enlisted to prevent rioting, and that companies should be made liable for deaths and injuries unless they could prove it was the fault of the workman. It would be another forty years before legislation was passed. By this time improvements had been made by some employers in other industries, enlightened industrialists who took a more responsible role in their employees' welfare. They built model villages and towns for their workforces to provide what they perceived to be the right environment for nurturing morally correct and healthy citizens, and an industrious workforce. The most famous of these were Titus Salt's Saltaire in Bradford, 1853, Cadbury's Bournville in Birmingham, 1879, and Lever Brothers' Port Sunlight near Liverpool, 1888. Each provided cottage-style houses and shops, canteens, schools, libraries, places of worship, children's playgrounds, allotments, village halls, and recreational areas. Grand communal public buildings stressed both the idea of community and the importance of the benevolent, patriarchal industrialist himself. These were ideals brought to the model navvy settlements of the late nineteenth and early twentieth centuries.

This resulted in the provision of planned, structured settlements with separate huts for married couples and families and the inclusion of community services such as hospitals, missions, recreation or reading rooms, shops and clean water supplies. The Forth Rail Bridge built between 1883 and 1890 and the Manchester Ship Canal, 1887 to 1894, were two of the first big construction projects to provide good accommodation. By the time the Upper Derwent dams were begun it was normal practice to do this, though at exactly the same time navvies working on the Kinlochleven dam had to build their own huts which were placed in a ring around a communal rubbish dump.

Tin Town: the navvy village

Do you know, we did not first relish the idea of playing these navvies, but now we agree with many other players in Sheffield, that the Birchinlee fellows are perfect gentlemen.

A visiting amateur footballer

Sorry people are just finding that fact out.

A navvy's reply

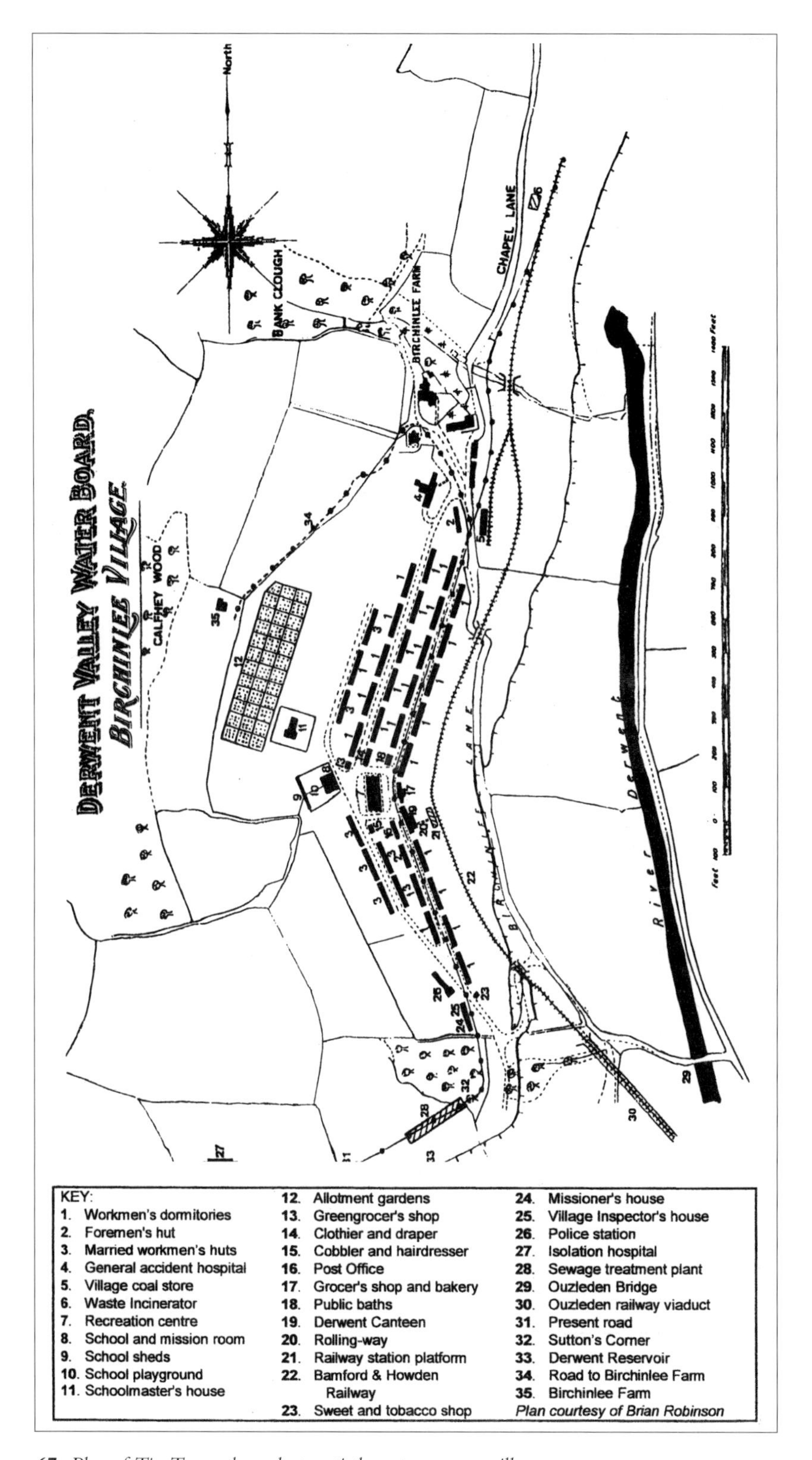

67 *Plan of Tin Town, the early twentieth-century navvy village.*

So this was how Tin Town came to be built – the village which for fifteen years was home to nearly 1,000 people and by far the biggest settlement ever to appear in the Upper Derwent (**67**). Surviving photographs, plans, documents, 'eye-witness' accounts and archaeological remains give us a clear insight into the life of the village. Most of the buildings occupied large artificial terraces. The village plan does not show that the valley-side location was terraformed in a huge earth moving operation to create four massive level terraces for the buildings. All of the buildings were constructed in the same way. Corrugated iron was used for the walls and roofs, which were lined inside with wood panels.

Village tour: an imaginary journey through Tin Town

The best way to explore Tin Town today is to approach along the main valley road from the south.This road was only made after the dams were finished and it was the line of a railway during the life of the navvy village. The original road, called Birchinlee Lane, crossed the River Derwent from the east side of the valley over Ouzelden Bridge and ran to Birchinlee Farm before continuing further up the valley. As it approached Tin Town, the lane took a large right-hand bend to climb the valley side at a gentle gradient. During the occupation of Tin Town, Birchinlee Lane was bridged by the Bamford and Howden railway line and by passing under the bridge you moved from the valley's rural landscape of fields and into Tin Town's streets.

SUBURBIA

Imagine yourself exploring the village in the distant past. The first buildings you see as you round the bend into Tin Town are two prominent huts situated on higher ground above. These are slightly detached from the rest of the village and form a sort of mini 'suburbia', housing the village inspector and navvies' missionary in one semi-detached hut and the policeman next door.

The village inspector was responsible for the maintenance of the village and the upkeep of services such as coal deliveries, and the sewage system. W.S. Lelliott of Langsett has held the position for most of the life of the village. While he has a position of responsibility, he is there to maintain the practical operation of the village rather than having authority over people. His work on the sewage system has obviously struck a chord with the navvies who call him 'Shit House Dick'. He may not be held in the high regard he perhaps thinks he deserves.

Next door, the missioner is George Sutton, familiar to some of the navvies from earlier public works. The Navvy Mission Society had been founded in the 1870s. He caters for their spiritual and social well-being, holding services in the school with a local vicar. He can be seen at the window, writing his history of Tin Town – called *The Story of Birchinlee: a memento of twelve years in the workmen's village, Derwent Valley Waterworks, Derbyshire.*

Next door to the first hut is the police station, which includes living quarters for Neil McLean, Tin Town's policeman, and a cell. The cell is rarely used and there are plans to convert it to a hut for a married workman and his family. There is little crime in Tin Town, though brawling is not perceived as a crime unless serious. When drunken workmen start a fight the policeman often takes them to a field to get on with it and wheelbarrows the loser home.

The physical distance of these huts from the rest of the village creates a social distance between the workmen and the village officers, copying the highly class-ridden structure of British society. Each officer's hut also has an inside toilet while all the workmen and their families have outside toilets. The commanding position overlooking the road to Tin Town also enables the officers to monitor 'outsiders' entering the village.

DORMITORIES

As you turn north towards the village you look down the two main streets, their gritstone cobbles and limestone chippings reminiscent of Pennine towns (**68**). The next building you pass, on the right-hand side of the road, is the small sweet and tobacco shop of Bessie Bateman. Beyond it you enter the regimented rows of workmen's dormitories, their austere corrugated iron exteriors facing both sides of the lower street. The rows of 'barrack-like' huts have an appearance similar to army, prisoner of war or early holiday camps. Each hut is divided into three sections and entering through the front door leads to a communal living room with a fireplace (**69**). To one side is the dormitory for up to eight men and to the other a private area for the hutkeeper and his family. What is most striking is the homeliness of inside compared to the simple façade. Framed prints and mirrors cover the wood-panelled walls, net curtains hang in the window, pot plants and gramophones sit on tables and embroidered cushions on the seats. If we are invited in on a Sunday you might join the occupants and guests sitting around the table with its brilliant white table cloth and fine bone china dinner service.

Being caught short, you would go outside and around the back of the hut to clamber up a slope to the outside toilet and might be amazed that it flushed waste away with water and piped it to a sewage treatment plant rather than dropping it down into an earth closet. A report from the village medical officer in 1908 claims that Tin Town was free of insanitary diseases – 'splendid evidence of the value of the water-carriage system of excrement removal in the prevention of filth disease'. The phrasing of the sentence implies that such a system was then a relatively new development. The outside toilets survive as small terraced platforms which are some of the most visible features surviving from Tin Town today.

The workmen are rent-paying tenants of the DVWB and are issued with a set of rules and regulations. These govern the cleanliness and safety of each hut, and while alcohol is permitted inside the huts it was limited to the daily amount

68 *Neil McLean, the village policeman, looks north along Tin Town's streets lined with rows of dormitories. Bessie Bateman's sweet shop and tobacconist is on the right. The carts are travelling shops. The Italianate cupola of the Recreation Centre is just visible in the distance.* Courtesy of Brian Robinson

69 *The men who built Derwent and Howden dams. Navvies, families and friends sit down for the wedding dinner of William Ashworth and Vinetta Dobson (far right) in one of the huts on Boxing Day, 1910. The road to Derwent church was roped-off with washing lines at many places and the best man paid 'tolls' for the wedding party to progress.* Courtesy of Brian Robinson

each workman can purchase from the canteen. Infringement of the rules results in a warning, then ejection from the hut and village. There is no mention of misconduct or violent behaviour.

HEART OF THE VILLAGE

Continuing north along the street we come to the physical and social centre of the village. On the right is one of the most important buildings, the all-male preserve that is the public house known as the Derwent Canteen. Its very presence scandalises the local temperance societies but it does focus most of the drinking in the village rather than surrounding inns. The canteen is operated by the People's Refreshment House Association Ltd which promotes sobriety and responsible drinking. Landlords sticking to this principle have quickly come and gone before the more relaxed approach of the present incumbent. Below the canteen lies the beer cellar which has its own railway platform connected by a rolling way for the beer barrels. The canteen and its beer cellar have already been enlarged twice due to overcrowding, and now there is a room provided for people, including women, not requiring alcoholic drinks.

Just beyond the canteen on the opposite side of the street is the towering bulk of the recreation centre. One of the largest buildings in the village, its large Italian-style roof-top bell cupola and imposing front façade (incorporating eight large windows and a set of massive doors) dominate the village. The centre hosts billiards, dances, concerts, cinema shows, whist drives, dinners and an annual horticultural show of produce grown in the village allotments. Many young people, especially women, from the surrounding area come to dances here, and though their parents may not approve, many a navvy has married locally.

Ringing the recreation centre are four streets and most of the other services in the village: the shops, post office, public baths and school. This is much like any other village green or public square. It is bustling with people shopping and chatting, while children play in gangs. Here you can buy most provisions or services from the grocer, the baker, the cobbler, the tailor, the draper, the hairdresser and the greengrocer. The shops are operated by shopkeepers from Bamford and Sheffield while milk is delivered every day by the farmer from Crookhill.

THE NORTH END

Leaving behind the frenzy of shopping, you continue north between further ranks of workmen's huts until we come to the northern end of the village. Here is one of two separate huts built to accommodate the site foremen, this one strategically placed to overlook the village coal store. Coal is used for all heating and cooking in Tin Town and is delivered in measured quantities to each hut by Tom Fletcher. Separate foremen's huts are a departure from previous construction projects where the foreman doubled as the hutkeeper. This separation helps to signify the different status of the foremen while preventing any exploitation

70 *Birchinlee Village looking south. It was the main settlement for navvies working on the Derwent and Howden dams between 1901 and 1915. Known as Tin Town because of the corrugated iron used to construct the buildings, it was home to nearly 1,000 people.* Courtesy of Brian Robinson

of the navvies that might result from having the same person control your working and living arrangements.

Here you turn by Birchinlee Farm to join the upper street (**70**). The farm is still occupied and village gossip says one of the daughters will marry her navvy boyfriend. Beyond the farm is Bank Clough where water is piped to the village and further away smoke rises from the brick-built waste incinerator.

Behind the foremen's hut at the northern end of the upper street is the imposing building that is the accident hospital. Here, a doctor and nurses treat industrial injuries sustained by workmen. Large windows make the spacious ward inside light and airy, as well as helping the many pot plants grow. Walking south from the hospital you pass the now familiar dormitories on our way back to the recreation centre and the school. There is another hospital, isolated to the south-west of the village, for infectious diseases. It was built when it was realised that outbreaks of scarlet fever amongst the children could infect navvies and affect the construction timetable.

SCHOOL

With the rear of the recreation centre on your left, the school is up a slope to our right. Its height and its bell tower make it another imposing building in the village. Many of the 110 pupils are in the playing field behind the school during break, making this the noisiest place in the village – though they still do not drown out the sound of the steam engines and hammers. The bangs, clangs and rumbles are constant during day and night and as both dams rise into view so the navvies and their families are constantly reminded of the reason they are here.

The school master has his own hut next to the school. This is relatively palatial compared to the other huts – with three bedrooms, a sitting room, living room, scullery, larder, coal store and inside toilet. The front door faces towards the school itself, so he is confronted every morning by his vocation before anything else.

MARRIED QUARTERS

The huts along upper street to the south of the school are very different to the dormitories you have passed so far (**71**). Here, each of the long huts is divided into four smaller 'houses' for married navvies and their families. This is effectively the married quarter. Demand for these houses is high, with the numbers of marriages between navvies and local girls, and another row of 'family' huts is planned to the north of the school.

ABBEY SPORTS FIELD

Before you leave Tin Town, it's worth looking over to below Howden Dam, where Abbey Farm still stands. There is another very important part of the social landscape of Tin Town. The field in front of the farm is the sports field where

71 *Looking along the upper street of Tin Town as it survives today. The terrace that held the married quarters is in the foreground, with the upper street to the right.* Photo by Bill Bevan

the village football team plays its home matches in the Sheffield Amateur League. The football team is vital to the village's identity and had huge support. The team telegraphs back results when playing away and once took a homing pigeon for a crucial game in 1912 where no telegraph was present. Here also, the village celebrated the coronation of Edward VII in 1903 with a traditional tea and sports day, which has since become an annual event. And here our tour ends, back where we started between the sweet shop and the police cell, between rock and a hard place.

A model village

The Derwent Valley Water Board had planted a model village into the rural landscape of the Upper Derwent (**67**). The utilitarian look of the huts emphasised conformity rather than individuality but the separation of village officers, foremen, families and single navvies into different zones reflected the highly stratified nature of contemporary British society. Edwardian ideas of civic pride created grand municipal buildings in the towns and cities of Britain, and Tin Town was part of the same trend. The recreation hall, school and hospital were all imposingly large buildings and the roads around the hall created a public square where groups of people would congregate and chat, and children would play.

Tin Town was not static but changed throughout its life and though extensively planned out in advance did not come into being ready formed. Most of the civic buildings and services were still being built nearly a year after the first accommodation was occupied. George Sutton, the missioner, instigated Sunday School and brought baptisms to the village rather than a nearby church. Sutton also commented that in the early years there was a lack of mutual knowledge and trust amongst the navvies but that this grew as they got to know each other and as they settled into the routines of living in such a settlement as Tin Town. As first aid courses, a fire brigade, Bible reading union and a football team were founded so more opportunities for strengthening group identity emerged.

The social impact of the village was widespread. Locally, the arrival of the navvies and their families temporarily changed the social structure of the valley. Tin Town was the largest settlement in the area and the first time a significant nucleation of a population had occurred in the area. Where previously the majority of people lived in dispersed farmsteads and the small Derwent and Ashopton hamlets, here nearly 1,000 people occupied a village. As far as the Upper Derwent was concerned this was a new way of living and, in effect, the planned nature of the village was an extension of urban ideals into the countryside.

Within and beyond the valley, the constant coming and going of navvies looking for work, and those going on rambles, picnics and shopping visits would have vastly increased the number of people travelling around the area. Events at the Recreation Hall also attracted people from Bamford, the Derwent Valley to the south and Hope Valley. Many of these were young women and there is today a large number of Welsh and Irish surnames in the locality from navvies marrying local women and settling in the region after the dams were completed. Those who died at Tin Town were buried in Derwent churchyard, with their remains moved to Bamford churchyard after the flooding of Ladybower Reservoir. At both graveyards, burials were made in areas set aside for navvies and their families so incorporating them into the wider local community but still with a degree of separation.

The occupants of Tin Town were the labour force who transformed the Upper Derwent according to the needs of the nearby cities. It was they who arrived in a pastoral upland valley where the largest building was Derwent Hall and left a landscape dominated by gigantic water reservoirs contained behind huge mock-gothic stone walls. When the job was done the village was cleared away, the majority of buildings being sold to the Ministry of Defence for use as a prisoner of war camp near Wakefield. Others were sold to individual buyers and at least one of the married huts still survives in the nearby village of Hope – where it is now a hairdressers.

Gardenesque: Ladybower Dam

The original plans for supplying water from the Upper Derwent and Ashop rivers did not include proposals for the construction of Ladybower Dam. Three smaller dams were favoured because they allowed the catchment area to be increased without flooding Derwent Hall, then owned by the Duke of Norfolk. Subsequently the Duke of Norfolk agreed to sell the hall to the Derwent Valley Water Board allowing the larger Ladybower Reservoir to be created between 1935 and 1944. This flooded the Derwent Valley between Yorkshire Bridge and Derwent Dam and a short stretch of the Woodlands Valley.

Ladybower Dam is very different to the first two dams. In thirty years dam fashion went from Gothic towers to country garden (**72**). A puddled clay and earthen core lined with stone forms its upstream edge, with the downstream covered by turf. Below the dam the valve houses, water management features and surrounding area were made in the style of garden terraces typical of nineteenth-century aristocratic houses including balustrades and formal garden plantings. Some features are unnecessary for the pure functioning of the dam but rather play on existing familiar images of landed estates to help 'naturalise' the impact of such a huge industrial construction on the landscape. The reservoir was formally inaugurated in 1945 by King George VI who planted a tree at the end of the road to the north of Howden Reservoir. That tree died, but its replacement still bears the name 'King's Tree' and is now a convenient 'roundabout' for turning vehicles.

72 *Architectural design and ornamental planting were used in the 1940s to give the works at Ladybower Dam a country estate look. This contrasts with the Gothic towers of the earlier two dams, but still shows a desire to give these monumental structures an architectural importance.* Photo by Bill Bevan

A second navvy settlement was built to house workers on the Ladybower project. Situated below the dam, it was on a much smaller scale than Tin Town. A surviving photograph shows a small compound comprising less than thirty huts, one of which was a cinema. Many labourers were lodged in the surrounding area.

Inundation and exodus

Society in the valleys was changed enormously through the depopulation of the area which was to be submerged. Eleven farmsteads were demolished during the flooding of Derwent and Howden reservoirs while another twenty-one farms, Derwent Village and Ashopton hamlet were lost under the waters of Ladybower (**73**). Derwent Village still holds the imagination of visitors today (**74**). During exceptionally dry weather the ruins can still be seen when the water levels drop. The church spire was originally left standing as a monument and rose above the reservoir but it also had to be demolished after it became unstable. Families displaced during the construction of Ladybower were resettled in a new, purpose-built village at Yorkshire Bridge. The rows of terraces were much closer together and more urban looking than the isolated farmsteads and irregular layout of Derwent Village. People moving in to the new houses would have had to get used to having closer neighbours than before. At least the village was built next to an inn. The dead were moved too. Burials from Derwent graveyard were exhumed and reburied in Bamford churchyard, where the Derwent vicarage was rebuilt.

The Upper Derwent landscape was dramatically changed. The three reservoirs replaced much of the farmed landscape of fields and dry-stone walls (**75**). Today, only eight functioning farms survive: Ashes and Old House in Derwent Valley, Rowlee, Hayridge, Blackden View and Upper House in the Woodlands Valley, and Crookhill and Two Thorn Fields on the ridge in between. The dams are monumental features and conifer forests have been planted around the reservoirs to reduce silting. The Gothic-style towers of Derwent and Howden dams, lake-like reservoirs and conifers give the area an Alpine feel which may partly account for its popularity with visitors today. There are now trails around the reservoirs and through the plantations, a museum in the west tower of Derwent Dam and a visitor centre built on one of the Dam's spoil heaps. Visiting the

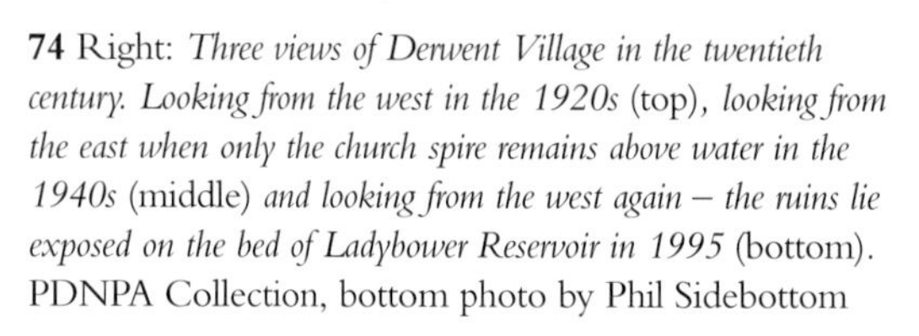

73 Left: *Fairholmes Farm. The farmhouse was still occupied in the 1930s* (above) *but was in the process of being demolished in the 1940s as the waters of the new Ladybower Reservoir ran up to its front door* (below). PDNPA Collection

74 Right: *Three views of Derwent Village in the twentieth century. Looking from the west in the 1920s* (top), *looking from the east when only the church spire remains above water in the 1940s* (middle) *and looking from the west again – the ruins lie exposed on the bed of Ladybower Reservoir in 1995* (bottom). PDNPA Collection, bottom photo by Phil Sidebottom

75 *Ashopton Viaduct under construction in the 1930s. The nineteenth-century Ashopton hamlet can be seen to the right of the picture. The original Snake Pass and valley roads run below the viaduct. Today, when Ladybower Reservoir is full, the waters reach to the bottom of the viaduct's arches.* Photo by R. Chaney

Upper Derwent for recreation also has a history that, like the reservoirs, began at the start of the twentieth century. As we shall see in the next chapter, the subsequent history takes in Communists and Anarchists, landowners and policemen, mass trespasses, pitched battles with gamekeepers, court cases and its own set of songs.

In 1900, a party of working class walkers from Sheffield organised their first Sunday ramble. At the Snake Inn they met one of the first navvies to be employed on the dams works. In this moment, two worlds met – the sepia bygone days of Tin Town and the visitor interest that would lead to the multi-colours of modern interpretation panels.

Fellows in arms, and my most loving friends,
Bruised underneath the yoke of tyranny,
Thus far into the bowels of the land
Have we march'd on without impediment.
Shakespeare, Richard III

No man is an Island, entire of itself;
every man is a piece of the Continent,
a part of the main.
John Donne

Our land is more valuable than your money.
As long as the sun shines and the waters flow,
this land will be here to give life to men and animals;
therefore, we cannot sell this land.
Blackfoot chief

We live in a land of 'weather forecasts'
and breakfasts that 'set in'.
Withnail & I

The real voyage of discovery consists
not in seeking new landscapes
but in having new eyes.
Marcel Proust

NINE

MODERN LANDSCAPES, MULTIPLE PERCEPTIONS

A journey into the past, present and future

The Derwent bus from Sheffield drops down into Ladybower Gorge along the A57, following the route of Thomas Telford's 1821 Sheffield to Glossop turnpike. To the right the broad sweep of Derwent Moor gently rises towards Derwent Edge on the skyline. Its surface is chequered by burning to improve heather for the grouse that have been shot on this moorland since enclosure in the nineteenth century. Heather is burnt on all the moors to renew old stems with new shoots that feed not only the grouse, but also the sheep, mountain hare, curlew and other wildlife. Walkers now have open access to all of the Upper Derwent's moors. Today the reds, yellows and greens of outdoor jackets are visible, strung out along a public right of way which follows the line of the medieval packhorse route between Derwent and Sheffield; the 'common way' and turnpike following each other in parallel.

Views of the moors are lost as we pass through the narrow Ladybower Gorge and then enter into the Upper Derwent Valley where it meets the Woodlands Valley. The confluence of the two rivers lies metres below Ladybower Reservoir. On the surface fishermen sit in small boats, a new recreational pursuit introduced into the area only because of the reservoir. The bus crosses the reservoir via Ladybower Viaduct, below which lie the remains of the nineteenth-century Ashopton hamlet now submerged and redundant. At this point Crookhill is a prominent landmark and views open up along both valleys.

As the bus turns off the A57 and onto the Upper Derwent road, the walkers who make up most of the passengers begin to get off at the start of walking routes. Car parks with historical place-names such as 'Derwent Overlook' and 'Hagg Side' have been built all along the road and are screened with trees from walkers on the moorlands above. Information panels tell the story of how the valley is managed today.

As we drive north along the valley, the left-hand side of the road is fringed with the dark-green and sometimes gloomy interior of conifer plantations. Planted by the Derwent Valley Water Board, they stabilise the ground and provide a supplementary income to water supply. The bus halts as the logging machinery of one of the forestry contractors turns off the road and into the woodland. A financial return is still important but conservation is also a major consideration. The contractor will have been briefed on the locations of hundreds of eighteenth-century charcoal burning platforms and the nesting sites of rare birds. Bright paint marks the trees; red for felling, yellow for avoiding. As mature conifers are felled, mixed planting with more native deciduous species replaces them to make the forests more in keeping with the natural landscape. Further upslope are smaller Forestry Commission plantations.

The level of the reservoir rises and falls with demand and rainfall. Dry summers leave a sandy shore exposed and every few years the level is low enough to reveal the remains of Derwent Village. Across the reservoir the land rises in a series of shallow slopes to Derwent Edge. The lower valley side is still farmland, crossed by dry-stone walls that form the small, irregular fields that originated in the medieval period. Some walls are ruined and their lines can be traced as lynchets which cast linear shadows on the grass when the sun is low on the horizon. The farmland is now all pasture and most is shared between two farms owned by the National Trust. This and the moorland above are managed to benefit the complex relationship between upland farming, recreation and conservation of heritage and wildlife. Stone needed to repair a gap in a wall is most easily obtained from ruined walls nearby but that diminishes the fabric of the historic landscape. Keeping sheep numbers low to promote heather regeneration and wildlife may threaten the financial viability of the farm. The National Trust attempts to juggle all of these through recourse to traditional forms of land use allied to land management plans, archaeological surveys and ecological assessments.

Leaving the bus at Fairholmes Visitor Centre, a walk through the packed car park leads to a hubbub of visitors eating, drinking, sitting, chatting and walking alongside ducks that quack hopefully for a handout. This is the nerve centre for managing the landscape and visitors in the Valley, housing Rangers, Cycle Hire and the Information Centre. Fairholmes is also where the valley 'management partners' – parish councillors, Park Authority, National Trust, Severn Trent Water and the Forestry Commission – regularly meet to discuss, negotiate and co-operate on policies and actions to manage the landscape for recreation, conservation and economic production.

Modern landscapes: multiple perceptions

Over the last 10,000 years people have lived in and shaped the landscape of the Upper Derwent in relation to its topography and environment. From the prehistoric clearance of forests, through the medieval to post-medieval enclosing of fields for agriculture, to the modern creation of huge reservoirs, the actions of people have created many different social worlds and landscapes. Now, in the early years of the twenty-first century, some of these past landscapes can be seen and interpreted through the palimpsest of many buildings, features and artefacts which survive in the present. One theme which has run through the history of the Upper Derwent since the thirteenth century has been the role that the relationship between landowners and tenants has played in the use and perceptions of this landscape. In the past the area was dominated by the Crown, Welbeck Abbey and the landed gentry. Now, in the twenty-first century, there is a new set of landowners with more specific objectives associated with farming, water supply and forestry, with recreation and conservation of scenic beauty, wildlife and heritage.

Severn Trent Water, the successor to the Derwent Valley Water Board, owns the reservoirs and surrounding woodlands. It has long realised the recreation potential of the area and more recently the conservation needs. The National Trust acquired most of the moorlands and all of the remaining farms to manage them for conservation and recreation. This brings with it economic demands of supporting upland farming. The Forestry Commission owns a small number of conifer woods in Alport, Westend and the Snake Pass, and has also taken a more recreation-minded approach to management. Each has its own objectives and its own way of perceiving the landscape which can potentially lead to tensions over land management. Conservation may conflict with the production of timber or livestock, while rambling and grouse shooting are not always seen as compatible uses of moorland.

Contemporary with this has been the foundation of National Parks, government bodies, pressure groups and societies who also greatly influence the countryside. The Peak District was the first National Park in England and Wales when it was formed in 1951. In 1981, the Park Authority designated the Upper Derwent as a Management Area. This aims to bring together the landowners, parish and district councils, and local community to further the Park aims of conservation, recreation, sustainable development and public interpretation of the landscape.

The multiple uses and perceptions of the rural landscape are not unique to the modern period. Since the medieval period there have been various official bodies and individuals occupying the land and legislating on its use. What characterises the twentieth century is the prominence given to recreation and conservation, hitherto absent or restricted to the ruling classes, and the way rural landscapes are now identified as countryside in contrast to the urban centres. During the late eighteenth and nineteenth centuries people like William Wordsworth and John Ruskin saw the countryside as representing a natural way of life defined by open spaces, peace and simple virtue while the city was seen as overcrowded, polluted and constantly changing. Recreation in and conservation of the countryside grew out of these ideals and the experience of life in cities. Urban populations looked to the countryside as an escape from the drudgery of congested living and industrial labouring, a place where they could participate in character-building activities such as walking and climbing. Others saw the countryside as needing to be preserved from the spread of urban conurbations, quarrying and from being overwhelmed by 'hordes' of urban tourists.

Rambling to recreation

To look at some of the first urban tourists we must step back to the beginning of the twentieth century and the year before work began on the Derwent and Howden dams. In 1900, a group of people were discovering the area for a new reason – walking, or as it was more commonly known at the time, rambling. In this history, rambling has a significant place in the way the modern Peak District landscape is managed and perceived. The identification of the region as the 'green lung' for the surrounding populations of Sheffield, Manchester, Leeds, Birmingham, Derby and other towns has informed the way we perceive the Peak District today. The region has a population of 38,000 people yet is surrounded by urban conurbations of over 17 million people within a 60 miles radius. The interest in the Peaks by this urban population has directly instigated access to moorlands privatised under Parliamentary Enclosure, the formation of National Parks in England and Wales and helped to define what constitutes 'appropriate' enjoyment of the countryside. It is no coincidence that the first National Park was the Peak District, the place where early ramblers were most active campaigners.

Some of the earliest ramblers took to the hills in the eighteenth century, which quickly generated guidebooks to tell them where to go! Walking guides to the Lake District were published in 1778 by Thomas West and 1810 by William Wordsworth. Walking was largely restricted to the upper and middle classes, and the odd laudanum-taking Romantic poet, until the spread of railways from the mid-nineteenth century onwards made it easier for more people to travel from cities to the countryside. This was about the same period that the creation of private grouse shooting estates was preventing people walking across open moorland. This would lead to conflict in the twentieth century (**77**). As walking became more popular, clubs were founded to promote rambling and to campaign for the preservation of footpaths. In Sheffield a group of workers in

77 *Two contrasting early twentieth-century public notices. Public access to footpaths and moorlands was a contentious issue and signs were used as part of the battle. Landowners tried to bar ramblers while ramblers often used archaeological information to campaign for the reopening of rights of way.* Left: PDNPA Collection, right: photo by Bill Bevan

the steel industry organised a ramble on Sunday 2 September 1900 around Kinder Scout, calling at Hayfield in the west and the Snake Inn in the north before continuing along Doctor's Gate down the Woodlands Valley and to Hope railway station. The ramble was organised by G.H.B. Ward, son of a Sheffield Little Mester, who placed an advert for the walk in the weekly *Clarion* newspaper (**78**). The *Clarion* promoted a particular brand of international socialism which emphasised culture as well as economics. The walk around Kinder Scout was pioneering at the time. On reaching the Snake Inn, tea was not readily available for a large group and the proprietor baked cakes. Here they also met one of the navvies employed on the very first stages of dam-building. Due to the popularity of the first walk, the Sheffield Clarion Ramblers were founded to enable more labourers to escape the drudgery and pollution of the city. They were one of the most prolific organisers of walks and campaigners for public access to the Dark Peak. Ward researched the history of the areas he walked over, including archival documents, archaeological sites and place-names. His aim was to educate Clarion Handbook readers about the moorlands and valleys, and to establish historical rights of access. He was the Upper Derwent's first archaeologist. One of the

78 *G.B.H. Ward of the Sheffield Clarion Ramblers addresses an access meeting at Winnats Pass in the 1930s. The early twentieth-century ramblers movement greatly influenced the way landscapes are managed and perceived today.* PDNPA Collection

79 *The Mass Tresspassers on their way to Kinder Scout in 1932. Many ramblers were members of sports clubs which promoted access to the countryside as an antidote to city life and industrial labouring.* PDNPA Collection

routes he was most keen on opening to walkers was the Duke of Norfolk's Road, which crossed the moors between Sheffield and Abbey Brook.

Between the wars the growing amount of leisure time, public transport and motor cars increased access to the countryside. Rambling, day tripping and charabanc touring gradually became more popular. The Ordnance Survey first issued their 'Popular' and 'Tourist' maps aimed specifically at drivers and walkers. The expansion of leisure was becoming more inter-linked with the conservation movement than in the previous century. Preservationists believed rambling improved moral spirit, good health and a culture of citizenship – developing internal order, discipline and the 'art of right living'. Campaigners for National Parks were eager to preserve the scenic beauty of hill areas for visitors. This was when the Youth Hostel Association and the Ramblers Association were founded. It was also the time of the Kinder Mass Trespass.

On 24 April 1932, the Manchester branch of the British Workers' Sports Federation, a communist affiliated sports and rambling organisation, organised an illegal ramble by hundreds of Manchester and Sheffield walkers across the private grouse moors on Kinder (**79**). Police and gamekeepers, the latter armed with pit props, confronted them and after a melee caused by the gamekeepers a number of ramblers were arrested. They were tried and convicted in Derby and during the hearing Benny Rothman, the leader of the trespass summed up their aims: 'We ramblers', he told the court, 'after a hard week's work and life in smoky towns and cities go out rambling for relaxation, a breath of fresh air, a little sunshine. We find, when we go out, that the finest rambling country is closed to us, because certain individuals wish to shoot for about ten days a year. For twenty-five years the Ramblers' Federation has carried on a campaign that has been futile. It was united action on the part of the ramblers that the well-known path, Doctor's Gate was opened.'

This was not the first trespass, as hinted at by Rothman's defence, and indicates that part, if not all, of the Doctor's Gate packhorse route had been closed by barring the way with field walls. The Peak District and Northern Counties Footpath Preservation Society was founded in the 1920s to lobby landowners to keep footpaths open and to publicise rights of way. Its large green signs can still be seen in the Upper Derwent. Along Doctor's Gate they advertise the Roman history of the route to justify access.

The Sheffield Clarion Ramblers organised 'Rakes' Rambles' – mass trespasses – over private grouse shooting moors at night, the first in 1907 being on Bleaklow where the Pennine Way now crosses. Though not greatly involved in the Kinder Mass Trespass, the Clarion club helped to organise a second trespass in 1932 which covered the three mile length of the Duke of Norfolk's Road. At Abbey Brook they were met by a large force of gamekeepers and a small number of police. On being confronted, the ramblers sat down for a picnic. They followed police orders to leave the moorland by turning around and walking back along the full length of the Road, much to the infuriation of the keepers. The pastoral Dark Peak was a landscape of conflict. A year later Ward spoke in front of 10,000 people at the foot of Winnat's Pass near Castleton, during the first of many access rallies. In 1945 the Sheffield rambling community raised money to buy the summit of Lose Hill above the Hope Valley which they named 'Ward's Piece' and presented to Ward in his honour. He immediately handed the deeds to the National Trust.

Campaigning by ramblers and conservationists led to the passing of the National Parks and Access to Countryside Act in 1949. This set the basis for the foundation of National Parks in England and Wales, and for access to moorlands. When the Peak District National Park was created in 1951, a special planning authority was set up to administer it, and wardens were employed to help provide an infrastructure for recreation. Local authorities also used the new powers of the Act to give public access along historical rights of way – and the Duke of Norfolk's Road was one of the first to be opened.

The southern stretch of the Pennine Way runs through the north-west of the Upper Derwent, crossing the Snake Pass and Bleaklow. The objective of the early rambling societies – freedom to roam, has been met by the National Trust's ownership of moorland since the 1950s, which guarantees open access in perpetuity. The Countryside and Rights of Way Act, 2000, gives public access for open-air recreation to moor, mountain, heath and down that has not been improved, and to registered common land.

Recreational use of the area has increased dramatically since the days the Clarion Ramblers and gamekeepers fought over the moorlands. Visitor numbers have increased since the 1960s due to the wider ownership of vehicles, and today, over two million people are attracted to the Upper Derwent's views, apparent 'wilderness' and relative solitude of the moorlands every year – making it one of the most heavily visited parts of the Park. This number of people has created a new feature in the landscape – footpath erosion caused by recreational walking. Erosion along packhorse routes and sledways has occurred before, as evidenced by hollow-ways, but it was the result of trade or local land-use.

The majority of visitors still come from the neighbouring cities of Sheffield and Manchester; today joined by people from further afield who are holidaying in the Peak District. The landscape is managed for their benefit, and in an attempt to control their impact, by the provision of visitor infrastructure. Fairholmes Visitor Centre is run by the Park Authority and Severn Trent Water as the hub for information and facilities. Built on a huge spoil heap created by the construction of the adjacent Derwent Dam, it is named after the nearby Fairholmes Farm which now survives as an archaeological ruin on the shore of Ladybower Reservoir. Car parks on the road between Fairholmes and the A57, provide access to moorland footpaths and give views across the landscape. Signs dot the landscape to direct people onto footpaths and to indicate the special characteristics of the area (**80**).

Conservation: National Parks, National Trust and national designations

The Peak District National Park Authority, the Department for Environment, Food and Rural Affairs (DEFRA), the Countryside Agency, the National Trust, Forest Enterprise and Severn Trent Water, lead conservation of the Upper Derwent landscape. After a government review of national parks at the end of the twentieth century, the aims of the Authority are now to 'conserve and enhance natural beauty, wildlife and cultural heritage – and to promote opportunities for the enjoyment and understanding of the special qualities' of the Park. How it carries out these aims is largely dependent on the Authority, working within national guidelines. The area is inside another national designation, DEFRA's North Peak Environmentally Sensitive Area. These areas were introduced in 1987 to offer incentives to encourage farmers and landowners to adopt agricultural practices that would safeguard and enhance parts of the country of particularly high landscape, wildlife or historic value.

Conservation of wildlife and cultural heritage is an important factor of estate management for all landowners and the National Park. The more commercially minded Forestry Commission and Severn Trent Water are both primarily working to make money from producing sustainable resources but they work with the Park to do so in as conservation-minded a way as possible. Both have conservation strategies. Severn Trent has a Biodiversity Action Plan and actively manages its woodlands to make them more attractive for wildlife. Tree felling is planned to avoid damaging archaeological and ecological features (**colour plate 17**). The National Trust owns most of the farmland and moorland, and is actively planting broadleaf trees. Founded in 1895, it acquired its Upper Derwent moorlands in separate grants from the Dukes of Devonshire and Norfolk in lieu of death duties during the 1950s. The farms have been acquired, mainly by purchase from Severn Trent, since 1980. The Trust, by its nature, has the strongest conservation-minded ethic of all the landowners. It

80 *A bench on a right of way along the line of the pipe that takes water from the reservoirs to the cities. Poetry with a sense of place interprets the recent past for visitors.* Photo by Bill Bevan

81 *Sheep from a National Trust tenant are shepherded along the valley road between Severn Trent Water's conifer plantations, swamping tourists in a sea of wool.* Photo by Ray Manley

tries to manage change so that those aspects of the landscape identified as being significant are conserved as far as possible in the evolving and developing landscape.

Production: water, timber and sheep

For all the recreation and conservation principles of the National Park Authority, the Upper Derwent is dominated by industrial-scale provision of water and timber (**81**). The three reservoirs continue to be important water sources for the cities – Derby, Nottingham, Leicester and Sheffield – that first promoted the Derwent Valley Water Bill in 1899. While Severn Trent is active in protecting and promoting to the public the wildlife and archaeology on its estate, this is undertaken within its primary purpose of supplying, and making commercial profit from, water.

Clear-felling, and changing water levels in the reservoirs, create the most visible temporary changes in the modern landscape. Felling creates opportunities to alter the landscape when species are replanted. Severn Trent and the Forestry Commission are now planting more mixed deciduous species to improve the wildlife habitats of their woods. The economic viability of some plantations is being re-evaluated and those in Alport Dale are now considered too remote to make a profit from their harvest. As a result the Commission and the National

82 *Archaeological survey in the Upper Derwent. Alice Ullathorne assists with the excavation of neolithic pits in Howden Reservoir.* Photo by Bill Bevan

Trust are drawing up a plan to fell many of the conifers and enable the regeneration of indigenous species in their place.

Despite the flooding of large tracts of land and the abandonment of the majority of farms, the valleys are still occupied. There are eight working farms, all of which are owned by the National Trust and let to tenants. All of the farms raise livestock within the enclosed pastures and open moorland grazing. Sheep dominate, usually to the exclusion of any other livestock, and both wool and sheep are sold on the national and European produce market. The sheep market has been depressed since the 1980s and upland farmers have found it difficult to make livelihoods from their flocks resulting in the abandonment of farms across the British uplands. The National Trust has supported its farmers to some extent, largely by helping with grant applications and estate maintenance, so softening the economic effects and helping to sustain the continuation of hill-farming in the Upper Derwent. Boundaries have been lost to neglect, or when walling stone has been taken from one wall to repair another, but there is still a coherence to the enclosed farmland of the valley-sides. Routeways continue in use to move flocks between the farms and moors. This is the remnant of the dominant land-use pattern and dispersed settlement which originated in the thirteenth century. The National Trust balances its agricultural, conservation and recreation aims through traditional land-use and modern practices. Grazing levels are one issue where decisions have to be made about the future of the landscape, the profitability of more sheep being weighed against moorland conservation requiring numbers to be kept low.

Historic landscapes and land management

This modern landscape, which is being managed for the benefit of visitors and its own preservation, with a substantial input of resources, is the current timeframe of a history of human activity which extends back into the past for approximately 10,000 years (**82**). Until the late twentieth century, many landowners and conservation bodies overlooked management of the historic landscape, concentrating more on the scenery, wildlife and specific monuments. This changed in the late 1980s with the rise in popularity of landscape archaeology. Both the National Park and the National Trust began to think of archaeological conservation as encompassing the whole landscape rather than just high-profile individual monuments.

In 1994 the Upper Derwent Officer Working Group, at the suggestion of the National Park Authority, initiated the Upper Derwent Archaeological Survey. Although a comprehensive ecological survey of the area had been undertaken in the 1980s, the only source of archaeological information was the Sites and Monuments Record compiled from existing information rather than a systematic search on the ground. The archaeological survey was the first time that most major landowners in the area obtained a comprehensive database of archaeological features. More fundamentally, it introduced a shift in perception: archaeology was not a group of isolated monuments surrounded by modern, archaeologically valueless land. Instead, the whole of the landscape should be recognised as a historic artefact in its own right. The survey has taken eight years to complete and it is feeding information into management plans, conservation activities, working practices and the local interpretation plan.

Futures: a pre-emptive archaeology of the next 100 years

Individuals can perceive such a landscape as the Upper Derwent's in many diverse ways. For example, the conifer plantations are many things to different people – an economic return, a livelihood, places of beauty and tranquillity, part of the thrill of a cycle ride, a threat to the countryside or an opportunity for wildlife conservation. None of these themes exist in isolation from the others. Farming maintains parts of the community and can contribute to conservation. Conservation can be an element in forest management and timber extraction. Recreational use is based on the physical landforms and the aesthetics perceived in the farmland, moors, commercial woodlands and reservoirs. The designation of the area as the Upper Derwent Valley Management Area (representing the National Park Authority, major landowners and local communities), was made in recognition of the inter-relationships between these themes and the need for a co-ordinated approach to the use and management of the Upper Derwent landscape.

What the Upper Derwent will look like in the future, how much of the 10,000 years of its past and what wildlife thrive in its valleys or on its moors, largely depends on the work of the landowners and the Park Authority. No one can predict how rural landscapes will be thought of in 100 years, never mind 10,000, but currently the prevailing view stresses the importance of marrying conservation, recreation, sustainable development and thriving local communities. If we can learn one thing from the past it is that there will always be differing uses and perceptions of any one landscape and that it never remains the same. Conservation is not about preservation in aspic but about managing change so that it is in keeping with the character of the area. Depending on how the various themes we have explored in this chapter develop we might see very different landscapes emerging over the next 100 years. Here follows some potential futures for 2100 AD (**83**).

Future scenario 1: wilderness

After the collapse of British farming in the twenty-first century, heavy costs made it impossible to keep any of the hillfarms working. Reluctantly, each one was allowed to come out of farming as the occupying tenant retired. Many of the enclosed pastures were allowed to regenerate as native, mixed woodland which spread along the cloughs and lower valley sides. Other pastures were maintained as grassland for birds and flower meadows through a combination of feral sheep and deer, the latter having arrived in the area from moorland to the south. Walls were allowed to fall into ruin except for those enclosing the native woodlands which were topped with high fences to stop the deer. Birch spread up from the cloughs to blanket the lower moorland, and visitors could no longer see the uninterrupted views that had attracted the ramblers and mass trespassers in the twentieth century.

As the oldest known farmstead in the valley, Crookhill was maintained as an agricultural heritage centre with rare sheep and cattle breeds kept in the old way of allowing them to graze outside. Dry-stone walling skills were demonstrated and taught. The remaining farmsteads were let out to tenants who worked in the area, converted to eco-tour guest houses, re-opened as environmental education centres or simply left to ruin. Timber production also fell because of cheap wood imports and most of the conifer plantations were managed as broadleaf woodlands.

Future scenario 2: development

The opening of the Derwent Quarry had been long fought by walkers but with Parliament's abolition of National Parks, there was little that could be done. The quarry company built its large headquarters by the A57 and the huge, bright quarry face could be seen from miles around as it bit through the moor towards Derwent Edge. On a dry day the dust from the huge dumper trucks covered the road and choked the air. The new traffic lights were essential to reduce the

83 *Three reconstructions of potential future landscapes*

numbers of accidents as the trucks continually pulled onto the road. The prehistoric settlement and field system had long been eaten away but could be seen as a holographic reconstruction in the quarry heritage centre by those who could afford the entrance fee. Grouse and mountain hare were not seen on the moors anymore.

Out of sight of the quarry, but only a short distance from the A57, the contractors were still building the new housing development for professionals working in the nearby cities who wanted a dream house in the country. All the houses were a pastiche of local architectural style, though there was more faux Tudor 'country house' styling than before. Severn Trent's objections to the estate because of pollution had been overturned by the Secretary of State for the Environment and the next phase for a further 150 houses had just been passed. The valley road had long been private access for the residents and CCTV cameras surveyed the A57 outside the electronic gate. Someone had rescued a fading interpretative panel about the archaeological remains and attached it to the fence by the gate, like a blue plaque proclaiming 'the past – used to live here 8,000 BC to AD 2100'. The Water Company was thinking of abandoning the reservoirs anyway as global warming had reduced rainfall in the area for so many years now that there was rarely any water left in them. The dams might become historical monuments, though the housing developers had an eye on converting the towers into apartments. The peat moorlands were often on fire in the dry summers and on a bad day the smoke could cloud the sun. Trees found it difficult to thrive except for the recent Eucalyptus plantations which supplied wood pulp for the dwindling paper trade. Ramblers who still came this way bemoaned the closing of Fairholmes Visitor Centre along with its café.

Future scenario 3: sustainability?

The rise of organic farming and farmers' markets made the sheep of upland Britain a popular product. This, and the changes in farm subsidies which promoted conservation rather than production, allowed every farm in the valley to thrive after the agricultural slump of the early twenty-first century. Visitors might think the farms and their fields probably looked much as they had always done without realising the work put into maintaining them by the National Trust. However, the public interpretation project let everyone know how the landscape was looked after and why. The CROW Act of 2000 had little impact on the Upper Derwent because most of its moors had already been open access. For those less able to explore the moors, the National Park and the landowners provided GPS-guided footpaths through woods and fields or along the reservoir-sides, so doing away with the need for signposts. A narration about the landscape was triggered at different grid references. Some people chose not to even visit the area in person, preferring the themed fly-through virtual reality tours that could be accessed on mobile 'electronic life assistants'.

84 *After the day is done.* Photo by Bill Bevan

Widespread congestion charging and the ubiquitous public transport routes had removed most cars from the valley and all but one of the car parks were converted to picnic areas next to bus stops. Visitor numbers had stabilised after the huge rise in numbers in the twentieth century. The mix of conifer and broadleaf forests provided a sustainable income while allowing wildlife to thrive. Every few years the reservoir levels dropped so much that the remains of Derwent Village were visible again, which always proved a popular sight for visitors. Management plans covered every aspect of the way the landscape was worked while conserving its historic fabric, enhancing wildlife habitats, ensuring local employment and providing plenty of opportunities for recreation.

Not endings but moments

These three scenarios are of course fantasy but all are potentially real. How the landscape of the Upper Derwent changes in the future will depend on how its' defining qualities are perceived and how these are put into practice through its management. So, where we are today is not so much the end of the landscape history as a small point somewhere in the middle (**84**). Here's to the story of the next 10,000 years.

PLACES TO VISIT

Some of the places mentioned in this book can be visited though many are private residences or located on private land without public access. Access to farmland is restricted to public rights of way, while the woodlands are open access. However, please remember that both are working landscapes and may be dangerous because of large machinery. All of the open moorland is open access with limited restrictions due to grouse shooting or, sometimes, when fires break out in dry weather. There are also regular guided walks led by National Park Rangers in the summer which often combine archaeology and wildlife. Please follow the Country Code and remember the hard-fought campaigns of early twentieth-century ramblers in gaining access to the moorlands.

There is a regular bus service from Sheffield to the King's Tree, at the top of Howden Reservoir, on summer weekends and bank holidays, and winter Sundays. Cars are only allowed as far as Fairholmes (SK 173893), where there is a car park, except during weekdays when the road to the King's Tree is open to traffic. Car parking is only possible at designated car parks such as Fairholmes, Heatherdene, near to Ladybower Dam on the Bamford road and smaller roadside car parks which are all marked on maps of the area.

Please check at the Fairholmes Visitor Centre (01433 650953) or the Peak District National Park Authority office in Bakewell (01629 816200) for further information.

What follows is a list of recommended sites which can be visited and a suggested walk which takes in much of the Upper Derwent's historic landscape:

Fairholmes Farm (SK 173892)
The ruins of a typical Upper Derwent farmstead are close to Fairholmes Visitor Centre.

Tin Town (SK 166915)
The original streets of the navvy village can be followed in a circular walk through beech woodland. This includes a trail which highlights some of the buildings.

Doctor's Gate (centred on SK 130897)
The medieval packhorse route and possible Roman road can be followed for most of its length between Hope and Glossop, though the busy A57 Snake Pass road follows part of it.

Derwent, Howden and Ladybower Dams (SK 173898, 170924, 200855)
The three imposing dams are all impressive sights, especially when water levels are high and water is flowing over the top of Derwent and Howden. You can walk across the top of Ladybower Dam and there is a small museum in the west tower of Derwent Dam, which is open most Sundays.

Derwent Packhorse Bridge (SK 169952)
The seventeenth-century stone packhorse bridge was moved from Derwent village to Slippery Stones when the valley was flooded for Ladybower Reservoir. It is near the start of Cut Gate, the medieval packhorse route to Penistone.

Pike Low Burial Barrow (SK 181898)
The barrow is situated on open access moorland at a little distance from marked rights of way. It comes into view as you approach it. From the barrow you can take in views of the surrounding moorland shelf and down the Derwent Valley.

Derwent Village (SK 185887)
The remains of the village lie mostly below the waters of Ladybower Reservoir but may be visible from this spot during dry summers. Impressive buildings built by the Duke of Norfolk, such as St Henry's School Room and the Shooting Lodge, can be seen from the road that runs from Fairholmes along the east side of the Reservoir.

Walking with archaeology

This guide walk begins and ends at Fairholmes Visitor Centre. It covers approximately 8km across rough ground and along reservoir-side tracks so is only recommended for those comfortable with moorland walking and steep gradients.

From Fairholmes Visitor Centre cross the car park and pass the opportunistic ducks toward Ladybower Reservoir and follow the waymarked footpath through woodland towards the main valley road. After 20 metres you will reach an interpretation panel about Fairholmes Farm from where you can look down on the remains of the farmbuildings. The farm may have medieval origins and was occupied until the 1940s when the Reservoir rose to the edge of its front garden and its fields were flooded or planted with conifers. This is also a good vantage point to look down the valley and maybe picture the scene in the nineteenth century when there were small pasture fields bordered by hedges and the main valley road ran straight towards where you are standing.

Backtrack to the Visitor Centre and head to its right-hand side where a signed footpath takes you to the road that passes below Derwent Dam. Follow the road. The dam is first hidden by trees but as these give way the castle-like towers and dam wall rise monumentally towards the sky. Built between 1901 and 1915, it is most impressive when the reservoir is full and water comes cascading over the dam. You can imagine the hard labour of the navvies who built the dam and excavated a 35m deep trench below it through unstable rock.

Keep on the road that runs in front of the dam as it takes a large right-hand bend and continue south along the east side of Ladybower Reservoir. After a few minutes you will pass Jubilee Cottage on the left which was built in 1896 by the Duke of Norfolk to accommodate domestic staff from Derwent Hall.

Old House then comes up on the left. This is one of eight surviving farms in the Upper Derwent owned by the National Trust. A farmstead has been recorded on this site since 1767, when it was called Hog Hill, but it may be much earlier. The existing farmhouse dates to the nineteenth century.

As you walk along the road two very different historic landscapes are visible on either side of the valley. Immediately above the road, small fields enclosed by dry-stone walls climb the valley side and give an idea of how most of the valley would have looked before the reservoirs were created. These are all pasture now but in the medieval period oats, barley and other cereals were also grown. Across the reservoir lie the dark green conifer plantations originally planted by the Derwent Valley Water Board in the early twentieth century to stabilise the ground. There were earlier woodlands here too, broadleaves that were used to make charcoal for Sheffield forges in the eighteenth century.

The next buildings on the left are two more survivors of the Duke of Norfolk's Estate, both of which were built in 1877. The first is the Shooting Lodge where guests were entertained and the second is St Henry's Schoolroom. Both are built in a mock-Tudor style which the Duke used to symbolise his ownership in the local area.

At this point you can take the public footpath which leaves the road to climb the valley side. Before doing so you may want to continue along the road a little way to the small inlet, passing the impressive gates of the nineteenth-century Vicarage in the woodland to your right. Here you can look across the site of Derwent Village which lies below the water. Here local medieval farmers brought corn to the mill and prayed in Welbeck Abbey's chapel. Derwent Hall was built in 1672 and the chapel replaced with the parish church of St James and St John in 1867. An interpretation panel of Derwent Village is located on the other side of the bridge.

By taking the public footpath you are walking on a traditional route connecting the valley and the moorland common. It also ran to Bamford House which we will come to later. Where the route runs through the valley side fields it is deeply incised into a hollow-way. As you walk along this path you will see changing views of the surrounding farmland and pass Lanehead Farm on your left. It was first recorded in 1614 but may be older.

About 200m beyond Lanehead you are on the moorland common of Derwent which local landowners enclosed by Act of Parliament in 1808. The

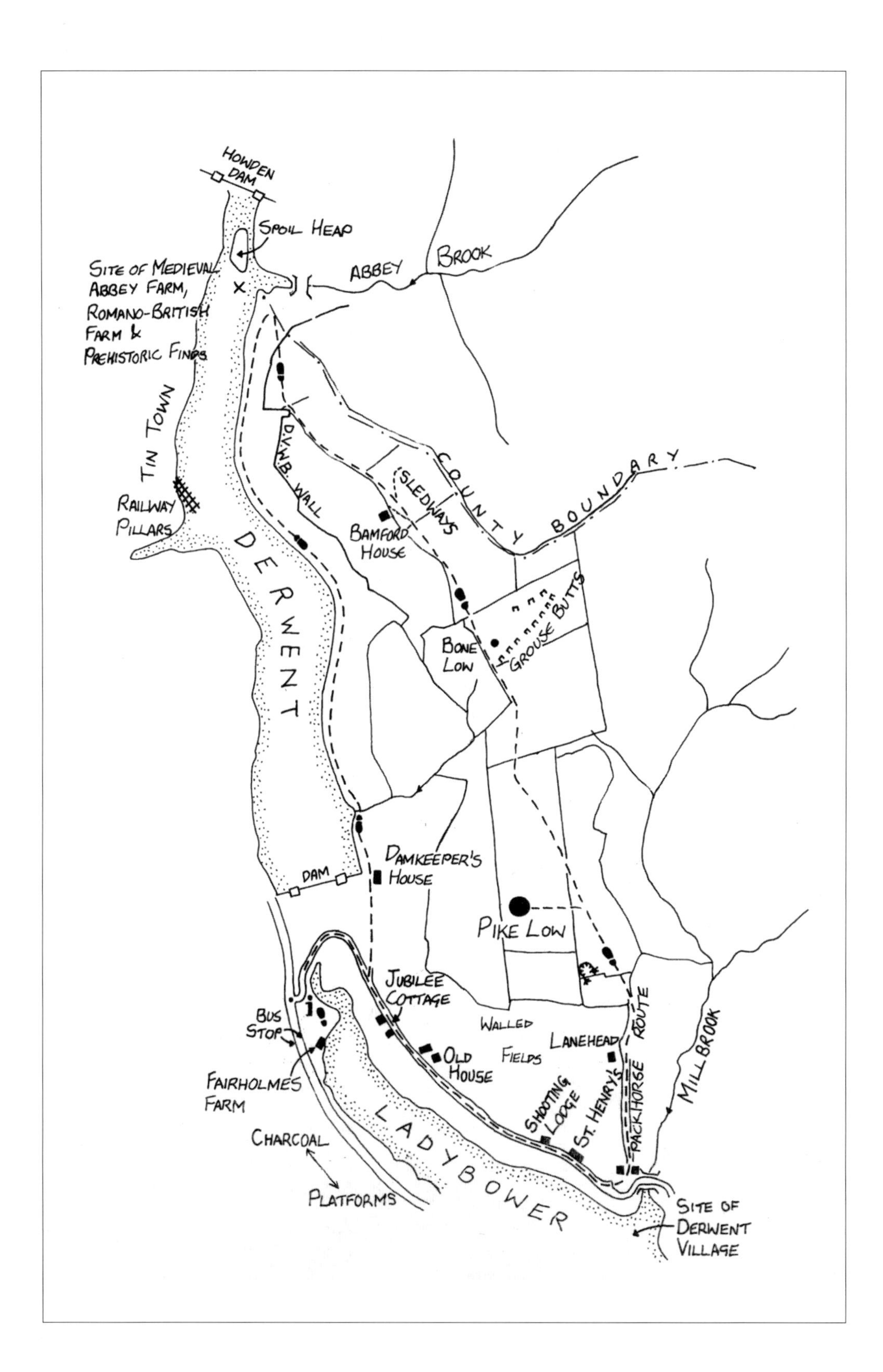

HOWDEN DAM
SPOIL HEAP
SITE OF MEDIEVAL ABBEY FARM, ROMANO-BRITISH FARM & PREHISTORIC FINDS
ABBEY BROOK
TIN TOWN
RAILWAY PILLARS
D.V.W.B. WALL
SLEDWAYS
COUNTY BOUNDARY
BAMFORD HOUSE
DERWENT
GROUSE BUTTS
BONE LOW
DAM
DAMKEEPER'S HOUSE
PIKE LOW
JUBILEE COTTAGE
BUS STOP
WALLED FIELDS
LANEHEAD
OLD HOUSE
FAIRHOLMES FARM
SHOOTING LODGE
ST. HENRY'S
PACKHORSE ROUTE
MILLBROOK
CHARCOAL PLATFORMS
LADYBOWER
SITE OF DERWENT VILLAGE

ruler straight walls are characteristic of Parliamentary Enclosure but were not built until 1830 when the landowners had finally agreed how the common was to be divided. The large mounds on the horizon to your left are the spoil heaps of stone quarries which may have supplied the stone to build the Enclosure walls and possibly buildings in Derwent Village.

As you walk onto the heather-covered moorland it is worth taking a small detour from the footpath to visit Pike Low burial barrow. The barrow only comes into view as you approach it. The large hole in the centre was made by unknown grave robbers some time ago. Pike Low was built sometime between 4,500 and 3,500 years ago to prominently mark burials in the landscape. This was done to remind the living of their ancestry, of their kinship with their community and of their association with a geographic location.

From Pike Low you can take in views of the surrounding moorland shelf and down the Derwent Valley. These views were important to the people who built the barrow to bury their dead, extending across the land that was important to their community. Many centuries before the barrow was built this area was scrubland and about 10,000 to 6,000 years ago people hunted game across it. To make clearings to attract animals people burnt the scrub slowly creating the open peat moorland you see today.

Rejoin the right of way which runs north through the Parliamentary Enclosure fields. You can see by the surrounding vegetation that improvement of this land was rather unsuccessful. If the sun is low and casting long shadows you might just see the faint traces of ridges to your right which might be the result of ploughing. Before Enclosure this was Derwent's common where livestock could be grazed and peat cut for fuel. The 1808 Act may have simply been used to privatise the common for sole use by selected landowners. There are no obvious peat cuts here but the peat is relatively thin over a large area which suggests it has been removed. Farms in the valley were also connected to this area by hollow-ways which were probably created by sleds carrying peat.

Another reason for Enclosure was to create grouse shooting estates for local landowners such as the Duke of Norfolk. The right of way takes you past two lines of grouse shooting butts. One is built into a large round mound which may be another prehistoric burial barrow known as Bone Low.

From here you can descend back towards the valley and after only a short time will come across the ruins of Bamford House on your left. It is one of the highest farmsteads in the valley and is first recorded in 1640 though may have medieval origins. The remains of the farmhouse, barns and the farmyard are all visible. Can you find the deep hollow-ways which run up the steep slope above the farmhouse? These were made by the wooden sleds used to carry peat down to the farm.

There are great views of the surrounding landscape from Bamford House including the reservoirs, plantations and moorland on the other side of the valley.

Carry on along the footpath down the steep valley side. You might see more sledways and wall builders' quarries on the way. As you approach the conifer plantation look closely at the wall which separates it from the moorland. It has a distinctive arrangement of coping stones which, in the Upper Derwent, is found only on the wall built by Derwent Valley Water Board at the edge of their land. It makes their boundary stand out from field walls and may be a style known to those navvies who came from Wales.

In the plantation turn left on to the wide track and join the road that runs along Derwent Reservoir. Turning right would take you into Yorkshire because here you are on the county boundary.

Howden Dam is just to the north and the wooded island in front of it is a spoil heap created during the building of the dam. Below the waters of the reservoir Abbey Brook meets the River Derwent and there is evidence that people lived in this area for 10,000 years. Stone tools have been found dating to between 10,000 and 3,000 years ago. Romano-British people ground corn and spun wool. In the thirteenth century AD, Welbeck Abbey was granted a meadow here on which they built a farmstead which became known as Abbey Farm. When the dams were being built the field in front of the farmhouse was re-used as the sports field for navvies and their families.

A few hundred metres to the south of Abbey Farm a barrow was built to mark the burials of the dead about 3,500 to 2,500 years ago. This barrow was probably positioned on the edge of a contemporary settlement and cairnfield.

As you walk back along the reservoir side look over to the other side of the reservoir. Stone pillars can be seen at the mouth of Ouzleden Clough. These carried the Bamford and Howden Railway line during the building of Howden Dam. Just north of the pillars and hidden in the woodland is the site of Tin Town.

On this side of the valley the reservoir hides the remains of medieval farmsteads which were demolished by the Derwent Valley Water Board in the early twentieth century.

You can see the towers of Derwent dam in the distance from the water side. They were used for some practice runs by the Dambusters squadron to train in use of the target range finders. Just before reaching the dam you pass the house of the damkeeper on your left. You can then either continue down the track or cut through the woodland on a narrower footpath. Both take you back to the road to Fairholmes Visitor Centre.

BIBLIOGRAPHY AND FURTHER READING

Geology and vegetation

Aitkenhead, N., Barclay, W.J., Brandon, A., Chadwick, R.A., Chisholm, J.L., Cooper, A.H. and Johnson, E.W. 2002 *British Regional Geology: the Pennines and adjacent areas.* Nottingham: British Geological Survey. 4th edition.

Anderson, P., and Shimwell, D., 1981 *Wild Flowers and Other Plants of the Peak District.* Ashbourne (Derbyshire): Moorland.

Johnson, R.H., (ed.) 1985 *The Geomorphology of North-West England.* Manchester: Manchester University Press.

Landscape archaeology

Aston, M., 1985 *Interpreting the Landscape: landscape archaeology in local studies.* London: Batsford.

Barrett, J.C., 1999 Chronologies of landscape. In Ucko, P.J., and Layton, R., (eds) *The Archaeology and Anthropology of Landscape: shaping your landscape*, 21-30. London: Routledge.

Bender, B., 1993 Introduction: landscape – meaning and action. In Bender, B., (ed.) *Landscape: politics and perspective*, 1-18. Oxford: Berg.

Bunce, M., 1994 *The Countryside Ideal: Anglo-American images of landscape.* London: Routledge.

Cornish, V., 1930 *National Parks, and the Heritage of Scenery.* London: Sifton Praed.

Daniels, S., and Alfrey, N., (eds) 1990 *Mapping the Landscape: essays on art and cartography.* Nottingham: University of Nottingham.

Fleming, A., 1990 Landscape archaeology, prehistory and rural studies. *Rural History*, **1 (1)**, 5-15.

Fleming, A., 1998 *Swaledale: valley of the wild river.* Edinburgh: EUP.

Hodges, R., 1991 *Wall-to-Wall History: the story of Roystone Grange.* London: Duckworth.

Hoskins, W.G., 1955 *The Making of the English Landscape.* London: Hodder and Stoughton.

Ingold, T., 1993 'The temporality of the landscape' *World Archaeology*, **25(2)**, 152-174.

Rackham, O., 1986 *The History of the Countryside.* London: J.M. Dent.

Shanks, M., and Tilley, C., 1987 *Social Theory and Archaeology.* Cambridge: Polity Press.

Tilley, C., 1994 *A Phenomenology of Landscape.* Oxford: Berg.

Upper Derwent

Bevan, B., 1995 The mysterious case of the Lost Lad. In Cumberpatch, C.G., McNeil, J. and Whiteley, S.P., (eds) *A Review of Archaeology in South Yorkshire 1994-1995*, 63-69. Sheffield: SYAS.

Bevan, B., 1999 Carry On Upper Derwent. In Cumberpatch, C.G., McNeil, J., and Whiteley, S.P., (eds) *Archaeology in South Yorkshire 1996-1998*, 15-23. Sheffield: SYAS.

Bevan, B., 1999 Medieval Leads: Archaeological Excavation and Conservation of a Lead Working Site, Howden Clough, Bradfield, South Yorkshire. *Transactions of the Hunter Archaeological Society*, **20**, 31-51.

Bevan, B., 2001 Town of Tin. *British Archaeology*, **59**, 20-23.

Bevan, B., 2003 Neolithic pits, Howden Reservoir, Hope Woodlands, Derbyshire: excavation and fieldwalking 1999. *Derbyshire Archaeological Journal*, **123**, 29-49.

Byford, J. S., 1981 *Moorland Heritage.* Wood Cottage, Snake Pass Road, Bamford: James S. Byford.

Chatsworth Archives. *Hope Woodlands Estate Papers.*

Derwent Community 1998 *Derwent Days.* Castleford: Yorkshire Arts Circus.

Fairbank, W., 1810 *Sketches and Numerical Survey of Derwent.* Sheffield Archives.

Gill, G.H., 1946 *The Story of the Lost Villages of Derwent and Ashopton.* Matlock: G.H. Hill.

Hallam, V., 2002 *Silent Valley.* Sheffield: Sheaf Publications. 3rd ed.

Jourdain, F., 1869-70 Notes on the Chapelry of Derwent in Hathersage, North Derbyshire. *Reliquary*, **10**, 29-32.

Potter, P., 1808 *Map of the District, or, Hamlet, of the Woodlands.* Chatsworth: Chatsworth House Archives.

Preston, F.L., 1961 A flat axe from Ashopton. *Transactions of the Hunter Archaeological Society*, **8(3)**, 162.

Robinson, B., 1983 *Birchinlee, the Workmen's Village of the Derwent Valley Water Board.* Manchester: Brian Robinson.
Robinson, B., 1993 *Walls Across the Valley: the building of the Howden and Derwent Dams.* Cromford, Derbyshire: Scarthin.
Robinson, B., 2002 *Memories of Tin Town.* Sheffield: Northend.
Senior, W., 1627 *Duke of Devonshire's Woodlands estates.* Chatsworth Archives.
Sheffield Archives. *Hathersage Estate Papers.*
Sidebottom, P., 1993 The Derwent Cross-Shaft: Discovery and Excavation, 1991. *Transactions of the Hunter Archaeological Society,* **17**, 9-18.
Sutton, G., 1914 *The Story of Birchinlee: a memento of 12 years in the workmen's village, Derwent Valley Waterworks, Derbyshire.*
Ward, G.H.B., 1925 The Duke of Norfolk's Road. *Sheffield Clarion Ramblers,* **24**, 130-148.
Ward, G.H.B., 1927a Cut-Throat Bridge, Lady Chair, Lady Bower, Moscar Moors and Farm. *Sheffield Clarion Ramblers,* **26**, 117-125.
Ward, G.H.B., 1927b Howden-Penistone Stile Track, Cutgate, North America Farm and Barnside Edge. *Sheffield Clarion Ramblers,* **26**, 97-102.
Whittingham, K., 1996 *The Recessed Earthen Platforms of the Woodlands and Upper Derwent Valleys, Derbyshire.* Unpublished dissertation for Division of Continuing Education, University of Sheffield.

Regional overviews

Barnatt, J., and Smith, K., 1997 *Peak District: landscapes through time.* London: Batsford.
Hart, C.R., 1981 *The North Derbyshire Archaeological Survey.* Chesterfield: North Derbyshire Archaeological Trust.
Hodges, R., and Smith, K., (eds) *Recent Developments in the Archaeology of the Peak District.* Sheffield Archaeological Monographs 2. Sheffield: University of Sheffield.

Prehistory

Barnatt, J., 1990 *The Henges, Stone Circles and Ringcairns of the Peak District.* Sheffield: University of Sheffield.
Barnatt, J., 1995 'Neolithic and Bronze Age radiocarbon dates from the Peak District: A review' *Derbyshire Archaeological Journal,* **115**, 5-19.
Barnatt, J., and Collis, J., 1996 *Barrows in the Peak District: Recent Research.* Sheffield: University of Sheffield.
Barnatt, J., 1999 Taming the land: Peak District farming and ritual in the Bronze Age. *Derbyshire Archaeological Journal,* **119**, 19-78.
Barnatt, J., 2000 To each their own: Later prehistoric farming communities and their monuments in the Peak. *Derbyshire Archaeological Journal,* **120**, 1-86.
Barnatt, J., Bevan, B. and Edmonds, M. 2002 Gardom's Edge: a landscape through time. *Antiquity,* **76**, 50-56.
Barrett, J.C., 1994 *Fragments From Antiquity: an archaeology of social life in Britain, 2900-1200BC.* Oxford: Blackwell.
Beswick, P., and Merrills, D., 1983 L.H. Butcher's survey of early settlements and fields in the Southern Pennines. *Transactions of the Hunter Archaeological Society,* **12**, 16-50.
Bevan, B., (ed.) 1999 *Northern Exposure: interpretative devolution and the Iron Ages of Britain.* Leicester: Leicester Archaeological Monographs.
Bevan, B., 2000 Peak Practice: what ever happened to the iron age in the southern Pennines? In Harding, J., and Johnson, R. (eds) *Northern Pasts: interpretations of the later prehistory of northern England and southern Scotland,* 141-156. Oxford: Archaeopress. BAR British Series 302.
Bevan, B., 2004 The early Iron Age in the Peak District, in Haselgrove, C. (ed) *Early Iron Age.* Oxford: Oxbow.
Coombs, D.G., and Thompson, H., 1979 Excavations of the hillfort of Mam Tor, Derbyshire 1965-69. *Derbyshire Archaeological Journal,* **99**, 7-51.
Edmonds, M., 1995 *Stone Tools and Society.* London: Batsford
Edmonds, M., 1999 *Ancestral Geographies of the Neolithic: Landscapes, monuments and memory.* London: Routledge.
Edmonds, M., and Seaborne, T., 2002 *Prehistory In The Peak.* Stroud: Tempus.

Garton, D., 1991 Neolithic settlement in the Peak District : perspectives and prospects. In R. Hodges and Smith, K., (eds) *Recent Developments in the Archaeology of the Peak District*, 3-21. Sheffield Archaeological Monographs 2. Sheffield: University of Sheffield.

Harding, J., and Johnston, R., (eds) 2000 *Northern Pasts: interpretations of the later prehistory of northern England and southern Scotland*. British Archaeological Reports, British Series 302. Oxford: Archaeopress.

Hicks, S., 1971 Pollen-analytical evidence for the effect of prehistoric agriculture on the vegetation of North Derbyshire. *New Phytologist*, **70**, 647-667.

Hicks, S. 1972 The impact of man on the East Moor of Derbyshire. *Archaeological Journal*, **129**, 1-21.

Hill, J.D., 1995 The Pre-Roman Iron Age in Britain and Ireland (ca. 800 B.C. to A.D. 100): an overview. *Journal of World Prehistory*, **9(1)**, 47-98.

Hind, D., 2000 *Landscape and Technology in the Peak District of Derbyshire: the fifth and fourth millennium BC*. Unpublished PhD thesis, University of Sheffield. 2 Vols.

Jacobi, R.M., Tallis, J.H. and Mellars, P.A. 1976 The Southern Pennine Mesolithic and the ecological record. *Journal of Archaeological Science*, **3**, 307-320.

Kitchen, W., 2000 *Later Neolithic and Bronze Age Land Use and Settlement in the Derbyshire Peak District: cairnfields in context*. Unpublished PhD thesis, University of Sheffield. 2 Vols.

Knight, D., 2002 A Regional Ceramic Sequence: Pottery of the First Millennium BC between the Humber and the Nene. In Woodward, A. & Hill, J.D. (eds) *Prehistoric Britain: the ceramics basis*, 119-142. Oxford: Oxbow.

Long, D., Chambers, F. and Barnatt, J. 1998 The Palaeoenvironment and the Vegetation History of a Later Prehistoric Field System at Stoke Flat on the Gritstone Uplands of the Peak District. *Journal of Archaeological Science*, **25**, 505-519.

Parsons, J., 1996 Stone mould from the Derwent Valley. *Derbyshire Archaeological Journal*, **116**, 60-67.

Pollard, J., 1999 'These places have their moments': thoughts on settlement practices in the British Neolithic. In Bruck, J. and Goodman, M. (eds) *Making Places in the Prehistoric World: themes in settlement archaeology*. London: UCL Press.

Radley, J., and Marshall, G. 1963 Mesolithic sites in South-west Yorkshire. *Yorkshire Archaeological Journal*, **41**, 81-97.

Radley, J. and Mellars, P.A. 1964 A Mesolithic structure at Deepcar,Yorkshire England, and the affinities of its associated flint industry. *Proceedings of the Prehistoric Society*, **30**, 1-24.

Riley, D.N., 1980 *Early Landscape From the Air*. Sheffield: J.R. Collis Publications.

Simmons, I.G., 1996 *The Environmental Impact of Later Mesolithic Cultures*. Edinburgh: Edinburgh University Press.

Spikins, P., 1999 *Mesolithic Northern England: environment, population and settlement*. British Archaeological Reports, British Series 283. Oxford: Archaeopress.

Tallis, J.H., 1964a The Pre-Peat Vegetation of the Southern Pennines. *New Phytologist*, **63**, 363-373.

Tallis, J.H., 1964b Studies on Southern Pennine Peats: I The General Pollen Record. *Journal of Ecology*, **52**, 323-331.

Tallis, J.H., 1991 Forest and Moorland in the South Pennine Uplands in the Mid-Flandrian Period III: The Spread of Moorland – Local, Regional and National. *Journal of Ecology*, **79**, 401-415.

Tallis, J.H., and Switsur, V.R. 1973 Studies on Pennine peats VI, a radiocarbon-dated pollen diagram from Featherbed Moss, Derbyshire. *Journal of Ecology*, **61**, 743-751.

Tallis, J.H., and Switsur, V.R. 1990 Forest and Moorland in the South Pennine Uplands in the Mid-Flandrian Period: II The Hillslope Forests. *Journal of Ecology*, **78**, 857-883.

Thomas, J., 1991 *Rethinking the Neolithic*. Cambridge: Cambridge University Press.

van der Veen, M., 1992 *Crop Husbandry Regimes: an archaeobotanical study of farming in northern England, 1000 BC–AD 500*. Sheffield: Sheffield Archaeological Monograph 3.

Whittle, A., 1997 Moving on and moving around: Neolithic settlement mobility. In Topping, P. (ed) *Neolithic Landscapes*, 15-22. Oxford: Oxbow.

Roman

Barrett, J.C., 1997 Romanization: a critical comment. In Mattingley, D.J. (ed.) *Dialogues in Roman imperialism: power, discourse and discrepant experience in the Roman empire*. Journal of Roman Archaeology Supplementary Series 23. Portsmouth: Journal of Roman Archaeology.

Bevan, B., 2004 The Peak District Romano-British Rural Settlement Survey. *Derbyshire Archaeological Journal*.

Branigan, K., (ed.) 1980 *Rome and the Brigantes*. Sheffield: J.R.Collis Publications.
Branigan, 1991 'Civilian Development in a Military Zone: The Peak AD 43-400' In Hodges, R. and Smith, K., (eds) *Recent Developments in the Archaeology of the Peak District*, 57-68. Sheffield Archaeological Monographs 2. Sheffield: University of Sheffield.
Dark, K. and Dark, P., *The Landscape of Roman Britain*. Stroud: Sutton.
Dearne, M.J., 1993 *Navio: the fort and vicus at Brough-on-Noe, Derbyshire*. British Archaeological Reports, British Series 234. Oxford: Tempus Reparatum.
Hingley, R., 1989 *Rural Settlement in Roman Britain*. London: Seaby.
James, S., and Millett, M., (eds) *Britons and Romans: advancing an archaeological agenda*. CBA Research Report 125. York: Council for British Archaeology.
Makepeace, G.A., 1998 Romano-British settlements in the Peak District and north-east Staffordshire. *Derbyshire Archaeological Journal*, **118**, 95-138.
Millett, M., 1990 *The Romanization of Britain*. Cambridge: Cambridge University Press.
Tyers, P., 1996 *Roman Pottery in Britain*. London: Routledge.
Wroe, P., 1982 Roman Roads of the Peak District. *Derbyshire Archaeological Journal*, **102**, 49-73.

Historical to modern periods

Ardron, P., 1999 *Peat Cutting in Upland Britain with Special Reference to the Peak District: its impact on landscape, archaeology and ecology*. Unpublished PhD thesis, University of Sheffield.
Aston, M., 2000 *Monasteries in the Landscape*. Stroud: Tempus
Bagshaw, B., 1869-70 'The Chapelry of Derwent' *Reliquary*, **10**, 91-96.
Bond, J., 1993 'The Premonstratensian Order: a preliminary survey of its growth and distribution in medieval Europe', in Carver, M., (ed.) *In Search of Cult: archaeological Investigations in honour of Philip Rahtz*, 153-185. Woodbridge: Boydell.
Cameron, K., 1959 *The Place-Names of Derbyshire*. Cambridge: Cambridge University Press. 3 Vols.
Chadwick, E., and Roberton, J., 1846 *Papers Read Before the Statistical Society of Manchester on the Demoralisation and Injuries Occasioned by the Want of Proper Regulations of Labourers Engaged in the Construction and Working of Railways*. Statistical Society of Manchester, Manchester.
Coleman, T., 1965 *The Railway Navvies: a history of the men who made the railways*. London: Hutchison.
Cooper, B., 1991 *Transformation of a Valley*. Derbyshire: Scarthin.
Cox, Rev. J.C., 1905 Forestry, in Page, W., (ed.) *The Victoria History of the Counties of England, volume 1, 397-426*. Folkestone and London: Dawsons.
Cox, Rev. J.C., 1877 *Notes on the Churches of Derbyshire*. Chesterfield: Palmer and Edmunds. Vol. 2 The hundreds of the High Peak and Wirksworth.
Cumberpatch, C.G., forthcoming Medieval pottery in Derbyshire: a review. *Derbyshire Archaeological Journal*.
Defoe, D., *Travels Through the Island of Great Britain*. London: Penguin. Reprinted 1979.
Dennis, R., 1984 *English Industrial Cities of the Nineteenth Century: a social geography*. Cambridge: Cambridge University Press.
Dodd, A. E., and Dodd, E. M., 1980 *Peakland Roads and Trackways*. Ashbourne: Moorland. 2nd ed.
Dodgshon, R.A., and Butlin, R.A., (eds) 1990 *An Historical Geography of England and Wales*. London: Academic Press. 2nd ed.
Frazer, B., 1999 'Common recollections: resisting enclosure 'by agreement' in seventeenth-century England'. *International Journal of Historical Archaeology*, **3(2)**, 75-100.
Hadley, D.M., 2000 *The Northern Danelaw: its structure, c.800-1100*. London: Leicester University Press.
Harrison, J., 1637 *Exact and Perfect Survey of the Manor of Sheffield with the Mannors of Cowley and Ecclesfield*. Sheffield Archives.
Hey, D., 1980 *Packmen, Carriers and Packhorse Roads*. Leicester: Leicester University Press.
Hey, D., 1998 *A History of Sheffield*. Lancaster: Carnegie.
Hill, H., 1980 *Freedom to Roam: the struggle for access to Britain's Moors and Mountains*. Ashbourne: Moorland.
Johnson, M., 1996 *The Archaeology of Capitalism*. London: Blackwell.
Kerry, Rev. C., 1893 'A History of Peak Forest' *Derbyshire Archaeological Journal*, **15**, 67-98.
Kiernan, D., 1989 *The Derbyshire Lead Industry in the Sixteenth Century*. Chesterfield: Derbyshire Record Society.

Kirke, H., 1925 'Monastic settlement in the Peak Forest' *Derbyshire Archaeological Journal*, **47**, 222-33.

Lichfield Record Office. *Probate inventories for the Diocese of Lichfield.*

Lowenthal, D., 1991 'British national identity and the English countryside' *Rural History*, **2(2)**, 205-230.

McCarthy, M.R., and Brooks, C.M., 1988 *Medieval Pottery in Britain AD 900 – 1600.* Leicester: Leicester University Press.

Morgan, P., 1978 *Domesday Book: Derbyshire.* Chichester: Phillimore.

Morris, M., 1994 'Towards an archaeology of navvy huts and settlements of the industrial revolution' *Antiquity*, 68, 573-584.

Newman, R., 2001 *The Historical Archaeology of Britain, c.1540-1900.* Stroud: Sutton.

PDNPA 2000 *National Park Management Plan: strategy 2000-2005.* Bakewell: Peak District National Park Authority.

Radley, J., and Penny, S.R., 1972 'The turnpike roads of the Peak District' *Derbyshire Archaeological Journal*, **92**, 93-109.

Roffe, D., 1986 *The Derbyshire Domesday.* Matlock: Derbyshire Museums Service.

Rosamond, M., 1970 'The sale of the Hathersage estates of the Fitzherberts in the 1650s' *Derbyshire Archaeological Journal*, **90**, 32-55.

Scurfield, G., 1999 'The Peak District in the Early Seventeenth Century' *The Peak District Journal of Natural History and Archaeology*, **1**, 1-12.

Sharpe, J.A., 1997 *Early Modern England: a social history 1550 – 1760.* London: Arnold. 2nd ed.

Sidebottom, P., 1999 'Stone crosses of the Peak and the 'sons of Eadwulf'.' *Derbyshire Archaeological Journal*, **118**, 206-219.

Sidebottom, P., 2000 Viking Age stone monuments and social identity in Derbyshire. In Hadley, D.M., and Richards, J.D., (eds) *Cultures in Contact: Scandinavian settlement in England in the ninth and tenth centuries*, 213-236. Turnhout: Brepols.

Sissons, D., 2002 *The Best of the Sheffield Clarion Ramblers' Handbooks.* Devon: Halsgrove.

Smith, H., 1993 *Mortimer Road: the Turnpike that Failed.* Sheffield: Howard Smith.

Stephenson, T., 1989. *Forbidden Land: the struggle for access to mountain and moorland.* Manchester: Manchester University Press.

Ward, G.H.B., 1931 'Derbyshire Moorlands and Production of Food' *Sheffield Clarion Ramblers*, **30**, 109-117.

Waterson, M., 1994 *The National Trust. The first hundred years.* London: The National Trust.

Williamson, T., 2002 *The Transformation of Rural England: farming and the landscape 1700 – 1870.* Exeter: UEP.

Williamson, T., 2003 *Shaping Medieval Landscapes.* Macclesfield: Windgather Press.

INDEX